Installing And Configuring File And Printer Services For Macintosh Under Windows NT

The first step in integrating Macintoshes into your Windows NT based network will be the installation of the Windows NT Services for Macintosh on your Windows NT server. Here are the steps that you will need to take to get Services for Macintosh installed on your Windows NT server.

1. Select Start|Settings|Control Panel. Then double-click on the Network icon to open up the Network Control Panel.

2. Click on the Services tab. The Services installed on my server are the standard ones that Windows NT installs.

3. To add the Services for Macintosh, click on Add, which brings up the Select Network Service dialog box.

4. Select Services for Macintosh from the alphabetical list and click on OK.

5. To add another Service, click on Add again, select the Service that you desire, and then click on OK again.

6. When you are all finished selecting all the Services you want to install, click on OK located in the Services Tab of the Network dialog box.

7. NT next asks you for the location of the files needed to install the new services. These are located on the Windows NT Server CD-ROM that you used to install the server originally. Insert the Windows NT CD-ROM into your server's CD-ROM drive and click on Continue.

Configuring Services For Macintosh

After the Services for Macintosh are installed, you then will be asked to configure them. Selecting the Services for Macintosh and clicking on the Properties button shows the default configuration dialog box for Services for Macintosh. To add an AppleTalk zone to your network, follow these steps:

1. Click on the Routing tab that is in the Services for Macintosh Properties dialog box.

2. Click on the Enable Routing checkbox.

3. Click on Use This Router to Seed the Network.

4. Enter the appropriate values in the Network Range boxes. If you have only one AppleTalk zone, then enter "1" in both boxes. Otherwise, in the To field, enter "1" and then in the From field enter a number that represents the total number of the AppleTalk zones you're adding.

5. Once you have entered the appropriate network numbers, click on Add to enter the zone name. Doing so brings up the Add Zone dialog box, in which you enter the name of your AppleTalk zone.

6. Once you have finished entering the name of your zone, click on Add. Notice that the AppleTalk zone you added is now listed at the bottom of the Microsoft AppleTalk Protocol Properties dialog box.

7. To add additional AppleTalk Zones, repeat steps 1 through 8.

8. After you've added all the AppleTalk zones you wish, select the zone you want to be used as the Default Zone and then click on the Make Default button. Doing so causes that zone to become the one that your server uses.

Setting Up A Printer Under Windows NT Server

To create a server that can be accessed by both your Windows-based clients and your clients running the Macintosh OS, you will need to complete the following steps:

1. Click on the Start menu.

2. Select Printers from the sub-menu located under Settings.

3. From the Printers window, double click on the Add Printer icon.

4. After the Add Printer wizard has finished launching you will choose between a printer that is locally connected to your server or one that is connected to a remote server. For this example, we will choose a printer that is connected to your computer.

5. Next, you will be asked to choose the port to which you will connect your printer. If the printer is directly connected to the server by a serial or parallel cable, then select the appropriate serial or parallel port.

After you have selected and or configured the port that the printer is connected to, you will be asked to determine which type of printer is being connected to the server. Since computers running Macintosh OS are limited to talking to network printers that use Adobe PostScript, you must be using a PostScript capable printer. To select the make and model of printer that you are using, follow these steps:

1. Locate the printer manufacturer's name, located on the left-hand side of the printer selection dialog box and click on it.

2. Once you have selected the printer's manufacturer, select the model of printer from the list on the right-hand side of the dialog box.

3. After you have selected the make and model printer you're configuring, click on Next to continue the process.

4. On the next Add Printer Wizard screen, you will be asked to enter the name that this printer will be known by on the network. While any name will do, it is usually best to choose a name that reflects ei-

6. Now, you are asked to enter the location of the printer and some comments about it. Although this is a completely optional step, it is a very good idea to do it, especially if you have many printers to manage. Entering the location and comments makes it easier to locate and keep track of printer resources. When you are done, click on Next.

7. After sharing your printer, click on Next to continue the setup process.

8. Congratulations, you are nearly done with the setup process. The Print Test Page screen of the Add Printer Wizard now asks you if you want to print a test page so that you can ensure the printer is configured correctly. Click on the Yes radio button to run your test page, which you can use to verify your configuration.

9. Once you have finished printing the test page and examined it to be sure your setup is correct, click on Next to go to the final portion of setup. Examine all the settings listed in the Completing the Add Printer Wizard screen. If they are all set the way you want, click on Finish complete the setup of your printer.

Installing DAVE

Installing DAVE involves essentially the same steps as installing most Macintosh software. To begin, you use the original installation disks that come with DAVE or download the most recent version of DAVE Installer from Thursby Software Systems at **www.thursby.com**. To install DAVE, follow these steps:

1. Double-click on the DAVE Installer icon to start the installation process.

2. Accept the license agreement to bring up the main Installer screen.

3. You can choose Easy Install to install all of the DAVE components or Custom Install to install just the components you desire. These components include the DAVE client components; the DAVE Sharing, Access, and messaging components; and the NetBIOS Control Panel. Unless you have a specific reason for installing only one or two of these components, we recommend the Easy Install (default) option.

4. Click on Install to perform an Easy Install.

5. Once all of the components have been installed, restart the Macintosh.

Configuring DAVE

After the Macintosh has finished the restart process, you are ready to configure the program to recognize your Windows NT or Windows 2000-based network. To configure DAVE, you must know the following:

- The NetBIOS name you wish to use for the Macintosh.
- The workgroup or domain that the Mac should be configured to use.
- Whether you will be manually configuring Windows Internet Name Service (WINS) or having your WINS configuration automatically configured for you by Dynamic Host Configuration Protocol (DHCP).

After you have this information at hand, you're ready to configure DAVE, by following these steps:

1. Open the NetBIOS Control Panel (located in the Control Panel folder). The first time you use the program, you enter the name and activation key information.

2. Enter the Macintosh's NetBIOS name and the Workgroup or Domain to which you wish the Mac to belong. You can also add a description of the Macintosh in the space provided.

3. Select TCP/IP as the desired protocol.

4. Depending upon your network, you may want to select the WINS and/or DHCP checkboxes. On most Windows 2000 networks, you should select only DHCP. If your DHCP server is not set to distribute WINS server information, you must select the WINS checkbox and then manually enter your primary WINS server's IP address and a secondary choice if it exists.

Working With DAVE

The process of connecting to a Windows shared volume with DAVE is very similar to mounting an AppleShare volume with the Macintosh Chooser or Network Browser application. You can mount Windows shared volumes by using either the DAVE client under the Chooser or by using the DAVE Access application. To connect to a Windows shared volume using the DAVE client, follow these steps:

1. Open the Chooser and select DAVE client.

2. Click on the name of the Windows computer that houses the shared volume that you wish to use and then click on OK.

3. From the list of volumes available on the Windows-based computer, select the one that you want and click on OK. If you want to mount the shared volume on your Mac's desktop when it's restarted, select the checkbox to the right of the volume's name.

4. Enter the username and password, as required.

5. Close the Chooser.

Using DAVE Access

To use the DAVE Access tool to mount a Windows shared volume, follow these steps:

1. Launch DAVE Access from the Apple menu.

2. Click on the Mount Share icon on the DAVE Access toolbar.

3. Enter the name of the Windows computer and the shared volume that you wish to connect to. You can also enter a name that you wish to use for this volume, for easy identification.

4. Select the type of network protocol you wish to use to connect to the remote computer. Unless you must use TCP/IP, it is generally best to select NetBIOS.

5. If you need to log onto the Macintosh-Accessible volume with a different username and password, select the Use Alternative Credentials checkbox.

6. Enter the username and password that you wish to use and then click on OK to finish the connection process.

CORIOLIS
Technology Press

©2000 The Coriolis Group. All Rights Reserved.

6. Examine the Subcomponents of Other Network File and Print Services list, select File Services for Macintosh, and then click on OK.

7. Once you have finished adding in File Services for Macintosh, click on Next.

8. Click on Finish to complete the installation of File Services for Macintosh.

Configuring AppleTalk Networking

When you have finished installing File Services for Macintosh, you are ready to configure it. On a network where there are already AppleTalk zones, Windows 2000 defaults to using the default zone configured for the network segment on which the server is located. To set this zone, follow these steps:

1. Open the Network and Dial-Up Connections window and then double-click on the Local Area Connection icon.

2. Click on the Properties button to display the Local-Area Connection Properties dialog box.

3. Next, select the AppleTalk protocol.

4. Lastly, click on Properties. Doing so brings up the AppleTalk Protocol Properties dialog box. You can click on the list of zones available on the network and then select the one that you wish to use.

To add an AppleTalk zone to your Windows 2000 network, follow these steps:

1. Click on Start|Programs|Administrative Tools|Routing And Remote Access. Doing so brings up the Routing And Remote Access plug in for the Microsoft Management Console.

2. On the left-hand side, click on the plus sign next to the server name to expand it. You then see all the options that you can configure.

3. Again on the left-hand side, click on AppleTalk Routing to list all the AppleTalk routers currently configured.

4. In the right-hand pane, double-click on Local Area Connection to open the Local Area Connection Properties dialog box.

5. Click on Enable Seed Routing On This Network. Now, enter the appropriate value(s) in the Network Range box(es). If you have only one AppleTalk zone, enter "1" in both boxes. Otherwise, in the To field, enter a number that represents the total of the AppleTalk zones you're adding.

6. After you have entered the appropriate network numbers, click on the New Zone to enter a zone name if one is not already present.

7. Once you have finished typing in the name of your zone, click on the OK. Notice that the AppleTalk zone you added is now listed in the Zones list at the bottom of the Local Area Connection Properties dialog box.

8. To add additional AppleTalk Zones, repeat Steps 6 and 7.

9. Once you have added all the AppleTalk zones that you want, click on the Default Zone pop-up menu and select the zone you want to be the default and then click on the Apply button.

Configuring A Printer Using Windows 2000 Server

Computers that run the Macintosh OS are limited to using network printers that support Adobe PostScript. Therefore, you must choose a PostScript-capable printer. In order to set up a printer that both your Windows-based users and those running the Macintosh OS can use, follow these steps:

1. Click on Start|Settings|Printers.

2. From the Printers window, double-click on the Add Printer icon

3. After the Add Printer Wizard has completed loading, click on Next.

4. Now, choose between a printer that is connected directly to your server or one that is connected t the network via a print sharing device (such as th Hewlett-Packard JetDirect card) and one that is being shared by another workstation or server o the network. For this example use a printer that locally connected to your server. Since we want go through all of the steps, uncheck the checkbo labeled Automatically Detect And Install My Plu And Play Printer. Once you have selected a loca printer and disabled the automatic printer setu click on Next.

5. Now, on the Select The Printer Port dialog box, yo are asked to select the port to which you will con nect your printer. If the printer is directly connecte to the server by a serial or parallel cable, select tl appropriate serial or parallel port.

6. If the printer is connected directly to the networ click on the Create A New Port radio button locate towards the bottom of the dialog box. Doing so ; lows you to create a new port for a network printe to use.

7. After you have chosen and/or configured the po to which your printer is connected, you are aske to choose the type of printer that you are connec ing to the server.

Selecting The Printer

To select the make and model of printer that you ar using, follow these steps:

1. Click on the printer manufacturer's name, locate in the Manufacturers list on the left-hand side of the Add Printer Wizard screen.

2. Then, choose the model of printer from the Printe list on the right-hand side of the screen and click o Next.

3. The Add Printer Wizard now asks you to type in th name by which this printer will be known on the network. Although you can use any name, it is gen erally best to select a name that reflects either th department that the printer supports or the locatio where it can be found.

4. Once you have typed in the printer's name, click o Next to continue.

5. You are then asked if you want to share this printe with the other computers on the network. Click c the Share As radio button and then enter the name of the printer.

ther the group that the printer supports or the location where it can be found.

5. Once you have entered the printer's name, click on Next to continue.

6. You will now be asked if you wish to share this printer with other computers on the network. Click on the Share As radio button and then type in the name of the printer.

7. After sharing your printer, click on Next to proceed to the final phase of the setup process.

Connecting To The Printer From Your Macintosh

After you have finished setting up the printer on your Windows NT server, then you are ready to use that printer from your Macintosh computers. To connect to and use this printer, do the following on each Mac in your network:

1. Click on the Apple menu and then select the Chooser.

2. When the Chooser screen appears, click on the LaserWriter 8 icon.

3. Next you will need to select the zone in which the server is located if it is not the same as your own.

4. After you have selected the proper zone, then you need to select the printer from the list in the upper right hand corner of the dialog box.

5. The next step is to click on Create to allow the driver to choose a proper PPD (PostScript Printer Description) file and set up a desktop printer.

6. The Auto Setup option is the first to try. Click on this button and your driver will examine the list of available PPD files to locate one that matches the make and model of your printer. If the correct PPD file is located, it will be automatically selected, and a desktop printing icon for the selected printer will appear on your Mac's desktop. If you cannot locate an appropriate PPD, then select the Generic PPD.

7. Click the close box on the Chooser, and OK the message that your printer selection has been changed.

Repeat the above steps for each Macintosh on your network. You are now ready to send your documents to that printer for output.

Installing File Services For Macintosh: The Beginning

The first step when you install AppleTalk and File Services for Macintosh is to add them to the list of Windows 2000 Network Protocols and Windows Components. These Protocols and Server Options enable the Windows 2000 server to provide multi-platform support when communicating with the various computers on the network.

Follow these steps to quickly install AppleTalk and File Services for Macintosh:

1. Click on Start|Settings|Control Panel. Or, double-click on the My Computer icon located on your Windows 2000 desktop and then double-click on the Control Panel folder located in the My Computer window.

2. Double-click on the Network and Dial-up Connections icon. Doing so brings up the Network and Dial-Up Connections window. You can examine every network connection that you have established on this computer directly from this window. The most common connections are Local Area Connection and Dial Up Connection.

3. Once you have the Network And Dial-up Connection window open, double-click on the Local Area Connection icon to open the Local Area Connection Status dialog box for your server's LAN connection.

4. Information about current network traffic is displayed in the Local Area Connection Status dialog box. This dialog box has two buttons: Properties, which allows you to configure all the networking options, and Disconnect, which shuts down your network connection. Click on Properties to see the adapter that is currently selected and the network options and protocols that are configured for that interface.

Installing AppleTalk And File Services For Macintosh: The Next Steps

Once you have the Network Control Panel opened, follow these steps to do to add AppleTalk to Windows 2000:

1. Double-click on the Local Area Connection icon and then click on the Properties button to display the Local Area Connection Properties dialog box. Alternatively, you can right-click on the Local Area Connection icon and then select Properties from the shortcut menu. The components installed on my server are the standard ones that Windows 2000 installs.

2. To add a Windows 2000 Network component, click on Install.

3. Double-click on Protocol in the Select Network Component Type dialog box.

4. In the Select Network Protocol dialog box, select AppleTalk Protocol from the list of available protocols and then click on OK.

Adding The File Services For Macintosh Service To Windows 2000

After you added AppleTalk to the list of available protocols, you must also add the File Services for Macintosh service to Windows 2000. To do so, follow these steps:

1. Open the Control Panel window by clicking on Start|Settings|Control Panel.

2. Next, double-click on the Add/Remove Programs icon.

3. From the Add/Remove Programs dialog box, click on the Add/Remove Windows Components option and wait for the Windows Components Wizard to start.

4. Once the Wizard has started. Look at the list of Windows components available, scroll down, and select Other Network File and Print Services.

5. Next, click on Details to see all the available options.

Windows 2000
Mac Support
Little Black Book

Gene Steinberg

Pieter Paulson

President, CEO
Keith Weiskamp

Publisher
Steve Sayre

Acquisitions Editor
Stephanie Wall

Marketing Specialist
Tracy Schofield

Project Editor
Tom Lamoureux

Technical Reviewer
Brad Harris

Production Coordinator
Wendy Littley
Meg E. Turecek

Cover Designer
Jody Winkler

Layout Designer
April Nielsen

Windows 2000 Mac Support Little Black Book

© 2000 The Coriolis Group. All Rights Reserved.

This book may not be duplicated in any way without the express written consent of the publisher, except in the form of brief excerpts or quotations for the purposes of review. The information contained herein is for the personal use of the reader and may not be incorporated in any commercial programs, other books, databases, or any kind of software without written consent of the publisher. Making copies of this book or any portion for any purpose other than your own is a violation of United States copyright laws.

Limits Of Liability And Disclaimer Of Warranty

The author and publisher of this book have used their best efforts in preparing the book and the programs contained in it. These efforts include the development, research, and testing of the theories and programs to determine their effectiveness. The author and publisher make no warranty of any kind, expressed or implied, with regard to these programs or the documentation contained in this book.

The author and publisher shall not be liable in the event of incidental or consequential damages in connection with, or arising out of, the furnishing, performance, or use of the programs, associated instructions, and/or claims of productivity gains.

Trademarks

Trademarked names appear throughout this book. Rather than list the names and entities that own the trademarks or insert a trademark symbol with each mention of the trademarked name, the publisher states that it is using the names for editorial purposes only and to the benefit of the trademark owner, with no intention of infringing upon that trademark.

The Coriolis Group, LLC
14455 North Hayden Road, Suite 220
Scottsdale, Arizona 85260

480/483-0192
FAX 480/483-0193
http://www.coriolis.com

Library of Congress Cataloging-in-Publication Data
Steinberg, Gene.
  Windows 2000 Mac support little black book / by Gene Steinberg and Pieter Paulson.
    p.   cm.
  Includes index.
  ISBN 1-57610-388-9
  1. Microsoft Windows NT.   2. AppleTalk.   3. Macintosh (Computer)   4. Local area networks (Computer networks)   I. Paulson, Pieter.   II. Title.
QA76.76.063S7368   2000
005.4'4769--dc21   99-43079
                                                              CIP

Printed in the United States of America
10 9 8 7 6 5 4 3 2 1

14455 North Hayden Road • Suite 220 • Scottsdale, Arizona 85260

Dear Reader:

Coriolis Technology Press was founded to create a very elite group of books: the ones you keep closest to your machine. Sure, everyone would like to have the Library of Congress at arm's reach, but in the real world, you have to choose the books you rely on every day *very* carefully.

To win a place for our books on that coveted shelf beside your PC, we guarantee several important qualities in every book we publish. These qualities are:

- *Technical accuracy*—It's no good if it doesn't work. Every Coriolis Technology Press book is reviewed by technical experts in the topic field, and is sent through several editing and proofreading passes in order to create the piece of work you now hold in your hands.

- *Innovative editorial design*—We've put years of research and refinement into the ways we present information in our books. Our books' editorial approach is uniquely designed to reflect the way people learn new technologies and search for solutions to technology problems.

- *Practical focus*—We put only pertinent information into our books and avoid any fluff. Every fact included between these two covers must serve the mission of the book as a whole.

- *Accessibility*—The information in a book is worthless unless you can find it quickly when you need it. We put a lot of effort into our indexes, and heavily cross-reference our chapters, to make it easy for you to move right to the information you need.

Here at The Coriolis Group we have been publishing and packaging books, technical journals, and training materials since 1989. We're programmers and authors ourselves, and we take an ongoing active role in defining what we publish and how we publish it. We have put a lot of thought into our books; please write to us at **ctp@coriolis.com** and let us know what you think. We hope that you're happy with the book in your hands, and that in the future, when you reach for software development and networking information, you'll turn to one of our books first.

Keith Weiskamp
President and CEO

Jeff Duntemann
VP and Editorial Director

Look For These Other Related Books From The Coriolis Group:

Windows 2000 Systems Programming Black Book
by Al Williams

Windows 2000 Registry Little Black Book
by Nathan Wallace

Windows 2000 Reducing TCO Little Black Book
by Robert Simanski

Windows 2000 Security Little Black Book
by Ian McLean

Also Recently Published By Coriolis Technology Press:

Access 2000 Client/Server Solutions
by Lars Klander

Java Black Book
by Steven Holzner

I wish to pay special thanks to my "muse" (she knows who she is) for always helping me to find the right things to say and the means to say it.

—Gene Steinberg

To my family, with without whose understanding this book would not have happened.

—Pieter Paulson

ᔰ

About The Authors

Gene Steinberg first used a personal computer while publishing a magazine in the 1980s and has never looked back. He originally studied broadcasting and worked for a number of years as a disc jockey and newscaster. Gene is now a full-time writer (of fact and science fiction) and computer software and systems consultant. He is the author of over a dozen books on computing, the Internet, and telecommunications. In addition, he has also written feature articles and product reviews for such magazines as *MacAddict, MacHome Journal, MacUser* and *Macworld*, and conducts a weekly segment for Craig Crossman's "Computer America" radio show on the Internet and strange and unusual computing tips.

Pieter Paulson is an experienced senior network engineer. He has managed Microsoft NT and Mac OS systems for over six years for several Fortune 100 corporations, including Nike. He has also provided extensive hardware system support to members of America Online, as a community leader in the service's Macintosh Hardware Forum. Paulson has received B.A. degrees in chemistry and English literature.

Acknowledgments

When I took on this project, I was under no illusions that it would be simple. Describing how complex computer operating systems can communicate with one another in an efficient, reliable manner was clearly a daunting task.

Thanks to a number of friends and colleagues, however, I was somehow able to get the task accomplished, and I hope you will find the results informative.

I would especially like to express praise to my co-author, Pieter Paulson, for agreeing to work with me on this project; his expertise and dedication to the arcane issues of networking were an inspiration to me. And I'd like to single out the expert staff at The Coriolis Group, including Stephanie Wall, Brad Harris, Tom Lamoureux, Wendy Littley, Meg Turecek, and April Neilsen, for seeing to it that what we wrote was both technically accurate and understandable to all of our readers.

And finally, a hearty thank you to my beautiful wife, Barbara, and my brilliant son, Grayson, for putting up with the long hours that I left them stranded as I labored on my keyboard to get this book out on time.

—*Gene Steinberg*

I would like to thank the following people for helping make this book a possibility: John "Bear" Stroud, David Swartz, Donna Sanclemente, Ilene Hoffman, Jim Galvez and Brian Chinn. I would also to thank Jeffrey Robbin, Judy Cziprian, Roman Kasan, Donald Beirdneau and Min Wang, all of whom have been of great help to me over the years. I also need to thank my co-author, Gene Steinberg, without whose drive and friendly persistence, this book would never have been written.

—*Pieter Paulson*

Contents At A Glance

Table Of Contents

Part II   Windows 2000

Chapter 6
Introduction To Windows 2000 And Mac OS Networking 167

Introduction

The scene is typical at offices around the world, both small and large.

You get a request from one of your department heads to purchase some Mac OS computers. However, your office's computer network is already based on Windows NT or Windows 2000.

Well, a personal computer is a personal computer, right? At least that's how the theory goes, but you've heard all the stories about Macs. They're difficult to set up on your network, they'll slow down performance, cause crashes, and tie up your office with endless hours of additional technical support issues. And then there are the questions about training your staff as well as buying and supporting hardware for that "other" platform.

And you've read all those news reports that Apple is an unstable company. What if they go out of business, leaving you with orphan computers that can't be fixed or upgraded?

Why saddle your business with all these uncertainties?

Is it really all worth it?

Myth Vs. Reality

The truth is that the Macintosh isn't going away. Apple Computer is not about to cease operations, and with its popular line of G3 and G4 Power Macintosh models, the stylish iMacs, iBooks and PowerBooks, these computers are showing up in more and more locales that previously shunned the Mac OS.

And Apple's growing profit margins, market share, and consistent operating system roadmap shows they are preparing themselves for a long, prosperous future.

Moreover, graphic designers and other content creators have traditionally preferred the Mac. While similar software may be found on the Windows platform, many users do not wish to give up their Macs.

And they don't have to.

Mac computers are perfectly capable of functioning at high efficiency in a mixed platform environment. As a matter of fact, Microsoft provides a rich array of tools designed to make it easy for you to configure your Windows NT/Windows 2000 computers to work just fine with Macs.

To the Mac user, in fact, the Windows computers will appear as just another computer on the network, readily accessible for print servers, file transfers, email and Internet access.

The Purpose Of This Book

Windows 2000 Mac Support Little Black Book is designed to demystify the process of configuring your Macs to function on your Windows NT or Windows 2000 network.

This book is designed for businesses large and small. The important elements of configuring your Macs and Windows computers to work in harmony will be outlined, step by step, complete with illustrations. There will also be extensive troubleshooting advice, so you know what to do in the event something goes wrong.

The Roadmap

The support issues for Windows NT 4.0 and Windows 2000 are different. In upgrading its premiere operating system, Microsoft has made a huge number of changes. Fortunately, some of those changes actually simplify the process of networking with Mac OS computers.

To make it easy for you to find the information you need, this book is divided into two parts. Part I covers how you can configure Apple to relate to Windows NT. Part II examines the Apple as it pertains to Windows 2000. In essence, what you have in your hands are two books in one.

Depending on whether or not you have deployed Windows 2000 in your company or you're sticking with Windows NT, you'll want to read Part I or Part II and the chapters that apply to your particular setup.

And, if you are planning to migrate from NT to Windows 2000, you'll be able to compare the two operating systems between Part I and

Part I and know what has changed in Microsoft's latest enterprise operating system and the preparations you'll need to make.

NOTE: *We have also provided an overview of the system-level security features that Apple has included in Mac OS 9. These features are extremely important, because they allow you to customize each Macintosh for individual users, and to block access of the System Folder and other components where necessary.*

Part I Windows NT 4

Part I includes five chapters that will take you through the process of mating your Windows NT 4.0 server with Mac OS computers.

- Chapter One is designed to cover the basic Windows NT services ("features") that support your Macs. You'll also learn about the common misconceptions about networking Macs and what the real facts are governing such setups.

- In Chapter Two, you'll receive easy instructions on how to set up the network for easy, transparent file sharing between the two platforms. You'll also learn how to set up network security as effectively as possible.

- Chapter Three will cover Windows NT 4.0 printing services, and how to make your network printers work seamlessly with your Mac OS computers.

- The arcane issues of managing an AppleTalk network are covered in Chapter Four. You'll also learn about setting up AppleTalk zones, giving each department in your office separate access to computers and printers.

- The final chapter in this section covers the setup of the Microsoft BackOffice environment, and covers Internet access, database exchange and how to use Microsoft Exchange for office and Internet email.

Part II Windows 2000

In Part II, you'll learn how to configure Windows 2000 to work with your Mac OS computers. The differences between Microsoft's newest operating system and Windows NT 4.0 will be described in each chapter, so you'll be able to quickly see the changes you need to make when you decide to upgrade to Windows 2000.

- Chapter Six is the Windows 2000 counterpart to Chapter One. You'll learn that the new Microsoft operating system offers new, Mac OS-friendly features that will help simplify the process of network management.

- In Chapter Seven, the basic steps to configure file sharing between your Windows 2000 server and your Macs are outlined. Mac OS security tools will also be covered.

- Chapter Eight covers printing services. You'll learn how to manage your printing workflow, and how to confront and solve problems should they arise.

- For Chapter Nine, you'll see how AppleTalk services are supported and how to configure your network servers to mate properly with your Mac computers.

- Chapter Ten covers integration of the BackOffice Environment under Windows 2000. You'll learn how to set up your Macs to interface with Microsoft Exchange, database software and how to handle Internet access.

Each chapter includes step-by-step setup instructions, as well as a complete set of troubleshooting tips, so if you run into any problems along the way, you'll find solutions that will help you cope.

Throughout the book, you'll be introduced to some new terms, so we've added a Glossary at the end, so you can get immediate practical definitions for the arcane, mysterious terminology that describes how to setup a personal computer network.

NOTE: *In order to get this book out in time for the official releases of Windows 2000 and Mac OS 9, we used prerelease versions of these operating systems. It's possible that some setup screens and even some setup procedures may differ in some minor respect between these versions and the final releases. However the basic instructions and troubleshooting steps will be as accurate as we can make them, and we've done our best to check into possible changes before this book went to press.*

How To Use This Book

Windows 2000 Mac Support Little Black Book is not necessarily meant to be read as a novel, from cover to cover (although we don't mind if you choose to do so). Instead, you'll probably want to read the chapters that specifically cover the tasks you wish to accomplish.

Each chapter includes an *In Brief* section, where you can learn the basic background information that covers the subject at hand. From there, the *Immediate Solutions* section will give you the step by step setup information and troubleshooting procedures you need to solve a specific problem or accomplish a specific purpose.

Working on a book of this sort is an ongoing process of learning, testing and discovering new insights into the very complex process of integrating computing systems with two different operating systems.

We welcome your comments, be they criticisms or compliments. Feel free to share your personal experiences and "war stories" with us. We'd like to consider them for possible future editions of this book.

Gene Steinberg
Scottsdale, AZ
email: gene@macnightowl.com
http: www.macnightowl.com

Pieter Paulson
Portland, OR
email: pieter@teleport.com

Part I

Windows NT 4

Chapter 1

An Introduction To Windows NT And Mac OS Networking

In Brief

Apple Macintosh computers are growing in popularity again, and more and more of these products are showing up in art departments and in front offices, running everything from desktop publishing software to the bookkeeping software required to manage your business. Although the Mac and Windows NT environments may have different rules, there's no reason to isolate Mac OS computers in the corner of the office or in a separate network. You shouldn't look at Mac OS computers as strangers or orphans when it comes to connecting them to your Windows NT 4 network. As we'll describe throughout this book, Macs are good corporate citizens; they provide great performance on your network as long as you follow a few basic setup choices.

Using Macintosh Support Options In Windows NT Server

Several Windows NT 4 services are designed to support the Macintosh in an NT environment. Other services are not designed to provide such support; however, you can use them if you follow some simple setup procedures. We will cover these support services in the remainder of this book—step-by-step—so you'll see exactly what you have to do to make them work properly. In addition, you'll discover troubleshooting tips and tricks that will help you quickly overcome problems as they arise.

The first services you'll want to become familiar with are known as Services for Macintosh. Under the Services for Macintosh banner, you'll find three basic features: File Services for Macintosh, Print Services for Macintosh, and AppleTalk networking.

Using File Services For Macintosh

File Services for Macintosh is a Windows NT 4 feature that allows Mac OS computers to easily log on to NT servers and mount Macintosh-enabled server volumes. You can then use these volumes to store your files and applications seamlessly on an NT server, as you would on your local Mac computer.

With File Services for Macintosh, Windows NT also allows you to set very specific file permissions so that you can prevent unauthorized use of your files; you can even track who used what file and when. In addition, Windows NT allows you to store all your critical Macintosh data in a central location where you can be assured that it will get backed up regularly. You will learn more about these features in Chapter 2.

Supporting Printers

Print Services for Macintosh lets your Macintoshes connect to and share printers that are attached to the Windows NT 4 network. You can select printers in the Chooser, just as you do when printers are connected directly to a regular Mac network.

The printing services that Windows NT provides allow you to access any PostScript-capable printer connected to your network. You can set up printing queues on the server to allow you to select among multiple paper sources; you can even set up a whole bank of printers that can be configured to appear as a single entry in the Mac OS Chooser. Windows NT also allows you to control your print jobs and prioritize them so that critical jobs are printed out first, whereas jobs of lesser importance are put on hold until the printer is free. You'll read about these features in more detail in Chapter 3.

Using AppleTalk Zones

AppleTalk networking support lets you establish AppleTalk zones for your network, and route AppleTalk traffic across the network. You can use this feature to connect multiple Macintosh network groups. These groups have separate zones, each of which can be restricted by password. This arrangement allows users in that group to efficiently share files and print documents without having to be aware that other computers and printers are on the network.

The ability to seed AppleTalk zones and route AppleTalk over the corporate network is also a major tool in helping tie together many disparate groups of Mac users over the network. If you create a zone, a Windows NT Server can connect a group of Mac computers, perhaps representing a single department in your organization. This allows them to easily share resources. By letting you route AppleTalk over the corporate network, Windows NT allows you to manage all of these various Macintosh groups. As a result, these groups can efficiently communicate across the network, and you can create the proper range of access privileges. Chapter 4 will cover this subject in complete detail.

A Quick Review Of Other Windows NT Services

Mac users can also use many different services offered by Windows NT Server to provide needed resources. With a little work, you can use Windows NT to provide everything from automatic Internet Protocol (IP), address configuration via a Dynamic Host Configuration Protocol (DHCP) server to using a Domain Name System (DNS) server to provide name resolution for accessing your corporate intranet. In addition, you can use Windows NT services, such as Microsoft Exchange and Proxy Server, to provide email services and Internet access to all of the Mac users in your environment. Here's a list of some of these services, which will be described in more detail in upcoming chapters:

- *DHCP*—This is a quick and easy way for you to distribute IP addresses to the various PCs and Macs on your network without having to visit each workstation. By configuring the DHCP server under Windows NT, you can have the DHCP server automatically distribute key network configuration information whenever users reboot their computers.

- *DNS*—This is another service that allows your Mac, in the background, to link a server's name to its IP address. By setting up the Windows NT DNS service, you can provide your Macs with a way to resolve the names of internal Web servers and other intranet resources for easy access across the network. You can also configure your Windows NT name servers to resolve names of servers on the Internet.

- *Microsoft Exchange*—This is one of the most powerful email systems available today and forms part of the core of Microsoft's BackOffice suite. Mac users can now take advantage of this great tool by using the Macintosh Exchange client that is included with Service Pack 2 (SP2) for Exchange 5.5. This tool allows both your PC and Mac users to share a common email infrastructure, saving you time and money.

- *SQL Server*—This is another part of the Microsoft BackOffice suite that Macs and Mac-based applications can easily utilize. By using the Open Database Connector (ODBC) data connectors, you can connect your FileMaker databases to SQL Server backends to enhance the capabilities of your database applications. You can also use SQL Server to augment other applications by providing them access to the databases that it houses.

- *BackOffice Microsoft Proxy Server*—This is another component of the BackOffice suite. You can use it to offer Internet access to your Macintosh clients. Proxy Server can be used as both a caching proxy (storing already retrieved Internet files locally) to speed up Internet access. As a security measure, you can also set up a firewall to help protect your network from unwanted intrusions. Proxy Server supports Macs via its standard Web proxy and by a socks-compliant proxy.

- *Applications such as DAVE (from Thursby Software Systems, Inc.) and MacLinkPlus Deluxe (from DataViz, Inc.)*—These allow Mac users on your network to seamlessly share data with their Windows counterparts. Mac users can easily collaborate and share data even if there is no support for Macs on the Windows network or a Mac version of a Windows program that you're using. Such tools can help a small group of Macs integrate themselves seamlessly into a larger Windows-based network. If Mac file translation of a Windows document isn't an efficient way to go, you can consider Connectix's Virtual PC and FWB's Soft Windows. These programs create Windows environments on a Mac and let you run most of your Windows programs with good compatibility, though at reduced performance levels.

Immediate Solutions

Debunking Common Myths About Mixing Macs And PCs

When Macs are first proposed for an office computer setup, objections to their presence—sometimes vociferous ones—may be raised. Some of these objections make sense because a new computer operating system and hardware may require additional support services and training. However, there are also a number of misconceptions about the presence of Macs on your network. Here are some of those misconceptions and the real facts:

- *Macs slow down Windows NT Servers*—In the old days, this was somewhat true. Macs would keep requesting information updates from the server that housed their remote volumes. These days, however, servers are much faster and the Mac clients do not request as many updates from the server.

- *AppleTalk clutters up the network*—In a poorly run network, AppleTalk traffic can cause some degradation of network performance. This is because AppleTalk is a "chatty" protocol, meaning that information is sent in lots of small packets, which ties up a greater percentage of network capacity than other network protocols, like IP. However, by setting up either dedicated routers, from Cisco Systems and other companies, or using properly configured NT Servers, you can limit the amount of AppleTalk traffic that is placed on the network. We will discuss this topic in more detail in Chapter 4.

- *Macs and PCs have trouble sharing files*—In the last few years, Mac and Windows versions of the same application have generally used the same file format. For example, the file format of a file created with Office 97 on a Windows NT workstation is virtually identical to that of a document created by a Mac running Office 98.

WARNING! *The introduction of Office 2000 has changed the compatibility equation, however. Although the file formats are the same, some of the custom formatting of an Office 2000 document will be lost when opened in Office 98 for the Macintosh. Among the features lost are Office 2000's advanced table and graphic handling capabilities. A comparable Mac version, possibly called Office 2001, is expected during the second half of 2000.*

- *You cannot share parts between Macs and PCs*—In reality, Macs and PCs can share a large number of components. Hard drives, CD-ROMs, removable devices (such as Zip drives), scanners, monitors, and a wide variety of Universal Serial Bus (USB) peripherals can be used on both platforms with little or no configuration changes. At worst, you may have to install new driver software when switching from one platform to the other.

- *Macs have to use Services for Macintosh to share files*—Actually, this isn't so. Macs using DAVE can easily connect to and authenticate with Windows NT Servers without the need for Services for Macintosh to be installed. These programs help you simplify cross-platform setups in a small company.

- *Macs are too hard to manage on a network*— Macs do not have all the network management tools available to Windows clients. However, you can use several utilities to help automate management of the Mac clients. We will discuss these in Chapter 4.

- *Macs have poor security features*—Many of the more conservative administrators believe that because you cannot limit access to the Mac operating system, Macs are inherently much harder to maintain. The reality is that Macs are far more resistant to user damage than are their Windows cousins because the Mac OS is not subject to major changes when you add or remove software. In addition, you can easily configure a number of Mac security programs to limit access to disks, files, and directories. Moreover, the newly released Mac OS 9 is designed to offer robust system-level security and file encryption measures.

Utilizing Windows NT Service Packs To Fix Mac Service Conflicts

No major operating system ships bug-free. Microsoft periodically releases service packs to add new functionality or to fix bugs. The first three Windows NT service packs focused heavily on bug fixing, and a few features were added to improve performance in graphics and security. Very few of the fixes covered Mac networking. These fixes were designed to address problems that may result in the apparent lock-ups of Macs networked to the Windows NT Server.

Service Packs are available for download direct from Microsoft's Web site, where you can also locate information about the various changes and bug fixes. The list of the changes wrought by Service Pack 3, for example, can be found at **ftp://ftp.microsoft.com/bussys/winnt/winnt-public/fixes/usa/nt40/ussp3/readme.htm#1.1**.

Using Windows NT 4 Service Pack 4

Service Pack Four focused a bit more heavily than Service Packs 1 through 3 on adding new features, specifically some of the features that were planned for Windows 2000 but were ready for immediate release. For instance, Windows NT now supports the new NT File System (NTFS) file format as well as the new security paradigm that Microsoft is adopting for use in the forthcoming Windows 2000. However, as with Service Pack 3, Service Pack 4 includes quite a few bug fixes. Some of these updates address ac support issues. They include:

- *Server crashes when you run Services for Macintosh on a system on which McAfee Anti-Virus is installed*—The solution to this error requires installing Service Pack 4.

- *Commenting Macintosh file changes date and time stamp*—If you add, change, or delete a comment in the properties dialog box of a Macintosh file on a Windows NT 4 computer, the date and time stamps are changed. This occurs despite the fact that the change doesn't actually alter the file's contents. Service Pack 4 fixes this bug.

- *Macintosh change password fails on down trusted domain Primary Domain Controller (PDC)*—Despite this arcane language, the bug simply means that if you have multiple user domains on your network, you need to specify a domain name when you try to change a password from a Mac client computer. Otherwise, you'll see this error message: Your Password Could Not be Changed. Please Try Again Or See Your Server Administrator.

- *Macintosh clients see files on Windows NT Server constantly moving*—This is a cosmetic, but aggravating, bug. You look at a large list of files located on your Windows NT Server from a Mac, and the directory keeps refreshing itself. Until Service Pack 4 is installed, the best workaround is to keep as few files in a folder as possible.

- *Services for Macintosh may cause startup crash during high load*—This symptom, addressed by Service Pack 4, occurs with systems that include more than one CPU with Services for Macintosh installed. The actual error message would produce a System crash at startup, displaying the error "STOP 0x0000000a (parameter, parameter, parameter, parameter)".

- *Windows NT Explorer hangs when creating a new folder on a Mac volume*—The symptom is a temporary freeze, for about 10 to 20 seconds, when you type a new folder name on a local volume or a remote volume accessible to the Mac. Once the system performance is normal, you can rename the folder without further trouble. The bug is fixed with Service Pack 4.

- *Windows NT Services for Macintosh may not start in desired zone*—The symptom results in the computer choosing a network zone at random, rather than the one configured. Thus, the computers and printers on the proper network are not visible.

Although you may have chosen to stick with Service Pack 3 for compatibility (with the rest of your network) reasons, we recommend upgrading Windows NT 4 to Service Pack 4 for good compatibility with the Mac. You can find the complete list of fixes and feature improvements at **http://support.microsoft.com/support/kb/articles/q150/7/34.asp**.

Using Windows NT 4 Service Pack 5

Service Pack 5 for Windows NT 4 focuses primarily on bug fixes rather than on offering new features, which are largely saved for the arrival of Windows 2000. Another serious bug that was fixed in Service Pack 5 involves systems upgraded with Service Pack 4. After the update, Mac clients cannot see the NT Server on the network. This is one of the reasons why some companies have been reluctant to use Service Pack 4, despite the huge number of fixes that affect use of Windows NT. You will find more information on Service Pack 5 changes at **www.microsoft.com/ntserver/nts/downloads/recommended/sp5/updates.asp**.

Understanding Mac OS 9.0's New Level Of Security

Beginning with Mac OS 9.0, Apple has provided Mac users greatly enhanced security that will help systems administrators keep tabs on network use and access.

These features, in essence, amount to the return and enhancement of the old Keychain feature that was part of Apple's PowerTalk, which first came out in System 7.1.1 (sometimes known as System 7 Pro). In addition to standard username and password access, Apple is introducing a robust Voice Verification system, which provides a new level of system security.

In addition, Apple's Multiple Users Control Panel allows you to give each user a specific set of access privileges, which lets you restrict their use of applications, files, System Folder items and mounted disks (such as removable media).

We'll cover this subject in more detail in later sections of this book.

Chapter **2**

File Sharing

(continued)

In Brief

When the time comes for you to connect Mac OS computers to your Windows NT 4 Servers, you'll find that you already have the proper tools to make the process work successfully, with the minimum amount of fuss and bother. Windows NT 4 Services for Macintosh includes a series of related components that provide Windows NT Servers with the tools and options needed to support Macintosh users. These tools allow Mac users to take advantage of many of the resources that are available to their Windows cousins without the need for software emulators or client software. Services for Macintosh are divided between two basic functions: file sharing and print services, and AppleTalk Networking Services. We'll focus on file sharing in this chapter, print services in Chapter 3 and AppleTalk networking in Chapter 4.

After you install Services for Macintosh, you can create and share Macintosh file volumes on Windows NT-based Servers. Once you install and configure Services for Macintosh, the Mac users on your company's network can use the Windows NT Server as if it were just another Macintosh running AppleShare file server software. You can store applications and files as you would on any Mac-based server as well as take advantage of all the benefits that Windows NT offers.

In addition, by storing your Mac files on a Windows NT file server, you can easily share them with your Windows-based co-workers. Mac users also benefit from being able to have their data backed up in a central location as well as to restrict access to their files based upon Windows NT's advanced file access permissions. Mac users can also store and run applications from the Windows NT Server. Therefore, you don't have to add and remove seldom-used applications at individual workstations—which reduces support time and expense—because whenever you add a program on a personal computer, you risk (if slightly) creating new opportunities for software conflicts.

WARNING! You make an application available from the server rather than the client computer so that you can provide more efficient support services. However, your company must still buy multiple user licenses for software that is used on more than one computer. You should contact the appropriate publishers about their license policies so that you can decide whether to have a program accessed from a networked server.

Windows NT also enables Mac users to restrict the access that users on the network have to their files and folders as well as to create a log of who has been accessing those files. The Windows NT File System (NTFS) and permissions features allow you to set access rights. This lets you decide which users or groups of users have the rights to view or manipulate the files that they store on the server. You can consult your log for details about which users have been accessing these files and if and when they have been changing them.

NOTE: *Mac OS 9.0 offers improved system security that allows you to configure each Mac workstation to handle multiple users, and give each user a specific set of access privileges. We will cover some of these features later in this chapter.*

You can also use Windows NT Servers to provide printer sharing between Windows and Mac workstations. We will cover this subject in more detail in Chapter 3.

Overall, the Services for Macintosh feature available with Windows NT Server offers an excellent solution to the problem of integrating your Macintosh and Windows workstations. Windows NT file volumes provide a common file storage area, so the Mac and Windows users on your network will have access to the same documents. Many programs are available in Mac and Windows versions, so it's easier for users from both platforms to work together on individual documents if they have a central file source. In addition, it's a lot easier to perform regular backups of your mission-critical documents because they are accessible from a central location.

Using DAVE To Establish Easy File Transfers

DAVE, from Thursby Software Systems, Inc., is another handy tool that allows you to connect Macintoshes to Windows NT-based networks. It can be a time-saver, especially if you have a smaller network and wish to make the setup process as easy as possible.

Unlike Microsoft's Services for Macintosh, DAVE lets you communicate using Microsoft's Network Basic Input Output System (NetBIOS) protocol directly, allowing Macs to access file and print resources on the Windows network without making any changes to the servers on the network. Additionally, DAVE has integrated the Windows NT Challenge Handshake Authentication Procedure (CHAP), allowing you to properly authenticate users against the Windows NT Workgroup or domain security systems.

Services for Macintosh makes the Windows NT Server talk the language of the Macintosh—AppleTalk—whereas DAVE makes your Macs talk the language of Windows. With this setup, Macs are not confined to communicating with servers where Services for Macintosh are installed.

DAVE can access any Windows-based files or printers shared on the network; it's not limited to Windows NT workstations. You can access shared files from personal computers running Windows 95, Windows 98, or even Windows for Workgroups 3.11.

NOTE: *To browse all the resources in a specific Windows NT Domain or Windows Workgroup, you need to specify the name of the Domain or Workgroup in the NetBIOS Control Panel.*

Using DAVE, you can log in using your standard Windows Domain or Workgroup username and password and have them authenticate properly with the Windows Domain server or the Workgroup server using the secure Microsoft CHAP authentication protocol. This protocol encrypts the conversation that occurs between your workstation and the server when it checks to see if your username and password are correct.

As a result, Windows can maintain a high degree of security and you are protected from people snooping around on your network trying to steal passwords. DAVE also allows you to access resources on the network using an alternate username and password. This feature is extremely valuable because it allows you to connect to resources that you normally don't have access to by using an account that does.

NOTE: *The best passwords are those that look like words or phrases with eight or more letters that you can remember but are deliberately misspelled. They should include upper- and lowercase letters as well as numbers and special characters. A good example is Mac$RcOOI. If you create passwords of this sort, however, be sure to write them down and keep this copy in a safe location. You will need to refer to it later if a user forgets a password.*

The major downside to using DAVE is that you must separately install and configure it on every Mac that you wish to use to access your Windows network. Although this can be a support headache, it is usually less of an issue than using Services for Macintosh if you have only a small number of Macintoshes in your company.

2. File Sharing

Using MacLinkPlus Deluxe To Translate Windows Documents

The Mac users on your network can access Windows-based document files as easily as Mac files. But that's only half the battle. For the files to run, you need to have a Macintosh program available that can use them. In many cases, this isn't a problem. Microsoft Office 98 for the Macintosh can easily read files created by Office 97 for Windows and older. And the Mac versions of such popular programs as Adobe PhotoShop, Adobe Illustrator, and QuarkXPress translate quite well across platforms. The question gets complicated when you attempt to translate a file for which you don't have the application. Apple provides basic system-level features for file translation, such as PC Exchange, and for Mac OS 8.5 and later, File Exchange.

Every time you translate a document, you could lose some critical formatting information. At minimum, font selections change, simply because Macintosh fonts and Windows fonts (even with the same name) have different metrics (width spacing values). In addition, line breaks in your document may change. Other formatting elements of your document may change as well. Fortunately, there's a solution that addresses many of these problems. It's MacLinkPlus Deluxe, a clever program from DataViz, Inc. Apple even bundled a version of the program in some of its operating system versions. The Deluxe version adds a number of useful features that make the document conversion process more convenient. They include:

- *File viewing*—If you don't have a suitable application to review translated Windows documents, MacLinkPlus Deluxe includes its own file viewing feature. This works best with picture files, which can come in many formats.

- *File decompression*—Files that are compressed in Windows-based compression software, such as Zip, can be expanded to their original form.

- *Email file viewing*—An all-too-common problem is using the files attached to email messages. MacLinkPlus Deluxe makes it possible to restore the attachments to their original form for easy viewing.

Immediate Solutions

Installing Services For Macintosh: The First Steps

In order to install the Services for Macintosh, you need to add them to the list of Windows NT Network Services. These Services enable Windows NT Server to provide multi-platform support when communicating with the various computers on the network.

Follow these steps to quickly begin setting up Services for Macintosh:

1. Select Start|Settings|Control Panels. Alternatively, you can double-click on the My Computer icon located on your Windows NT 4 desktop and then double-click on the Control Panels folder, located in the My Computer window.

2. Double-click on the Network icon. Doing so brings up the Network Control Panel.

TIP: *A really quick way to open the Network Control Panel is to right-click on the Network Neighborhood icon that's located on your Windows NT 4 desktop. Then, select Properties from the drop-down menu.*

The Network Control Panel has several tabs. Clicking on these tabs allows you to reach the Services dialog box, where you add, remove, and control the various available networking options, briefly described here:

- *Identification tab*—This is shown in Figure 2.1. It shows you the name of the computer as well as the name of the domain or Workgroup it belongs to.

- *Services tab*—This shows you the different Services that you have installed. We will cover this tab in detail later in this chapter.

- *Protocols tab*—This is used to configure all of the various network protocols, like AppleTalk and TCP/IP or IPX/SPX that you have installed.

- *Adapters tab*—This is used to control the various network adapters that are installed in your server.

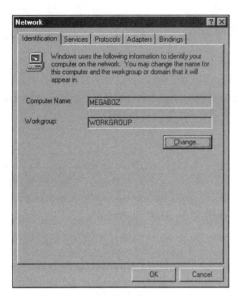

Figure 2.1   The Network Control Panel is used to configure your various network protocols.

- *Bindings tab*—This is where you can select which protocols are used or bound to each network adapter. For instance, you might find it useful to have two of your network adapters handle both TCP/IP and AppleTalk while having only TCP/IP on a third network adapter. This allows you to bind only some network protocols to some interfaces and thus to control what network protocols go out each network adapter. This can be extremely useful when you are setting up your network segments.

About Windows NT Network Services

Windows NT Network Services are various components that you can add to your Windows NT Server to provide the specialized features that you need. The Services that are installed by default when you install Windows NT Server are:

- *Computer Browser*—Talks to the other Windows NT Servers and NT or Windows 3.11, 95, and 98 workstations on your network and allows you to connect to them

- *NetBIOS Interface*—Allows for easy networking between Windows based-computers, much like AppleTalk does for Macintosh computers

- *Remote Procedure Call (RPC) Configuration Service*—Provides the tools needed to control the Locator and Security remote procedure calls that the server handles

- *Server Service*—Handles all of the options that are used to control how the server optimizes itself when serving up files

- *Workstation Service*—Is responsible for accessing remote servers and other workstations through Windows networking

Installing Services For Macintosh: The Next Steps

Once you have the Network Control Panel opened, follow these procedures to complete the installation of Services for Macintosh:

1. Click on the Services tab, shown in Figure 2.2. The Services installed on this server are the standard ones that Windows NT installs.

2. To add another NT Networking Service, click on Add, which brings up the Select Network Service screen. One Windows NT Service that is frequently installed is Windows Internet Name Service (WINS), which is used to reconcile a computer's

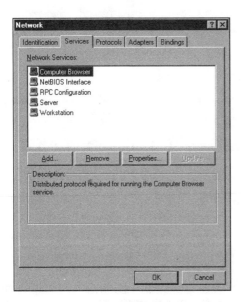

Figure 2.2   You can configure Network Services from this screen.

NetBIOS name to its TCP/IP address. Two other very popular options are Gateway Service and Client Service for NetWare, which allow Windows NT Servers to talk to NetWare servers and clients, much like Services for Macintosh offer support for Macintosh-based computers.

3. Select Services For Macintosh from the alphabetical list and click on OK.

4. To add another Service, click on Add again, select the Service that you desire, and then click on OK again.

5. When you are all finished selecting the Services you want to install, click on OK located on the Services dialog box.

6. NT next asks you for the location of the files needed to install the new Services. These are located on the Windows NT Server CD-ROM that you used to install the server originally. Insert the Windows NT CD-ROM into your server's CD-ROM drive and click on Continue. The NT Installer then displays the Services For Macintosh Setup dialog box, which updates you on the status of the installation of the various components of the Service you've selected.

NOTE: *To avoid the CD-ROM request, just copy the i386 or Alpha directory on the Windows NT Server install CD-ROM onto your hard drive. This way, you never have to hunt down an install CD-ROM when you want to install a new Service. Another good idea is to copy onto this server's hard drive the Installer for the latest Service Pack (SP) that you have installed. Doing so allows you to always make sure to reapply it after you have finished making changes to your server.*

Configuring Services For Macintosh By Adding AppleTalk Zones To Your Network

After all the Services files are installed, you are then asked to configure them. Figure 2.3 shows the default configuration dialog box for Services for Macintosh. Notice that Default Zone is blank. Once zones are added, you'll see the available choices listed in this display window.

AppleTalk Zones And Windows Workgroups Compared

AppleTalk zones are very similar to Windows Workgroups because they group the Mac computers on your network into a single, easily accessible group. However, unlike Windows Workgroups, AppleTalk

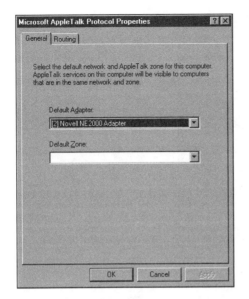

2. File Sharing

Figure 2.3   Use this dialog box to set up your configuration options for Services for Macintosh.

zones are assigned based on which portion of the network they are located. This means that you can select only from among those zones that are present on that section of the network.

Windows Workgroups, on the other hand, are assigned by the person that is configuring the workstation. In both the AppleTalk zone and the Windows Workgroup, all the shared resources that are available on the computers belong to that zone or Workgroup. Windows NT domains, on the other hand, are a type of super Workgroup that can include hundreds or thousands of computers, all coordinated by a single Windows NT Server known as a Domain controller. This arrangement allows for centralized user authentication and security management.

To add an AppleTalk zone to your network, follow these steps:

1. Click on the Routing tab, shown in Figure 2.4.

2. Click on the Enable Routing checkbox.

3. Click on Use This Router To Seed The Network.

4. Enter the appropriate value in the Network Range boxes. If you have only one AppleTalk zone, then enter "1" in both boxes. Otherwise, in the To column, enter a number that represents the total of the AppleTalk zones you're adding.

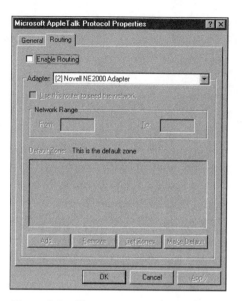

Figure 2.4   Choose your routing options from the Routing tab.

NOTE: *Network numbers are the numeric identifiers used for each zone. For example, you set up a network number range of 1 through 3 and then create corresponding zones. You can label them ZoneA, ZoneB, and ZoneC (or something that more clearly identifies the zones' purposes or locations). ZoneA is assigned network number 1, ZoneB is assigned network number 2, and so on. Zone numbers can range from 0 through 65,297 and must be coordinated so that no two routers or NT Servers contain the same network numbers.*

In old AppleTalk networks, called Phase-1, supported in Macs made before 1988, you could have only one network number per network segment and a maximum of 127 AppleTalk devices per network segment. In Phase-2 AppleTalk, which is supported by all the Macs you are likely to use, you can have from 1 through 65,297 zones per network segment. However, Cisco Systems (the largest manufacturer of network routers) recommends you set up a maximum of 50 zones for networks built using its products. In each Phase-2 AppleTalk network zone, you can have up to 253 AppleTalk devices.

---

5. Once you have entered the appropriate network numbers, click on Add to enter the zone name. Doing so brings up the Add Zone dialog box, in which you enter the name of your AppleTalk zone.

6. Once you have finished typing in the name of your zone, click on Add. Notice that the AppleTalk zone you added is now listed at the bottom of the screen shown in Figure 2.5.

7. To add additional AppleTalk Zones, repeat the procedure.

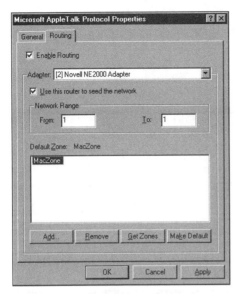

Figure 2.5 *The AppleTalk zone you've added is shown at the bottom of this screen.*

8. After you've added all the AppleTalk zones you wish, select the zone you want to be the Default Zone and then click on Make Default. Doing so causes that zone to become the one that your server uses.

Letting Windows NT Server Help You Find Existing AppleTalk Zones

If your network already has AppleTalk zones, you can click on Get Zones and have Windows NT Server automatically scan for all the available AppleTalk zones. The only limitation to this process is that Windows NT can see only those AppleTalk zones that are available on the same network segment as the server.

WARNING! Once you click on the Get Zones option, you see a warning dialog box letting you know that all the zones that you have entered will be replaced by any zones that Windows NT finds on the network. If you've already manually added AppleTalk zones to your network, you may prefer to avoid using this feature.

If no AppleTalk zones can be found on your network, Windows NT informs you that it cannot find any and asks you to verify your network configuration.

Finding Missing AppleTalk Zones

If you know that there are AppleTalk zones present on the network but Windows NT cannot find any, you most likely have a network-related problem. The most common cause of such a problem is a bad or poorly seated network cable. To check for this condition, follow these steps:

1. Look at the network adapter on your server to make sure that the Link light on the Network Interface card is on; this light indicates that the network connection is live.

2. If the Link light is visible, go into the Network Neighborhood window and check to see if you can locate any of the Windows-based computers on your network. If you can see other Windows-based computers, the problem may lie with either your Network Adapters settings or with something else on the network that is blocking the AppleTalk traffic.

Fixing Misconfigured Network Routers

The principal causes of missing AppleTalk zones are routers that are not configured to pass AppleTalk network traffic (packets). You need to make sure that AppleTalk routing has been properly enabled as well as whether you are trying to restrict AppleTalk traffic to only one segment of your network. If you are trying to connect to an AppleTalk device on another segment of the network, AppleTalk routing must be activated on all the routers between you and the remote segment. Otherwise, you won't be able to communicate with that device.

One way to configure routers to block specific AppleTalk traffic is to use access lists. You can configure these access lists to block specific network numbers, which are the numeric numbers used to represent a zone. Thus, if a router has an access list that blocks computers on your zone, you cannot connect to an AppleTalk device beyond that router.

Configuring Networks: The Next Stage

Once you get all of your AppleTalk settings properly configured, you need to restart your computer. To do so, follow these steps:

1. Click on OK to close the Network Control Panel.

2. In the Network Settings Change dialog box, click on Yes to restart your server.

3. After your Windows NT Server has completed the restart process, log in and then run the installer for the latest Microsoft Service Pack that you previously installed. You should be running Service Pack 3 at minimum; we recommend you use Service Pack 4 or Service Pack 5 instead. Each successive Service Pack generation includes bug fixes that are very important to making sure that the Services for Macintosh are robust and reliable. The need to be using an up-to-date Service Pack for Windows NT is covered in more detail in Chapter 1.

When the computer has completed restarting, Services for Macintosh start automatically. If they do not, you should first check Event Viewer, located in Start|Programs|Administrative Tools. Event Viewer has an entry that details the problem encountered when you try to start Services for Macintosh. This information should help you isolate the problem that caused the Services to fail on startup. The most common causes of the startup failure include incorrectly configured network number settings, the failure of another Networking Service, or—more rarely—a conflict with another Windows NT Service.

Installing Microsoft User Authentication Module (UAM)

If you want to use the Microsoft authentication system to allow for secure login to your Windows NT Server, you need to install the Microsoft UAM into the AppleShare folder, which is located in the Extensions folder inside the Mac's System folder. To install Microsoft UAM on your Mac, do the following:

1. Open the Chooser and click on AppleShare.

2. From the list of servers, select the Windows NT Server and click on OK.

3. From the list of shares, click on OK and then select Guest Access.

4. Open the Microsoft UAM Volume and then open the AppleShare folder within that volume.

5. Drag the Microsoft UAM file onto the System folder and when it informs you that this file needs to be placed in a special folder, click on OK. The file is placed in the correct location.

6. Restart your Macintosh.

Using The MacFile Control Panel

Once the Services for Macintosh have started up successfully, you will notice that several additions have been made to your Windows NT installation. For instance, in the Control Panels folder, you will now find a Control Panel named MacFile. You'll also find that the MacFile menu has been added to File Manager (we'll discuss the MacFile menu later in this chapter). The MacFile Control Panel, shown in Figure 2.6, provides the tools you need to administrate Services for Macintosh. Using this tool, you can monitor which Mac users are connected to the Windows NT Server, which files they have open, and how they are allowed to connect to the Windows NT Server. The buttons at the bottom of the MacFile Control Panel—Users, Volumes, Files, and Attributes—are used to provide additional information and control various aspects of network management.

Using The Macintosh Users Dialog Box

When you click on Users in the MacFile Control Panel, the Macintosh Users dialog box which shows you a detailed look at all of the users that are currently connected to your server, what files they have open,

Figure 2.6   Consult the MacFile Control Panel to check on the status of the Macs connected to your network.

and on what volume each file is located. You can use the tools in this dialog box to manage the network connections:

- *Disconnect and Disconnect All buttons*—These are very useful when you need to have all of your users get off the server and one user has kept a connection to your server open after he or she left. Although disconnecting a user in this manner can cause data loss, it is a useful tool if you cannot disconnect the user any other way.

- *Send Message button*—Allows you to send a message of up to 255 characters in length. This is very useful when you need to do maintenance on the server or make some other change that will cause users to lose access. By sending a message to all of the Mac users currently connected, you can warn them to close out of all the files they currently have open lest they lose them when you shut down the server.

Using The Macintosh-Accessible Volumes Dialog Box

When you click on Volumes, you see the Macintosh-Accessible Volumes dialog box, shown in Figure 2.7. This gives you another view of the volumes that are currently available on your server along with what users are currently connected and if they currently have files in use. As with the Macintosh Users dialog box, you have the option of disconnecting a single user or all the users from your server.

Using The Files Opened By Macintosh Users Dialog Box

As with the Macintosh-Accessible Volumes dialog box, clicking on Files affords you a view of which users are connected to your server and what files they have open. This dialog box also allows you to disconnect users from the files that they opened on the file server.

Figure 2.7   The Macintosh volumes on your network appear in this dialog box.

Using The Attributes Dialog Box

Clicking on Attributes brings up the Attributes dialog box, shown in Figure 2.8. This dialog box allows you to set a variety of session and security options on your NT Server. You can set the message, if any, that is displayed when a Mac user connects to your server as well as the various authentication options that are used when you allow a user to connect to the server. You can also limit the number of users that can connect at any one time as well as the name of the server that is displayed to your Mac clients.

The three security options available to Mac users are:

* *Allow Guests To Logon*—This option allows your Mac users to connect to the server as a guest. It is useful if you have an open server that is not protected by file permissions.

* *Allow Workstations To Save Password*—This option lets your Mac users save their usernames and passwords on their Macs when they connect to the server. Although enabling this option allows them to reconnect to the server easily, it represents a potential security risk because you cannot be certain that the user accessing the computer is the one authorized to do so.

* *Require Microsoft Authentication*—This choice tells the Mac to use Microsoft encrypted authentication when logging on to the server.

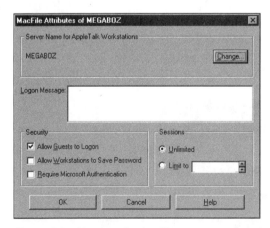

Figure 2.8   You can change file access settings in the Attributes dialog box.

Using The MacFile Menu In Windows File Manager

Another change that results from installing Services for Macintosh is that the MacFile menu is added to File Manager (see Figure 2.9). To run File Manager, select Start|Run, type "Winfile.exe", and then hit Return. File Manager is the old Windows 3.1/Windows NT 3.51 file management application; however, it is still quite useful under Windows NT 4 for managing your directory tree.

The new MacFile menu allows you to do the following:

- Create, modify, and delete Macintosh file volumes

- Set file permissions of the files and folders on those volumes

- Associate Windows file extensions to Macintosh file and creator types, allowing seamless access to PC files from your Macintosh applications

Creating A New Macintosh Volume From The MacFile Menu

To create a new volume for your Macintosh users, follow these steps:

1. Select the folder or volume that you wish to share.

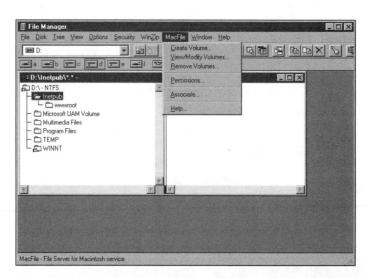

Figure 2.9   The venerable Windows File Manager returns with a new option, for managing Macs on your network.

2. Select Create Volume from the MacFile menu. The Create Macintosh-Accessible Volume dialog box, shown in Figure 2.10, appears. When setting up this volume, you should pick the various options that you want to use.

3. If you want just authorized users to connect to this volume, uncheck the Guests Can Use This Volume option.

4. To limit the number of Mac users who can connect to the server at any one time, click on the Allow radio button in the User Limit box and then set the number that you want to allow.

5. You can even set a special password for this file volume only. To do so, enter it in the Password text box. You'll need to retype the password in the Confirm Password text box to activate it. This special password is valuable only if you want to allow guests to connect to the file volume.

Viewing And Modifying Macintosh Volumes From The MacFile Menu

To view or modify an existing Macintosh volume on your server, simply follow these steps:

1. Select the View/Modify Volumes option under the MacFile menu, which brings up the View/Modify Macintosh-Accessible Volumes dialog box.

2. From this dialog box, select the Macintosh-Accessible volume that you want to examine or modify and then click on Properties. Doing so produces the Properties Of Macintosh-Accessible Volume dialog box.

3. As with the Create Macintosh-Accessible Volume dialog box described in Steps 3 through 5 in the previous section, the

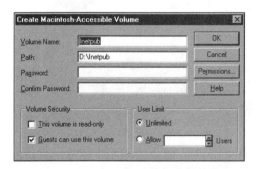

Figure 2.10 You can configure options for the selected Macintosh-Accessible volume in this dialog box.

Properties Of Macintosh-Accessible Volume dialog box allows you to set a Password, Volume Security, and User Limit for the listed volume. Enter your settings here before continuing.

4. Click on OK to store your settings, or click on Permissions to continue on to the next step and modify the access of your Macintosh-Accessible volume.

Setting Directory Permissions Of A Macintosh-Accessible Volume

The Macintosh View Of Directory Permissions dialog box (shown in Figure 2.11) is used to apply a very rudimentary set of file permissions on the Macintosh file volume. Unlike with a standard Windows file volume, you cannot have an unlimited number of users and groups in the Permissions list.

Mac permissions are limited to three groups. These are:

- *Owner*—The administrator(s) of the system

- *Primary Group*—The users specifically designated as having access to the Macintosh-Accessible volume

- *Everyone*—The remainder of the users on your network who can see the Macintosh-Accessible volume

Unlike with Windows, the granularity of the file permissions is significantly reduced because you have only a limited number of access settings. These settings allow you to permit or deny users from seeing files, seeing folders, or making changes. Additionally, you can lock the file volume so those who access the volume cannot move, rename, or delete files and folders.

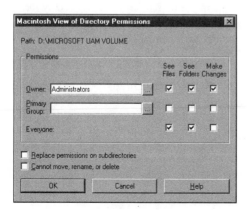

Figure 2.11   Use this dialog box to set permissions for the selected Macintosh-Accessible volume.

NOTE: *Although the permissions that you can set for the Mac appear to be very limited, they do not affect the permissions that you can set for your Windows clients. A good idea for administration purposes is for you to create a Windows Domain group with all of your Mac users listed in it. Then you can use this group or special groups of just a few Mac users to set the file permissions appropriately. For example, you might want to leave the Owner of a volume as the Administrators group and then set the Mac Users group as the Primary Group. As a result, you can deny access to the rest of the users on the network (those that fit the Everyone category), making sure that only the Administrators and Mac Users have access to the file volume.*

Removing Macintosh File Volumes

You can easily remove Macintosh files by following these steps:

1. Select Remove Volumes from the MacFile menu. Doing so displays a dialog box that lists the Macintosh-Accessible volumes on your server.

2. First, select the volume that you wish to delete and click on OK.

WARNING!   *Deleting the file volume in the Remove Macintosh-Accessible Volumes list does not cause the actual volume on the server to be deleted. This operation simply removes the volume from the list of resources available to Mac users. It is very important to make sure that you remove the Mac volume before you actually delete the volume from the server; otherwise, you can cause serious problems on the server.*

Associating Windows File Extensions To Macintosh File And Creator Types

The Associate dialog box, shown in Figure 2.12, is used to match up the three letter extensions used by Windows to tell which file belongs to which application and the file and creator types that are used on the Mac to perform the same function. You can even use this feature to map file types of applications that do not exist on the Mac onto applications that can read these types of files.

By default, the Associate dialog box should have most of the file associations you need. It is configured with many popular programs (such as Adobe Illustrator, Adobe PageMaker, Adobe PhotoShop, QuarkXPress, and Microsoft Office) with their Mac equivalents in mind. If you have a special-purpose program that has no Mac equivalent, you may choose an association of a Mac program that performs a similar function.

On the other hand, you may also wish to consider using Apple's PC Exchange (or File Exchange for Mac OS 8.5 and later) or DataViz's MacLinkPlus Deluxe to handle your file translations. We will cover MacLinkPlus Deluxe briefly later in this chapter.

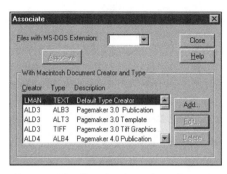

*Figure 2.12   Use the Associate dialog box to match up Windows file
extensions with the matching Macintosh applications.*

Installing DAVE

Installing DAVE involves many of the same steps as installing most
Macintosh software. To begin, you use the original installation disks
that come with DAVE or download the most recent version of the DAVE
Installer from Thursby Software Systems, Inc., at **www.thursby.com**.

NOTE: *If you are unsure whether to deploy DAVE across your Macintosh network, you may
want to try the time-limited demo version available at the publisher's Web site. If you do find it
useful, you can purchase a copy direct from the Web site.*

---

1. Double-click on the DAVE Installer icon to start the installation
   process.
2. Accept the license agreement to bring up the main Installer
   window, which is shown in Figure 2.13.

Figure 2.13   The DAVE Installer window.

3. From the install window, you can select Easy Install to install all of the DAVE components or Custom Install to just the compo-nents that you want. These components include the DAVE client components, the DAVE sharing, the DAVE access and messaging components, and the NetBIOS Control Panel. Unless there is a specific reason for only installing one or two of these compo-nents, we recommend the Easy Install (default) option.

4. Click on OK to perform an Easy Install.

5. Once all of the components have been installed, restart the Macintosh.

Configuring DAVE

After the Macintosh has completed restarting, you are ready to con-figure the program to recognize your Windows-based network. In or-der to configure DAVE, you need to have the following information:

• The NetBIOS name of the Macintosh.

• The Workgroup or domain that the Mac should be configured to use and whether you are using WINS or Dynamic Host Configura-tion Protocol (DHCP). WINS is a system that maps a computer's NetBIOS name to its IP addresses so that other computers can access it over the network. It is a Windows NT Service that you frequently find installed on Windows NT Domain controllers. DHCP is a system that automatically distributes IP addresses to the computers on the network. DHCP is another Windows NT Service that is commonly installed on Windows NT Domain controllers.

Once you have this information at hand, you're ready to configure DAVE, following these steps:

1. Open the NetBIOS Control Panel (located in the Control Panels folder). The first time you use the program, you'll enter the name and activation key information, which brings up the screen shown in Figure 2.14.

NOTE: Before opening the NetBIOS Control Panel, be sure you have configured the TCP/IP Control Panel to reflect the kind of network you are using, such as Ethernet built-in.

2. Enter the Macintosh's NetBIOS name and the Workgroup or Domain to which you wish the Mac to belong. You can also add a description of the Macintosh in the space provided.

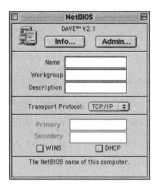

Figure 2.14   Use this Control Panel to configure DAVE to work on your Windows NT network.

3. Select TCP/IP as the desired transport protocol.

4. Depending upon your network, you may want to select the WINS and/or DHCP checkboxes. On most Windows NT networks, you should select only DHCP. If your DHCP server is not set to distribute WINS server information, you must select the WINS checkbox and then manually enter your primary WINS server's IP address and a secondary choice if it exists.

Related Solution:	Found on page:
Installing And Configuring DHCP	115

Using The DAVE Client

Using DAVE is very similar to mounting an AppleShare volume with the Macintosh Chooser or Network Browser application (which first appeared in Mac OS 8.5). You can mount Windows shared volumes by using either the DAVE client under the Chooser or the DAVE Access application (which can be easily accessed via the Apple menu). To connect to a Windows shared volume using the DAVE client, do the following:

1. Open the Chooser and select DAVE Client, which displays a screen similar to that shown in Figure 2.15.

2. Click on the name of the Windows computer that houses the shared volume that you wish to use and click on OK.

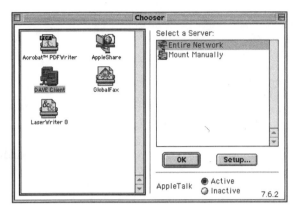

Figure 2.15   Choose your Windows-based volume from the list.

3. From the list of volumes available on the Windows-based computer, select the one that you want and click on OK. If you want to make the shared volume open when you restart your Mac, select the checkbox to the right of the volume's name.

4. Enter the username and password, as required.

NOTE: *If you are trying to connect to a hidden shared volume, click on Add Share once you have selected the Windows computer on which the volume is installed and then add the name of the shared volume.*

---

5. Close the Chooser.

The shared Windows volume that appears on your Mac's desktop is just another Mac volume, with files and folders readily accessible.

Using The DAVE Access Application

To use the DAVE Access tool to mount a Windows shared volume, do the following:

1. Launch the DAVE Access application from the Apple menu.

2. Click on the Mount Share icon on the DAVE Access toolbar.

3. Enter the name of the Windows computer and the shared volume that you wish to connect to. You can also enter a name that you wish to use for this volume, for easy identification.

4. Select the type of network communications that you wish to use to connect to the remote computer. Unless you must use TCP/IP, it is generally best to select NetBIOS.

The next two options allow you to disable the automatic update feature. This feature allows you to see changes that are made on the remote shared volume as well as to disable the creation of a desktop database file on that volume. Disabling the automatic update lessens the performance impact on the remote computer, but it does make it more difficult to see changes occurring on the remote volume. If you also disable the creation of the desktop database on the remote shared volume, your Mac is prevented from creating the two hidden desktop files that are used to map icons to the various file types.

5. If you need to log on to the Macintosh-Accessible volume with a different username and password, select the Use Alternative Credentials checkbox.

6. Enter the username and password that you want to use.

Accessing Your Windows Volumes From A Macintosh

Accessing a Macintosh-Accessible volume from your Macs involves the same basic steps you use when bringing up a networked disk via File Sharing:

1. Open the Chooser and select AppleShare.

2. Click on the name of the Windows computer that houses the shared volume that you wish to use and click on OK.

3. From the list of volumes available on the Windows-based computer, select the one that you want and click on OK.

4. Enter the username and password as required.

5. If you want to make the shared volume open when you restart your Mac, select the checkbox to the right of the volume's name.

6. Close the Chooser.

NOTE: *If you're using Mac OS 8.5 or later, you may also call up shared volumes, Macintosh- or Windows-based, using the Network Browser application. When you launch the application, which is available from the Apple menu, you'll see the listing of shared volumes that you can access.*

Installing DataViz MacLinkPlus Deluxe

DataViz MacLinkPlus Deluxe is a convenient solution to the problem of running Windows files on a Mac for which there is no matching program. The program comes with three different types of installers, depending on your purchase options. The boxed version includes either floppy disks or a CD. You may also purchase and download the installer file direct from the publisher's Web site at **www.dataviz.com**.

To install the program, follow these steps:

1. Place the installer CD or floppy disk in your drive, if this applies. If you downloaded the installation software from the publisher's Web site, locate the installer application.

2. Double-click on the Installer application.

3. Enter your name and company information, and the registration number and activation key provided by the publisher.

4. Follow the prompts to continue the installation.

5. Once the installation of MacLinkPlus Deluxe is complete, restart your Macintosh.

Setting Up MacLinkPlus Deluxe For Convenient File Transfers

Once the program is installed, you may simply launch the MacLinkPlus application by double-clicking on it to translate available files. But the easiest method is simply to let the program do its work automatically, by following these steps:

1. Locate and double-click on the Windows file you want to translate.

2. You will see a dialog box that lists available file translation options. Choose an application from the list that includes the words "with MacLinkPlus translation". MacLinkPlus Deluxe goes to work translating the file to an appropriate Macintosh format and then the document is opened in the selected application.

NOTE: If you have a number of similar programs with which to open a Windows file (such as several word processors), you should choose the one that you use most often. Another option is to use the Mac equivalent of the Windows program, if available (such as Office 98 for the Macintosh to open an Office 97 for Windows file). Use desktop publishing, graphic, or spreadsheet programs to open files in those formats.

TIP: *Mac OS 8 and later offer a great feature, Contextual Menus, which is basically borrowed with some changes from the Windows right-mouse menu feature. You can quickly call MacLinkPlus Deluxe into operation in a selected file by holding down the Control key and then clicking to bring up the Contextual Menu. Then choose Send To MacLinkPlus.*

Controlling File Access With Mac OS 8.0 File Security Options

Users running Macintosh OS 8.0, 8.1, 8.5, 8.5.1, and 8.6 have a small number of security options that they can use to limit access to shared volumes and folders. While these security options are very limited in their scope, they are capable of protecting your files from unauthorized users. When comparing file security under Macintosh OS to Windows NTFS file security, the first thing that you will notice is that you have far fewer choices in the number of users and the types of file access that you can assign.

By selecting the icon of the folder or volume that you are sharing, and the clicking on the File menu and selecting Sharing from the Get Info sub-menu, you can see all the security settings on the shared volume or folder, (see Figure 2.16). Unlike Windows NTFS file security where you can grant different access rights to a large number of users and groups, under Macintosh OS 8.x, you are only able to grant rights to

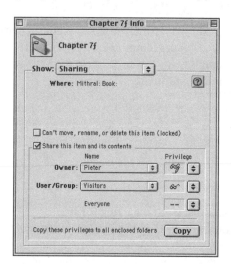

Figure 2.16   The Get Info window shows you the various security options that you have set.

the owner of the file or folder, a group of users defined on the Macintosh, and everyone. While this is considerably more limiting than the options available to you when using Windows NT with NTFS, it does give you the basic tools that you need to protect your files.

Looking at the type of access that you can set on files using Macintosh OS 8.x, you will see that you can give users read and write access, read only access, write only access, and no access. Another limitation of Macintosh OS 8.x file security is that you are only able to set permissions on shared volumes and the folders that are on them or upon folders that you share by themselves. This means that you must build your security policy around the folders and volumes and not individual files like you can under Windows NT using NTFS security.

One other option that is available to you, is the ability to prevent users connecting to the volume or folder from moving, deleting, or renaming it. This gives you a bit more security for your files and volumes that you choose to share. To prevent folks from moving, renaming, or deleting your volumes, or folders, select the volume or folder and then select Sharing from under the Get Info sub-menu located under the File menu. Looking at the Sharing portion of the Info dialog box for the folder or volume, click on the "Can't move, rename or delete this item (locked)" check box.

Using Mac OS 9.0 File Security Options

For Mac OS 9.0, Apple has introduced a robust set of system security tools that make it possible to provide a greater degree of control over the files and Mac volumes (including removable devices) the Mac users on your network can access and manipulate.

In this section, we'll introduce you to the new features of Mac OS 9. These features are expected to be continued and expanded when Apple moves towards its industrial-strength operating system, Mac OS X client.

Keychain Access

This feature allows you to establish a secure place for user password information. This information includes keys, passwords, and certificates. You can use this feature to attach a digital signature to such things as email and files. Once the digital signature is attached, the document cannot be opened until you enter the correct user password.

Here's how you go about creating a keychain:

1. Click on the Apple menu, select Control Panels, and choose the Keychain Access Control Panel.

2. If you haven't already made a keychain, you'll see a prompt asking if you wish to make one. Click the Create button.

NOTE: *If you've previously created a keychain, you'll want to click the Cancel button, then go to the File menu and choose the New Keychain command.*

---

3. Type in the new information for your keychain, then click the Create button. Be sure to follow our suggestions about creating and keeping a record of the passwords you create. Your first keychain will become your default.

4. If the program you're using supports the keychain feature, you can add items to the keychain from within the program. But you should not expect to find this feature available too often, as very few Mac programs support keychains (it'll be obvious from the program's documentation or the presence of a login dialog box).

Multiple Users

You can customize the user experience for each person who works on a specific Mac. This feature gives you full control over their access to applications, files, folders, System Folder items, and mounted volumes.

Here's a brief description of how to create a custom user profile under Mac OS 9:

1. Click on the Apple menu, select Control Panels, and choose Multiple Users from the sub-menu. This brings up the Control Panel shown in Figure 2.17.

2. If it's not already turned on, click the On radio button under Multiple User Accounts. If you leave it unchecked, the multiple user features will not operate.

3. To select global access features for the users on this Mac, click the Options button, which brings up the screen shown in Figure 2.18.

4. Choose your Log-in settings by checking the appropriate box.

5. If you wish to grant you or your users Voice Verification, check the "Allow Alternate Password" option. You'll be asked to speak your password, then repeat it for verification.

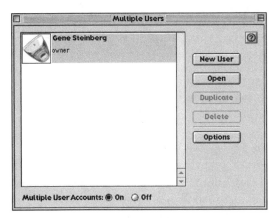

Figure 2.17   The name you entered when you set up this Mac is shown is the "owner."

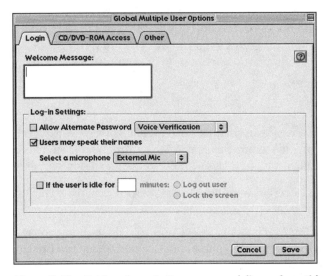

Figure 2.18   Set Log-in and other access privileges from this screen.

NOTE: *In order to use the Voice Verification feature of Mac OS 9, you need a Mac with a built-in mike, or one of Apple's so-called "PlainTalk" microphones, which are provided with almost every recent model.*

6. To restrict access to specific CDs and DVD-ROMs, click the appropriate tab and mount and choose the volumes to which you wish to provide access.

7. Click the Other button to access additional setup features, such as the ability to allow guest accounts, notification when new applications are installed, and whether or not users can select their own passwords.

8. To add users to this Macintosh, click the New User button, which brings up the screen shown in Figure 2.19.

9. Enter a User Name and Password in the text fields.

10. Click on the icon representing the appropriate user account. Here are some of the options a Normal account gives you:

   • You can, if you wish, prevent the new users from changing their own passwords.

   • The user's ability to manage similar accounts can be restricted.

   • You can limit access by others to the user's documents.

NOTE: *Apple provides a choice of several dozen custom pictures to be attached to a user's account. Just click the up and down arrows to pick the ones you like. You can also drag and drop small graphic files to the New User screen to provide additional choices.*

---

11. If you wish to restrict a user's access even further, click either the Limited or Panels icon, which will bring you to the Applications screen shown in Figure 2.20. These two account choices give you a much wider range of restrictions.

12. Once the applications to which a new user has access have been checked from the scrolling list, click on the Privileges button to control additional levels of access. See Figure 2.21 for a typical example.

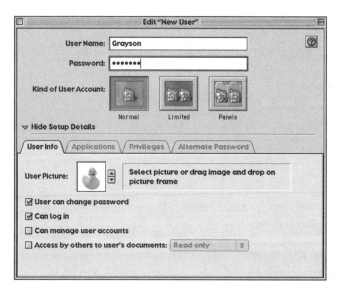

Figure 2.19   You can create a New User on this setup screen.

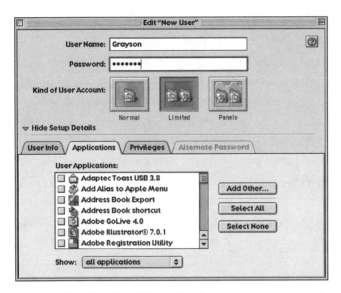

Figure 2.20   Specify which applications a user can access from the scrolling list.

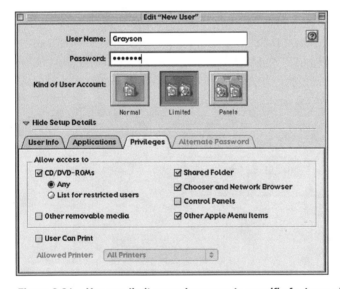

Figure 2.21   You can limit a user's access to specific features via this screen.

13. Click the appropriate checkboxes to select specific user privileges. Here's a brief description of what's available.

   • Access to CDs and DVD-ROMs can be restricted. The owner of the Macintosh (usually the system administrator) can provide a list of accessible disks, as explained in Step 6.

- Access to shared folders, printers, and networked volumes can be limited.

- You can also restrict access to Control Panels and other items in the Apple Menu.

14. Once you've made your settings for a specific user, click to close the box to activate those settings.

When you or another user finishes using that Mac, just choose Logout from the Finder's Special menu. If another user wishes to work on that Mac, he or she will have to pick his or her username from the list and enter (or speak) the correct password when the prompt appears.

If you choose to Restart or Shut Down the Mac, the username selection screen will appear after the Mac has completed its normal startup routine.

Troubleshooting Services For Macintosh

Troubleshooting Services for Macintosh can be broken down into two major areas: problems with authentication and file access problems. Authentication problems are usually the result of people forgetting their passwords or having their passwords expire without their realizing it. File access problems generally focus around problems with user access rights and the configuration of the Windows server that is running Services for Macintosh. In the next two sections, we have outlined common problems and their solutions.

Dealing With Macintosh Users Who Cannot Log In To The Server

The first question you need to ask when you have a Mac user who cannot log into a server is: "Can anyone log into this server?" If the answer is yes, you should check to see if the user can log into any other NT Servers on the network. If not, then the problem is most likely due to the login privileges that are set on the NT Server in question.

If the logon permissions are preventing the user from connecting, then you should use Windows File Manager to examine the permissions on the specific Macintosh-Accessible volume, following the steps described earlier in this chapter.

Check to see that the permissions are set correctly. If those in the Everyone category can connect to this volume, be sure that permissions are set appropriately. If this is a secure server, be certain that the user in question is a member of one of the two Windows Workgroup or Domain groups that have permission to log in to the Macintosh-Accessible volume.

If the user cannot connect to any other NT Server, then it is likely that the user has forgotten his or her password or used the wrong password, or the password has expired.

On the other hand, if the user is certain that he or she has not forgotten or mistyped the password, you should follow these steps to ascertain the problem:

1. Open the Windows NT User Manager For Domains tool.

2. From this User Manager For Domains dialog box, locate the user's account and make sure that the password has not expired and that the account has not been disabled due to too many failed logon attempts.

3. If the user has simply forgotten his or her password, consider just resetting it to the default one used on your network and then click on Must Change Password to force the user to change it when he or she logs in next. If the user cannot log in using the default password, check his or her keyboard to make sure that the CAPS LOCK key is not depressed and that it is functioning correctly.

Another common problem that you may see occurs only when you are using Microsoft authentication for logon. If a user reports that he or she is allowed to log on only as a guest and that the Registered User radio button is grayed out, you should check to see if the user has the Microsoft UAM option installed on his or her Macintosh. If it is not, install the Microsoft UAM module (following the steps described earlier in this chapter) and have the user restart his or her Mac.

Dealing With Macintosh Users Who Cannot See Servers Or Files

When a user is having trouble, you first need to determine if this is a problem seeing a specific server and its resources or if it is a problem seeing or accessing files on an NT Server. Here are some basic problems and solutions:

• *If users cannot locate a specific Windows NT Server or its Macintosh-Accessible volumes*—You should see if the server is currently available. If the server is functioning properly, then you will need to narrow down the problem a bit more.

- *If the server can be seen, but certain Macintosh-Accessible volumes aren't visible*—You need to use Windows NT File Manager to examine the volumes on that server to make sure they are all active. Check to make sure that all the shares are currently active and that the folders on the volume are present and located where they should be. If they are not, you should delete the existing Macintosh-Accessible volume and re-create it following the steps described earlier in this chapter.

- *If everything looks normal, but users cannot see the file share*—Delete the Macintosh-Accessible volume from the server and re-create it. If you still have trouble, try deleting the volume again and then create it with a new name.

- *If the user cannot see a specific server*—You need to determine if everyone is having this problem. If other users cannot see this server, you have to determine if this is a problem with AppleTalk or if the server is having connectivity problems. If you can see the server from a Windows-based workstation, you should go to the server and check its AppleTalk configuration. Make sure the AppleTalk zones are set correctly and that the Default Zone has not changed. If these settings are not correct, reset them to your preferred settings and restart the server.

- *If the AppleTalk configuration and Default Zone are all set correctly*—You should check with other members of your network team (if this applies) to make sure that they haven't made any changes to your network configuration that might cause this failure. If no network problems are blocking the server from reaching the Macs, you should try rebooting the server. If rebooting your server does not fix the problem, then try removing and reinstalling Services for Macintosh.

- *If a user is not able to see a file or folder on a Macintosh-Accessible volume*—This problem is almost always tied to the access permissions granted on the file server. The first thing that you should check when a user is having problems accessing a file or folder on a Windows NT Server is the actual file permissions you have granted on the affected volume. You should make certain that these users can see the files and folders they should see and that proper access rights have been granted. In particular, you should determine if users are members of the appropriate groups and that they are logging on using the proper accounts. If users have multiple NT accounts, then it is very easy for them to find themselves unable to access certain files simply because they are logged in using the wrong account.

2. File Sharing

- *When users attempt to save files using the short, 8.3 Windows file names*—This refers to the fact that older versions of Windows, pre-Windows 95, could only handle names that were 8 characters long followed by a period and then the three-letter file extension. Windows NT Services for Macintosh blocks Mac users from seeing the 8.3 names of files if they also have long file names. If you try to save a file with an 8.3 file name from your Mac that matches the hidden 8.3 name of another file, Windows NT will refuse to allow the file to be saved. If this happens, try changing the eight-character name slightly and see if the document can be saved in the normal fashion.

Chapter 3

Printing

In Brief

A Brief History Of Networked Printers

In the not so recent past, when you wanted to print a document, you had to either purchase a separate printer for each computer in your office or put your file on a disk and take it over to a computer that had a printer attached to it. As computer networks became more pervasive, it became less and less necessary to have a printer on every computer. By sharing a single printer among multiple computers, all connected by a network, you could purchase larger, more advanced printers that could handle the printing needs of an entire workgroup, not just those of a single person. These days, it is common for one or more large printers to be available on the network, allowing users to choose between printer types (such as color and monochrome). You can also easily take advantage of specific options that one printer may have (such as *duplexing*, the ability to print on both sides of the paper in a single operation).

In Chapter 2, you learned how to configure your Windows NT Servers to share files with the Macintosh computers on your network. You also discovered some handy utilities that make such file transfers more seamless. These include DAVE (from Thursby Software Systems, Inc.), which lets your Macs access files from a Windows network without special configuration, and MacLinkPlus Deluxe (from DataViz, Inc.), which simplifies the translation of files created with Windows applications for use on the Macs in your company.

In this chapter, we will discuss the various available options that allow you to share printers between Windows and Windows NT computers and those running the Mac OS. We will also describe another useful option that will help simplify the process, again employing the resources available through DAVE. This program makes it easy for your Macs to access PostScript printers available via your Windows NT network. As an added bonus, DAVE can allow you to make printers that are connected to your Macintosh available to users on the Windows NT network.

As you will see in the following pages, the process of sharing printers among computers running the Mac OS, Windows NT, and Windows 95/98 is pretty straightforward. Sharing printers helps you better utilize your network's printing resources by speeding up performance and lessening the need to purchase extra output devices.

Immediate Solutions

Setting Up A Printer Under Windows NT Server

To create a printer that both your Windows-based clients and your clients running the Macintosh OS can access, complete the following steps:

1. Click on Start|Settings|Printers.

2. From the Printers window, double-click on the Add Printer icon. This brings up the screen shown in Figure 3.1.

3. Once the Add Printer Wizard has finished launching, click on Next.

TIP: *Throughout the installation process, you can refer to a previous setup by using the Back button (when it isn't grayed out).*

---

4. At this point, you choose between a printer that is locally connected to your server or one that is connected to a remote server. This server is the one with Services for Macintosh installed, so you should select a printer that is locally connected. Refer to Chapter 2 for more information on setting up Services for Macintosh.

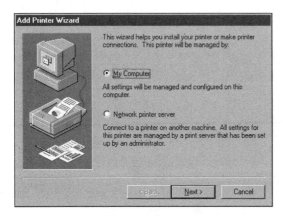

Figure 3.1   *The Add Printer Wizard program is used to configure your printer settings.*

NOTE: *Specifying that a printer is locally connected simply means that you have specified that your server is in control of the printer and its associated output queue. The printer can be located across the building, on another floor, or next to the server, attached by a standard printer cable, and still be considered "locally connected."*

5. The next screen of the Add Printer Wizard asks you to choose the port to which you will connect your printer. If the printer is directly connected to the server by a serial or parallel cable, select the appropriate serial or parallel port. If you are connecting to a network-based printer, select Add Port and configure it to connect to your network printer.

NOTE: *Serial printer connections are very similar to those you use when hooking up your PC to a modem. Serial ports send data one character at a time. As a result, they can be slow in transferring your data to a printer. Parallel ports, on the other hand, transfer a whole word at a time and thus are much faster than serial connections at moving data. On Windows NT-based servers, serial ports are listed as COM ports, of which there are normally four. Parallel ports are referred to as LPT ports, and there are normally only two of these on a server. When creating a network-based port, all you are really doing is creating a virtual port on the NT Server to which the printer resources can be linked. You then configure this port to have a network connection between the server and the network-based printer that you wish to control.*

6. Once you have selected and/or configured the port to which the printer is connected, the wizard asks you to determine which type of printer is being connected to the server. Computers that run the Macintosh OS are limited to talking to network printers that use Adobe PostScript, so you must be using a PostScript-capable printer.

NOTE: *There is one exception to the requirement of using a PostScript network printer for the Macs on your network. Infowave, a manufacturer of cross-platform printer connection solutions, offers a product that can provide a suitable alternative. It's called PowerPrint for Networks and is designed to allow Macs to access non-PostScript printers across an Ethernet network. The package includes printer drivers as well as a fast 10/100BaseT Ethernet print server and printer cable, and is said to support over 1,600 inkjet, laser, and specialty printers. You can get information about this product from the publisher's Web site: www.infowave.com. However, if the documents you prepare in your company are destined for professional printing, you will probably be better off using a PostScript printer on your network. PostScript printers, which may cost only a couple of hundred dollars more than their non-PostScript counterparts, provide more consistent, high-quality output for color and graphics.*

Selecting The Printer

To select the make and model of printer that you are using, follow these steps:

1. Click on the printer manufacturer's name, located on the left-hand side of the printer selection dialog box.

2. Then, select the model of the printer from the list on the right-hand side of the dialog box and then click on Next.

NOTE: *If your printer's manufacturer or model number does not appear on either list, you should click on Have Disk and then load the printer drivers from the installation disk provided with the printer. If you do not have drivers for the printer, you may want to check the manufacturer's Web site or contact the manufacturer's technical support department for the software you need or suggestions on choosing an alternate printer driver that may provide similar functionality.*

---

3. On the next Add Printer Wizard screen, you are asked to choose the name by which this printer will be known on the network, as shown in Figure 3.2. Although any name will do, it is usually best to choose a name that reflects either the group that the printer supports or the location where it can be found.

4. Once you have selected the printer's name, click on Next.

5. You are now asked if you wish to share this printer with other computers on the network, as shown in Figure 3.3. Click on the Shared radio button and then type in the name of the printer in the Share Name box.

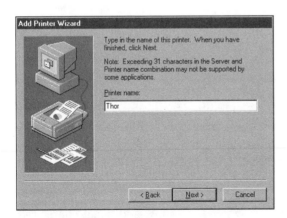

Figure 3.2   Name your printer here.

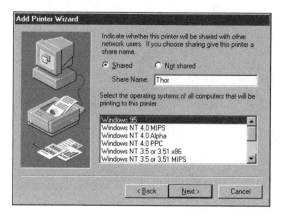

Figure 3.3   Use this screen to enable sharing on your selected printer.

6. After sharing your printer, click on Next. Note that the only operating systems listed are those made by Microsoft. By selecting these operating systems, Windows NT server will keep copies of the appropriate printer drivers for these operating systems on the server and will download them automatically when a workstation using one of the operating systems you selected connects to the printer hosted by this server. Macintosh OS-based computers are not supported by this feature and as such must have their printer drivers manually configured.

7. Congratulations, you are nearly finished with the setup process. The Add Printer Wizard now asks if you want to test your new printer by printing a test page. Click on the Yes radio button to do so.

TIP: *It is always a good idea, especially with network printers, to print a test page right after the setup process to be sure they are properly configured. Doing so avoids nasty surprises later on, when users attempt to print their documents.*

---

8. Once you have finished printing the test page and examined it to be sure your setup is correct, click on Finish.

Printing A Test Page If One Fails To Print

If your network printer fails to print a test page, it's a good idea to turn it off and then on again, to reset the memory. Depending on the make and model, you may need to follow additional configuration steps to enable the test page feature. Some Hewlett-Packard network printers, for example, provide different types of test pages, from configuration to font display, all accessed from the Control Panel display on the unit itself.

Despite being compatible with Windows, Apple laser printers do not offer a similar array of Control Panel settings, but do generate an automatic test page when the printer is turned off and on again (unless you turn off that option with a LaserWriter print program).

Solving Common Test Page Problems

Here are some suggestions on how to generate and review a test page:

- *You still can't generate a test page from your computer*—Go directly to the printer and engage the test print option. This process varies a bit from printer to printer; however, you can usually find a button on the front panel that generates a test page when you press on it. Or just turn the printer off and on, which will generate a test page on many models.

TIP: *When you look at the test page, pay particular attention to the interface that is currently selected and, if the printer has a network card in it, the network configuration. Check to see that the currently selected interface is the same one you have selected when setting up the printer in the server.*

- *The wrong network interface is active*—Make sure that you change it to match the settings on the server. Looking at the network settings, check the address of the printer to confirm that it is the same as the one you configured on the server.

- *The printer is using TCP/IP and the server cannot ping (contact) the printer*—Open a command prompt on the Windows NT Server and then type "PING XXX.XXX.XXX.XXX", where "XXX.XXX.XXX.XXX" is the IP address of the problem printer. If the printer responds properly to the PING command, double-check the network settings that you specified when you first set up the printer.

- *You do not get a response from the printer*—Make sure that your network server is properly connected and configured.

Related Solution	Found on page
Using A Sniffer On Your Network	87

3. Printing

Setting Permissions On Your New Printer

To set the access permissions on your new printer, do the following:

1. To open the Printers dialog box, click on Start|Settings|Printers, or open the Printers folder from the My Computer window, right-click on the icon of the printer you wish to examine, and then select Properties, as shown in Figure 3.4.

2. From the Properties dialog box, click on the Security tab to display the security options, shown in Figure 3.5.

3. Click on Permissions to open the Printer Permissions dialog box, shown in Figure 3.6.

Figure 3.4   Right-clicking on a printer allows you to open its Properties page.

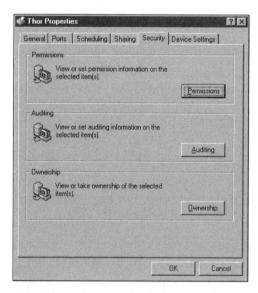

Figure 3.5   The Security page allows you to examine a variety of security options.

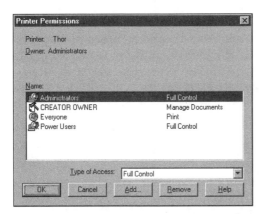

Figure 3.6   The Printer Permissions dialog box allows you to examine and set a user's or group's permission levels to use this printer.

4. From the Printer Permissions dialog box, you can view all the users who currently have access rights assigned on this printer and what those access rights are. If there is a user on your network who is having printer problems, simply select the user's name and then make sure the proper access rights are selected from the Type Of Access pop-up menu.

5. If the user is not listed, click on Add, which brings up the Add Users And Groups dialog box, shown in Figure 3.7.

6. Select the users and groups that you wish to add to the list of those with permissions to use this printer.

7. Choose the access levels you wish to grant to users of this printer and then click on OK. Clicking on Show Users adds a listing of all the users to this list.

8. Once you have made sure that the permission levels are correct for the users on your network, click on OK to close the Printer Permissions dialog box.

9. If you wish to configure the auditing function so that you can keep track of who is printing or who is trying to access the printer properties, click on Auditing in the Security tab of the Properties dialog box (refer back to Figure 3.5). (If you don't want to use the auditing feature, click on OK to close the Properties dialog box, and you're done.)

10. To set up the auditing properties on this printer, simply select the user or group that you wish to be audited and then choose which events you wish to audit, as shown in Figure 3.8. You can opt to have any success or failure logged for accounting or troubleshooting purposes.

11. When you are done, click on OK to close the Printer Auditing
     dialog box, and then click on OK again to close the Properties
     dialog box.

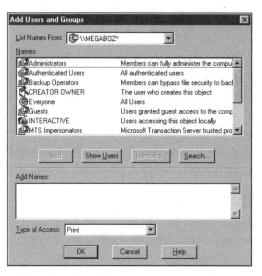

Figure 3.7   Select the users and groups you wish to add to the printer.

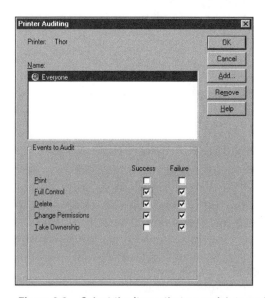

Figure 3.8   Select the items that you wish to audit.

Connecting To The Printer From Your Macintosh

Once you have finished setting up the printer on your Windows NT Server, you are ready to configure that printer from your Macintosh computers. This process enables your Mac users to use a printer's special features for best performance. To connect to and use the printer you have just set up, do the following on each Mac in your network:

1. Click on the Apple menu and then select the Chooser.

2. When the Chooser screen appears, click on the LaserWriter 8 icon.

NOTE: Depending on the particular system installation on the Macs in your network, you may have different sets of printer drivers installed and displayed in the Chooser. However, for Mac OS system version 8.5 or later, the most recent iteration of LaserWriter 8 is recommended. Some Adobe software packages offer an alternate driver, labeled Adobe PSPrinter, but this driver is not guaranteed to be compatible with the newest Mac operating systems.

3. Next, select the zone in which the server is located if it is not the same as your own.

4. You next need to select the printer from the list in the upper right-hand corner of the Chooser dialog box, shown in Figure 3.9.

5. The next step is to click on Create, which allows the driver to choose a proper PostScript Printer Description (PPD) file and set up a desktop printer icon, as shown in Figure 3.10.

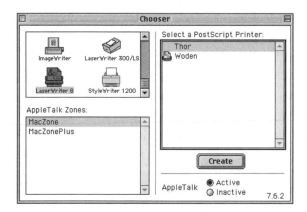

Figure 3.9   Choose the printer you wish to configure from the Select A PostScript Printer list.

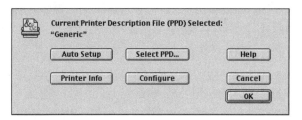

Figure 3.10   Clicking Auto Setup allows the driver to do the work for you.

NOTE: *A PPD file is a text file that contains information about your printer's special features. It defines such properties as the maximum image size, resolution settings, screen settings f or graphics and photos, the amount of memory installed in the printer, and the kinds of paper trays installed.*

---

6. Click on Auto Setup and your driver examines the list of available PPD files to locate one that matches the make and model of your printer. If the correct PPD file is located, it is automatically selected, and a desktop printing icon for the selected printer appears on your Mac's desktop.

7. Click on the Close box on the Chooser, and OK the message that your printer selection has been changed.

8. Repeat Steps 1 through 7 for each Macintosh on your network. You are now ready to send your documents to that printer for output.

Choosing The Proper PPD For Your Printer

The Auto Setup option isn't perfect, and sometimes it fails to select the right PPD file. This is common with printers that are available in a range of similar models. In some instances, you'll simply be asked to choose a set of installed printer options from a dialog box. If you are uncertain what these options are, you may wish to print a test or con-figuration page for the printer, or check the documentation to see which memory and tray options are installed.

If you cannot locate an appropriate PPD file, follow these steps:

1. When a PPD file suitable for your printer isn't found, you'll see a dialog box such as the one shown in Figure 3.11. Select your printer from the list of printers displayed.

2. Click on Select to activate this setting.

3. Finally, click on the Close box on the Chooser and then click on OK in the dialog box, which indicates your printer selection has changed.

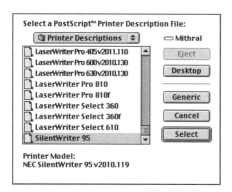

Figure 3.11   Select the correct Printer file from this listing.

You should now be ready to continue the setup process on other Macs in your network.

Using Other Options To Use The Networked Printer

If your printer's correct PPD is not listed, then you have to consider using other options to use the networked printer. Here are a couple of ways to do so and how they might affect printing your documents:

- *Click on Generic (refer back to Figure 3.11) to activate a default PPD file*—This option, though, prevents you from using the custom options of your printer such as special paper sizes, custom paper trays, and even such accessories as paper sorters or other advanced options. For simple letter-sized text documents, this may not have a big impact, but if you are going to be printing more complex files regularly, you should take steps to locate and install the correct PPD file.

- *Check your printer's installation disks to see if the correct PPD file is available*—Sometimes, PPD files are available from a manufacturer's Web site or from its support department. Another resource is Adobe's Web site (**www.adobe.com/supportservice/ custsupport/LIBRARY/pdrvmac.htm**). This site contains PPD files for a large number of popular and not-so-popular models.

NOTE: Most printer manufacturers offer PPD files without explicitly referring to them as being for the Macintosh. If you have a difficult time finding printer descriptions, look for items labeled "PageMaker Printer Descriptions"; they usually work just fine.

Installing A Macintosh PPD File

Once you've located the correct PPD file, it's very simple to add it to the list available in the Chooser. Just follow these steps:

1. Open your Mac's System Folder, then the Extensions Folder, and finally locate and open the Printer Descriptions folder.

2. Drag the PPD file to the Printer Descriptions folder.

NOTE: *If you're using one of the recent Mac OS 8- or 9-based systems, you can simply drag the PPD file to the closed System Folder icon. The Finder will recognize the proper file type and automatically drop it into the Printer Descriptions folder.*

---

3. To configure your printer to use the PPD file, follow Steps 1 through 7 in the "Connecting To The Printer From Your Macintosh" section earlier in this chapter. Use this setup procedure for each Mac on your network that needs a PPD file.

NOTE: *If you are configuring more than one printer for use by the Macs on your network, you need to follow the same range of setup procedures described above to configure them via Windows NT and then via the Macintosh Chooser.*

NOTE: *Once you've set up your printers and your Macintosh computers, you should run a test page and short text document (such as a Macintosh ReadMe file) to be sure performance is satisfactory.*

Using DAVE To Set Up Printers For Your Mac Computers

As described in Chapter 2, DAVE is a handy utility that lets your Windows NT computers work with Macs without your having to perform any special setup under Windows NT. Macintoshes with DAVE installed can use printers available on the AppleTalk network as well as all of the PostScript-based printers that Windows- or Windows NT-based computers are sharing. Having DAVE installed allows you to connect to a PostScript printer attached to a friend's NT Workstation or to the big laser printer connected to the departmental server without having to do any special configuration in Windows.

To configure DAVE to use PostScript printers on the Windows network, do the following:

1. Click on the Apple menu and then select the Chooser.

2. When the Chooser screen appears, click on the DAVE Client icon.

3. You will see the Select A Server list of available servers in the right-hand corner. From this list, select the server that supports the printer to which you wish to connect, as shown in Figure 3.12.

4. Log on to the network by entering the correct User Name and Password.

5. You will see a list of resources that the selected Windows server is sharing. From this list, select the PostScript printer to which you want to connect, as shown in Figure 3.13. Once you have selected the proper printer, click on OK to continue.

6. Next, a printer dialog box, where you need to select the correct PPD file for the selected printer, appears. Choose the correct PPD file. If the correct PPD file isn't available, follow the steps described in the "Choosing The Proper PPD For Your Printer," "Installing A Macintosh PPD File" and "Using Other Options To Use The Networked Printer" sections to make the proper choice available. Clicking on the Allow AppleTalk Access By

3. Printing

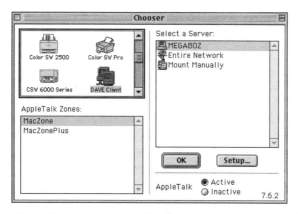

Figure 3.12   Select from this list the server that is sharing the correct network printer.

Figure 3.13   Choose a printer from the list of those shared by the server.

65

Others checkbox allows other AppleTalk-based computers on the AppleTalk portion of your network to connect to the network printer being accessed by DAVE and print to it, just as you would with a printer shared by a Windows NT server.

7. Once a PPD file has been selected, you will see a dialog box in which you can rename your printer. You can use a more descriptive or user-friendly name than the one originally selected when the printer was configured on the Windows network. This step may be useful if you are using several printers (some Mac, some Windows) with similar default names.

8. Once you have selected and (if needed) renamed the printer, click on OK to complete the setup process.

Using The DAVE Printing Utility To Manually Configure A Printer Connection

One particularly useful method of setting up a printer under DAVE is to manually configure the printer's attributes using the DAVE Print Client Control Panel. This manual process offers these advantages:

- You can choose to use a different user account and password to gain access to printers to which you do not normally have access.

- Creating a printer connection using the DAVE Printing Utility actually creates a printer gateway on your Macintosh that forwards printer requests from the other Macintoshes on your AppleTalk network. Manually configuring your printer connection also allows you to act as a gateway to the Windows network-based printer. This allows Macintoshes to print to it as well as if it were actually located on a Mac's network.

NOTE: *DAVE is not intended to be used as a way to bypass your network's security features. It is simply being offered as a convenient way to handle printer sharing on a small cross-platform network.*

To manually configure a printer connection using DAVE Printing, follow these steps:

1. Click on the Apple menu, and choose Control Panels from the list.

2. Select DAVE Print Client from the list of available Control Panels.

NOTE: *If the DAVE Print Client Control Panel is missing, you should first check the list under Extensions Manager to see if it has been disabled by mistake. If this Control Panel has been disabled (unchecked), enable NetBIOS, clicking on the checkbox, and restart your Macintosh. If DAVE Print Client is missing, you should reinstall the program from your original DAVE installer disks or installer application.*

NOTE: *If you get a NetBIOS error, check to see that the NetBIOS Control Panel is present. If it is, you should first check the list under Extensions Manager to see if it has been disabled by mistake. If it has been disabled (unchecked), check to enable DAVE NetBIOS and restart. If the NetBIOS Control Panel is present but not active, open the NetBIOS Control Panel. The most common cause of the NetBIOS Control Panel not being active is that it does not have a proper registration code installed. Double-check to see if the NetBIOS Control Panel is registered by clicking on the NetBIOS icon in the upper left-hand corner of the NetBIOS Control Panel. If NetBIOS is missing, reinstall the program from your original DAVE installer disks or installer application.*

3. Make sure that the DAVE Print Client Control Panel has been activated. If it is not on, you can activate it by clicking on the On radio button in the DAVE Print Client dialog box, shown in Figure 3.14.

4. Next, look at the list of available DAVE Print Gateways currently running and see if the printer you wish to add has already been defined. If the printer you want to access is not shown on the list, click on New to begin the process of adding the networked printer.

5. If the printer already exists, select the printer in the DAVE Print Client dialog box and then click on Edit. You are presented with a list of all the configuration options and their current values, as shown in Figure 3.15.

6. In the DAVE Printer dialog box, enter the name of the printer that appears on your Macintosh and on any other Macintoshes that access this printer through your Macintosh, as shown in Figure 3.16.

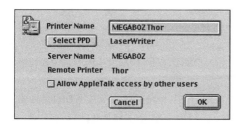

Figure 3.14 *Check the DAVE Print Client dialog box to be sure DAVE is running.*

Figure 3.15   Your printer settings are shown in this dialog box.

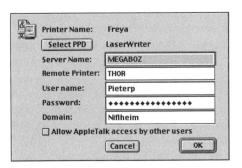

Figure 3.16   Check the Allow AppleTalk Access By Other Users to allow the printer to be accessed without special setup by other Macs on the network.

7. Once you have named the printer, enter the name of the server or workstation that controls the printer you wish to use.

8. Next, enter the name of the shared printer to which you want to connect.

NOTE: *Allowing too many users to connect to a Windows-based printer via your Macintosh's AppleTalk network can hurt performance on your Macs. In general, you should use the Allow AppleTalk Access By Other Users option only if you have a small number of AppleTalk users who might take advantage of a simple way to access the networked printer. If you have a larger number of Macintosh users, such as in a computer lab or large graphics department, you may want to consider using a dedicated printer gateway, following the steps described above.*

---

9. Next, you should select the printer's PPD for your printer. If the printer PPD selected is not correct, or one cannot be found, click on Select PPD.

10. Choose the proper file from the list and then click on Select (refer back to Figure 3.11). If the right PPD file isn't available, follow the steps described in the "Choosing The Proper PPD

For Your Printer" and "Installing A Macintosh PPD File" sections to make the proper choice available.

11. After you are sure that all of the printer's information is set correctly, click on OK to place the settings into effect.

NOTE: *You cannot have duplicate resource names on an AppleTalk zone. For instance, should a printer named Gutenberg already exist on the local zone, DAVE does not allow you to add a new printer with the same name. Should duplicate names be found, use the DAVE Print Client program to rename one of the printers.*

---

12. DAVE now asks you for the Windows NT domain or workstation account that you wish to use when accessing this printer. Enter the User Name, the Password, and the Domain or Workstation to which this user account belongs, as shown in Figure 3.17, and click on OK to activate the settings.

13. Once you have finished configuring your settings, the selected printer is displayed in the DAVE Print Client Control Panel, as shown in Figure 3.18.

14. To finish, click on the Close box to close the DAVE Print Client.

Related Solution	Found on page
Configuring DAVE	36

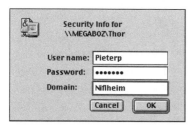

Figure 3.17   Log in to Windows NT using this dialog box.

Figure 3.18   The configured printer is shown here.

Sharing AppleTalk Printers With The Windows Network

DAVE lets you make printers on the AppleTalk network available to computers on the Windows network. This allows Windows- or Windows NT-based computers to access AppleTalk-only printers that would not normally be available to them. Using DAVE sharing, you can also limit the access that you grant to these printers by Windows NT domain or workgroup usernames or groups.

The only problem that you may encounter when sharing printers on your AppleTalk network is that the load on your workstation may increase to the point where it begins to slow down.

Configuring DAVE Sharing

To configure DAVE sharing to share AppleTalk-based printers with Windows- and Windows NT-based computers, follow these steps:

1. Click on the Apple menu and then select the Control Panels.

2. In the Control Panels display, double-click on the DAVE Sharing Control Panel to bring up the screen shown in Figure 3.19.

NOTE: *If the DAVE Sharing Control Panel cannot be found, you should first check the list under Extensions Manager to see if it has been disabled by mistake. If it has been disabled (unchecked), enable it and restart. If DAVE Sharing isn't displayed, you should reinstall the program from your original DAVE installer disks or installer application.*

---

3. The first thing you need to do is make sure that the Dave Sharing Control Panel is activated. If it is not active, click on the On radio button to start sharing.

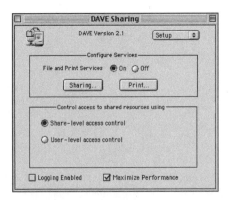

Figure 3.19   The DAVE Sharing Control Panel is used to allow your Windows computers to access AppleTalk printers.

4. Once sharing is running, click on Print to set up the printer that you are making available to the Windows and Windows NT users.

NOTE: *DAVE Sharing allows you to share only one printer at a time. You should set up your shared printers in such a way as to maximize their efficiency. Popular printers such as a Tektronix Phaser color printer should probably be shared by either a very fast Macintosh or by an older Macintosh that has been dedicated for use as a printing server. Likewise, a less-utilized printer could be shared by any of the Macintoshes on the network.*

---

5. If no printers are currently being shared, click on Add in the Printer Resources dialog box (shown in Figure 3.20) to begin the process of setting up the shared printer. If a printer already exists, the Add button is grayed out and the Edit button is made available.

6. Click on Edit to change the printer being shared.

7. To remove the shared printer, click on Remove.

8. From the Available Zones list shown in Figure 3.21, select the zone in which the printer you wish to share is located.

9. Click on the name of the printer that you want to share from the Available Printers list.

10. Once you have selected the proper zone and printer, click on OK.

11. You are next asked to enter the share-level access control for the printer. This step is optional, and it depends on the level of security you need in your installation. When you are done setting a password, if any, click on OK.

12. Once the printer has been configured, you'll see the Printer Resources dialog box, which shows the Shared Printer and the Shared Name. If you wish to delete the currently shared printer, click on Remove. Otherwise, click on OK to close the dialog box.

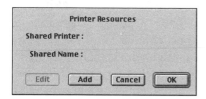

Figure 3.20   Use this dialog box to add a shared Macintosh printer to your Windows network.

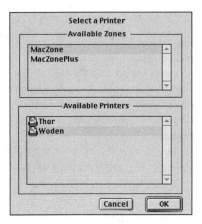

Figure 3.21   Choose a printer for sharing from this list.

Connecting To This Printer From Windows

On the Windows side, to connect to this printer, follow these steps:

1. Open the Printers folder from the My Computer window and then double-click on the Add Printer icon.

2. From the Add Printer Wizard screen, click on the Network Printer Server radio button, shown in Figure 3.22, and then click on Next.

3. You now must select the printer that you wish to use. If you want to see all the printers available on a certain server, simply double-click on any server whose name is preceded by a + sign, as shown in Figure 3.23.

4. A Macintosh that is sharing a certain printer does not automatically provide the proper printer driver to Windows and Windows NT workstations, as an NT Server would. Thus, you need to make sure that your Windows- and Windows NT-based computers have the proper printer drivers available when they use a printer being shared from a Macintosh. The warning notice you'll see is shown in Figure 3.24.

5. Next, you should select the proper printer driver for the remote printer from the list of all makes and models that NT supports. If you cannot find the make and model of the printer you need listed, then click on Have Disk and load the proper drivers from the installation disk (or check the manufacturer's Web site or support personnel for updates).

6. Once you have selected the proper printer, click on Next.

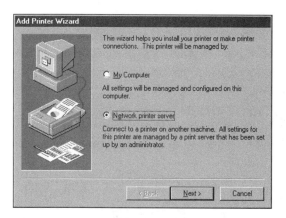

*Figure 3.22   The Add Printer Wizard shows you your choice of
printer connections.*

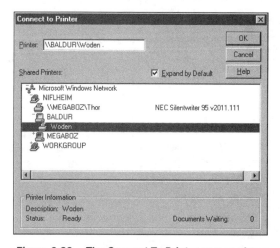

*Figure 3.23   The Connect To Printer screen shows you your choice of
network printers.*

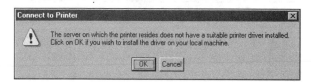

*Figure 3.24   If you don't have the proper printer driver, you'll see
this warning.*

73

7. The Add Printer Wizard next asks you if you want to use this printer as your default printer. This printer is most likely not the best suited to your normal printing needs, so it would probably be best not to select this printer as your default. Click on Next to continue.

8. Finally, the Add Printer Wizard informs you that the printer setup is complete. Click on Finish to complete the process of adding a new printer. You'll see an acknowledgment dialog box.

Once you've completed sharing your Macintosh printer, you will see it displayed in the Connect To Printer dialog box, shown in Figure 3.25, from your Windows workstation.

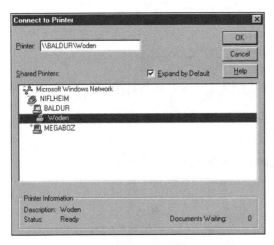

Figure 3.25   This dialog box shows that your Mac printer is correctly shared.

Troubleshooting Shared Printing Problems

Troubleshooting printing problems with Windows NT shared printers or printers that you access through DAVE is a relatively simple procedure. Such problems break down into two general areas: problems with the network or printer, and problems with the user's printer configuration or the configuration of the printer. Problems with the network and printer hardware are the simplest to diagnose and solve because they are usually very easy to spot. Problems with a user's printer connection on that workstation or the configuration of the printer are more difficult.

Isolating A Printer Problem

When trying to solve a printing problem, you first need to determine if it is a hardware problem or if it is related to the software or configuration of either the user's desktop or the printer itself. You should first check to see what type of problem the user is having. Here is a list of problems and troubleshooting procedures:

- *The user cannot print at all*—Determine which printer the user is printing to by clicking on the file menu and then selecting the Page Setup menu item.

- *The printer is visible on the network, but the user still cannot print*—Check the printer queue that controls the printer on the NT Server.

- *You can't see any documents from the user in the queue waiting to be printed*—This symptom tells you that it is a problem on the user's workstation. You will want to check the appropriate setups on that user's computer.

- *The printer is not visible on the network or a document appears to be stuck in the printer queue*—Examine the printer to make sure that it is not broken. Printing a sample sheet, if you can do so via a control on the printer, is a sure way to determine if the printer works properly and if the settings are correct.

- *The printer appears to be in working order, but the user still cannot print*—Check to make sure that the network is functioning by checking the printer's status display indicators, if the printer is network-based. The printer's manual defines the various display messages and what needs to be displayed.

- *The printer is directly connected, but the user still cannot print*—Check the server's connection to the printer to make sure that it is still good. It's not a bad idea to swap printer cables, as it is not always possible to visually determine if the cable is damaged.

- *All the printer's connections look good and the cable checks out okay, but the user still cannot print*—Clear the print job, if there is one, out of the print queue by highlighting the print job and then pressing Delete to see if it was just a bad print job. Sometimes, sending the document to the print queue a second time produces satisfactory results.

- *The printer still does not respond*—Try turning the printer off and on to see if you can clear the problem.

- *A print job from a Macintosh- or a Windows-based workstation captures the network printer and refuses to release it*—Try to print to the printer and see if you get an error message. If you get a message back that indicates that the printer is not responding, the simplest solution is to turn the printer off and on. This causes the printer connection to be reset. You should then try to identify which Macintosh refused to release the printer when it was done. Quite often, using an out-of-date or incompatible LaserWriter driver is the culprit. For best performance, we recommend you use the latest version of LaserWriter 8 that ships with your Macintosh system software (unless your printer manufacturer requires a special, customized driver).

Troubleshooting A PostScript-Based Printer Problem

Unless you are using PowerPrint for Networks from Infowave to share printers on your Macintosh workstations, Macs can access PostScript-based printers on the network by using Services for Macintosh for Windows NT Server or DAVE only. Sometimes, a user reports that he has connected to a printer on the network but that he cannot print to it. Should that occur, follow these steps:

1. Check to see that the printer to which the user has connected is actually a PostScript-based printer (unless you're using Infowave's software).

2. If the printer supports PostScript, make sure that the printer is functioning and that other users can print to it.

3. If it is not a PostScript printer, you need to let the user know that he or she cannot use this printer on a Macintosh network.

Troubleshooting A Printer That Has Access Rights Configured

Not all printers are for public use and as such are configured so that only certain users can access them. A user may report that he or she does not have the rights to print to a printer that he or she normally uses or should be using. In that case, you should examine the actual access setup on the shared printer to make sure that this user has the appropriate rights to use the printer. To examine and change the user rights applied to a printer, do the following:

1. Open the Printers folder from the My Computer window, right-click on the icon of the printer you wish to examine, and then select Properties (refer back to Figure 3.4).

2. From the Properties dialog box, click on the Security tab to display the security options (refer back to Figure 3.5).

3. Click on Permissions to open the Printer Permissions dialog box (refer back to Figure 3.6).

4. From the Printer Permissions dialog box, you can view all the users who currently have access rights assigned on this printer and what those access rights are. If the user who is having printer problems does not have the proper rights, simply select the user's name and then choose the proper rights from the Type Of Access pop-up menu.

5. If the user is not listed, click on Add, which brings up the Add Users And Groups dialog box (refer back to Figure 3.7).

6. Select the users and groups that you wish to add to the list of those with permissions to use this printer, select the permissions you wish to give them, and then click on OK.

7. Clicking on Show Users in the Add Users And Groups dialog box adds a listing of all the users to this list.

8. Once you have made sure that the permission levels are correctly set, click on OK to close the Printer Permissions dialog box.

9. Then, click on OK to close the Properties dialog box.

Dealing With A User Who Does Not Have Access Rights

If the user does not have the proper access rights to print to this printer, follow these steps to give them the proper access rights:

1. Verify that the user can access that printer, and then add the user back into the list of users with permission to use the printer.

2. If the user does have the proper permission to access the shared printer, have the user drop the connection to the printer and re-create the connection to the printer so that the user can log into it again. This helps make sure that the user logs in with the proper user account and password.

3. If Step 2 doesn't work, remove the user from the permission list for the printer and then re-add the user. For more information on setting permission levels on your printer, see the "Setting Permissions On Your New Printer" section earlier in this chapter.

Related Solution	Found on page
Setting Directory Permissions Of A Macintosh-Accessible Volume	33

Diagnosing And Handling Font Mismatches

The most common problems with editing and printing files created on another personal computing platform are font-related. You carefully format a document on the Windows computers on your network, transfer them to the Macs for further editing, and things change. Line breaks are different, and the fonts do not appear the same as on the screen. This is a problem that's especially troublesome if you designed your document text to fit a specific amount of space, and it runs too short or too long.

Here are some suggestions on how to handle this problem:

- *Match fonts on both platforms*—It's not enough to use fonts of the same name, such as Times or Helvetica. Different font manufacturers usually provide different versions of even the most common fonts, even if they have the same name. Font metrics, the values that control width spacing, may differ. The "cut" of the font may be different as well, making the actual size of the letterforms slightly smaller or taller, even if you choose the same font size. The best solution for this is to purchase fonts for both platforms from the same manufacturer. We are not going to recommend one firm above another, but Adobe fonts, for example, are an industry standard. When you choose all your fonts from a single vendor, you help ensure the maximum level of compatibility across platforms. In addition, with its Internet Explorer browser, Microsoft provides many Mac-equivalent fonts for the ones used under Windows. These include Arial, Courier New, and Times New Roman.

- *Proofread carefully*—Despite all the precautions you may take to ensure font compatibility, you should carefully compare the output of documents from both platforms to make sure that they look essentially the same. The way that lines break is often evidence of a potential problem; pay particular attention to this aspect of your document.

- *Watch out for font substitution*—If a font of the same name is not available when you open a document in another computing platform, you may find that a similar font—or an entirely different one—has been substituted. For example, on a Mac, you may find your document outputs in Courier, a mono-spaced font that looks much like that used on an old typewriter.

- *Use the same programs where possible*—It's not uncommon to find a document created from one program on one computing

3. Printing

platform translated to a different program on another platform. An example of this would be taking a WordPerfect Office document for Windows and opening it in Microsoft Office 98 on your Mac OS computers. Different programs may use various methods to calculate the values of the space between words—or even the actual space between letters—so even a careful matching of fonts may still provide unexpected surprises when you convert the document. The best choice here is simply to use (where possible) equivalent programs on both sides of the computing aisle. If the same programs are not available on both platforms, or the choices of individual users differ, take care in examining the printed output to be sure the results are satisfactory and meet your requirements.

NOTE: *Some publishers, such as Microsoft, provide documentation about compatibility between computing platforms with native and converted documents. Consult this information, where available, to see how your documents are impacted when you prepare or edit them on one platform and open and/or print them on the other. Fonts are not the only areas where disparities may occur. Sometimes, basic document formatting, such as styles for paragraphs and document size, may also be affected.*

3. Printing

Chapter 4

AppleTalk Networking

In Brief

Introduction To AppleTalk And Windows NT Networking

Adding AppleTalk to your Windows NT network is both a very simple and potentially complex endeavor. Although actually installing AppleTalk involves the same basic steps as installing Windows NT Services for Macintosh, it can be a bit more demanding to fine-tune your network to handle AppleTalk efficiently.

The first step to adding AppleTalk to your Windows NT network is to install Services for Macintosh, which is included with Windows NT Server. The complete installation process is covered in detail in Chapter 2. After you install and configure Services for Macintosh, your Windows NT Server can communicate to your Macintoshes in their native language, AppleTalk. In fact, if you want, you can use Windows NT Server to control all aspects of your AppleTalk network.

For more advanced control of your AppleTalk networking capabilities, you can use the tools built into your Cisco router. (We are assuming you are already using Cisco's products because they command a huge share of the router market.) Using Cisco's Internetwork Operating System (IOS), you can distribute routing information, restrict specific network traffic, and control which zones are present on each segment of your network. Although using the Cisco IOS is more complicated than configuring Services for Macintosh on your Windows NT Server, it's usually worth the extra effort because the Cisco IOS allows you to fine-tune your AppleTalk network. In this chapter, we delve deeply into the Cisco IOS. We show you examples of common configuration options that you may want to take advantage of when setting up your AppleTalk network.

DAVE from Thursby Software is simple to use and allows you to avoid complex Windows NT setup rituals. For those of you who prefer to use DAVE over the Macintosh Services available under Windows NT, we will also talk about the fine points of configuring DAVE's NetBIOS networking. We will examine all the significant options that you can select when configuring DAVE's NetBIOS client and the impact they have on your networking performance.

AppleTalk's Impact On The Network

The biggest challenge that most people run into when wanting to connect Macintoshes to the corporate network is the perception that AppleTalk can seriously degrade network performance. The origin of this myth, like most myths, is rooted a bit in fact and a bit in fiction. Back in the early days of computing, AppleTalk was devised as an easy way to network a bunch of Macintoshes on small workgroup-oriented networks. As such, Macintoshes were designed to discover as much about their network environment as possible when they were first connected. This meant that they generated a lot of AppleTalk traffic trying to determine what resources were available on the network.

To network administrators, this traffic caused congestion on the network and slowed the network for the other computers. In addition, Macintoshes, unlike their PC cousins, like to get regular updates from all the file servers that they are connected to. These frequent requests for updates commonly caused the servers of those days to have performance problems. Needless to say, both of these problems did not tend to make fans out of many network administrators.

However, as time and technology have improved, many of these issues have fallen by the wayside. Modern high-speed network hubs and switches have largely resolved the issue of Macintoshes consuming too much bandwidth on the network. Likewise, modern operating systems like Windows NT 4 are much better at handling the update requests generated by the Macintoshes connected to them. And yet, the myth of AppleTalk's impact on the network still remains strong in the minds of many network engineers.

AppleTalk In-Depth

AppleTalk is a robust routable network protocol that was developed by Apple Computer in the mid-1980s to provide networking capabilities to its Macintosh family of computers. The initial form of this protocol, now known as *AppleTalk Phase-1*, was limited to one network segment and 127 AppleTalk devices. Although AppleTalk Phase-1 was great at supporting small workgroup networks, Apple soon realized that it would need to make changes if it wanted to build larger networks. In 1988, Apple introduced the current version of AppleTalk that is used in all Macintoshes today, AppleTalk Phase-2. AppleTalk Phase-2 extended AppleTalk to include the concept of sub-networks as well as expanding the number of AppleTalk devices that can be present on a single network segment.

Unlike AppleTalk Phase-1, which was only able to handle one network segment, AppleTalk Phase-2 is capable of handling up to 65,298 networks, or as Apple calls them, *zones*. These zones are used to break up your AppleTalk network into a bunch of smaller networks, which may be located on the same physical segment of the network or may be located on remote network segments. By dividing the network in this way, you can now have more than 253 AppleTalk devices on each zone of the network. Additionally, having multiple zones allows you to break up your Macintoshes into smaller workgroup-oriented segments that are easier to manage.

In the Open Systems Institute, or OSI, model, AppleTalk is considered a protocol. This means that AppleTalk is defined by a specific type of network packet on the network, just like IP, the Internet Protocol, and many others. Also, like IP and other protocols, several different types of transport ride on top of AppleTalk. Like TCP and UDP (Transmission Control Protocol and Universal Datagram Protocol), the two primary transports that are used with IP, AppleTalk is the host to four major transport types:

- Datagram Delivery Protocol, DDP
- Printer Access Protocol, PAP
- AppleTalk Transaction Protocol, ATP
- AppleTalk Data Stream Protocol, ADSP

DDP and ATP are very similar to UDP because they are *connectionless transports*. This means that no connection is formed between the sending computer and the one receiving the DDP or ATP packets. Since no connection is formed, these transports are really designed to transfer only a small amount of data between computers. Also like UDP, DDP does not contain any error correction capability, relying instead upon what is known as *best effort delivery* of the packets. ATP, on the other hand, sends an acknowledgment for every packet to ensure that all the packets arrive at the destination and in the right order.

Like TCP, PAP and ADSP are *connection-oriented transports* because they form a connection between the sender and the receiver. ADSP, like TCP, is designed to transfer data between computers in a reliable fashion so that lost or damaged packets can easily be retransmitted preventing data loss. However, unlike TCP, ADSP utilizes DDP to handle the actual data transfer and then adds error correction and flow control capabilities to the connection. PAP likewise is a connection-oriented protocol that uses ATP to actually transport the data to the printer.

Understanding DDP Packet

DDP, the principal packet type used by AppleTalk, has two types. The first is the DDP type 1 packet, whose structure is shown in Figure 4.1. This type of packet exchanges data among Macintoshes located on the same zone.

Here is a detailed description of the makeup of the DDP Type 1 packet:

- *Flag Byte*—These two fields are set to 01111110. This binary number is the flag that tells the Macintosh that this is an AppleTalk packet and that it should see if the destination address matches that of the Macintosh.

- *Destination Node*—This number is the AppleTalk network address of the Macintosh for which this packet is destined.

- *Source Node*—This number is the AppleTalk network address of the Macintosh that actually sent the packet.

- *Protocol Type*—This field defines the type of DDP packet that this is. For the short DDP packet described here, the value is 1.

- *Length*—This field tells the receiving Macintosh how long the packet is. This information is critical because the amount of data carried in each packet can vary.

- *Destination Socket*—This number is the AppleTalk socket on the destination Macintosh that this packet is destined for.

- *Source Socket*—This number is the AppleTalk socket on the source Macintosh that originated this packet.

- *DDP Protocol Type*—This field defines which DDP protocol this packet uses.

- *Data*—This field, also known as the *payload* of the packet, can range from 0 bytes to 586 bytes of data.

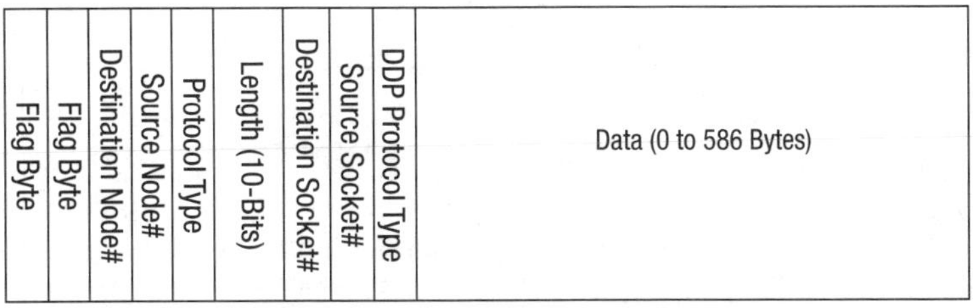

Figure 4.1   The structure of the DDP type 1 packet.

The second type of DDP is the longer Type 2 packet whose structure is shown in Figure 4.2. It is used for communication between Macintoshes located in different zones. These packets are longer because they have to carry information about their home zone, the destination zone, and the source and destination Macintoshes.

Here's a detailed description of the makeup of the DDP Type 2 packet:

- *Flag Bytes*—These two fields are set to 01111110. This binary number is the signal that tells the Macintosh that this is an AppleTalk packet and that it should see if the destination address matches that of the Macintosh.

- *Source Node*—This number is the AppleTalk network address of the Macintosh that actually sent the packet.

- *Protocol Type*—This field defines the type of DDP packet that this is. For the long DDP packet described here, the value is 2.

- *Length*—This field tells the receiving Macintosh how long the packet is, this is critical because the amount of data carried in each packet can vary. Also in the Length field is a 4-bit Hop Counter that is incremented by the various routers that direct the packet from network to network. This tells the routers how many networks this packet has traversed and if it reached 15 to discard the packet.

- *DDP Checksum*—This field is a numerical value that can be used to verify the contents of the data portion of the packet. This checksum ensures that the information contained in the data portion of the packet is not corrupted during the process of being routed over the network.

- *Destination Network*—This number is the numeric identifier assigned to the zone in which the destination Macintosh resides. As with all network numbers, these are defined by the routers that seed the AppleTalk zones on the network.

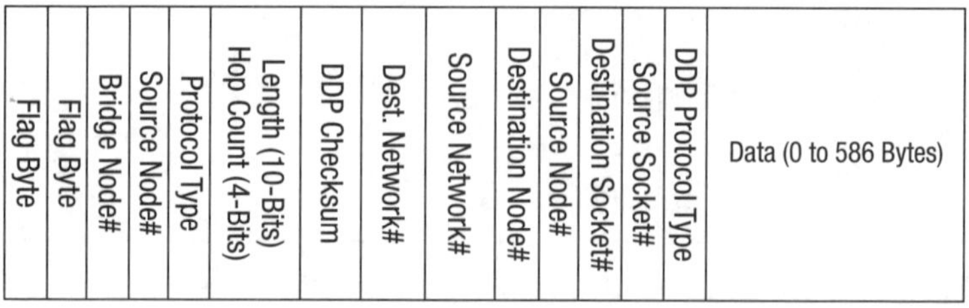

Flag Byte	Flag Byte	Bridge Node#	Source Node#	Protocol Type	Length (10-Bits) Hop Count (4-Bits)	DDP Checksum	Dest. Network#	Source Network#	Destination Node#	Source Node#	Destination Socket#	Source Socket#	DDP Protocol Type	Data (0 to 586 Bytes)

Figure 4.2   The structure of the DDP type 2 packet.

4. AppleTalk Networking

- *Source Network*—This number is the numeric identifier used by the zone in which the source of this packet resides.

- *Destination Node*—This number is the AppleTalk network address of the Macintosh for which this packet is destined.

- *Source node*—This number is the AppleTalk network address of the Macintosh that actually sent the packet.

- *Destination Socket*—This number is the AppleTalk socket on the destination Macintosh that this packet is destined for.

- *Source Socket*—This number is the AppleTalk socket on the source Macintosh that originated this packet.

- *DDP Protocol*—This field defines which DDP protocol this packet uses.

- *Data*—This field, also known as *payload* of the packet, can range from 0 bytes to 586 bytes.

Using A Sniffer On Your Network

A *sniffer* is a piece of software or hardware that allows you to examine the network traffic on your network. Using a sniffer, you can look at individual network packets and see what values are present in each portion of the packet. You can also use a sniffer to provide information on the number of packets that are on the network and which computers are generating them. Using this information, you can develop a better understanding of how the AppleTalk traffic is flowing on your network and which computers or other devices are generating it (which is why we went into so much detail in the previous section).

For Windows NT 4.0 users, a slightly crippled sniffer called Network Monitor is bundled with the operating system. This version of Network Monitor can only read network traffic to and from the Windows NT-based computer that it is running on. Although this limitation is annoying, Network Monitor does do a good job of letting you look at the AppleTalk traffic that is going to and coming from the server that you have configured to support Macintosh clients.

For those of you who have Microsoft's Systems Management Server 1 or 2, you can install the full version of Network Monitor. This version of Network Monitor can listen to all the traffic on the network, not just traffic destined for the server or workstation that it is running on. You can, therefore, set up a workstation with Network Monitor on it and have it record all the traffic on the network for a certain period of

4. AppleTalk Networking

time. You can then go back and review the packets that Network Monitor collected to look for problems on your network and to help trace back to the computer or other device that might be causing them.

Getting To Know Your Router

We will not pretend that working with a network router is a piece of cake. If you have not configured a router before, you should have this book and the product's manual at hand, and follow each step carefully. Be sure to check and double-check each command.

Once you've followed the process a few times, however, you should be able to manage it without much difficulty. Here are some setup basics:

- When you first start to work with a router, you should know the Internet Protocol (IP) address of the router, the console password, and the secret password that allows you to enter enable mode.

- The IP address of the router is set in the configuration installed on the router. To see the configuration that is currently running on the router, log in to the router and then type "enable" and the secret password to enter enable mode.

- Once you see the pound sign (#) cursor, which signifies that you are in the enable mode, type "show running-config" to see the configuration that is running on the router. This configuration is customized for each individual router based upon the type of router, the version of the Cisco IOS that it is running, and which network interfaces it has installed.

For more information about your router's configuration, contact the organization or department that installed the routers and maintains them.

Getting To Know Caches And Counters

Caches and *counters* are the areas where your router stores information about the network environment around it. Your router uses caches to keep lists of information that it needs to access rapidly. Routers cache information such as the routes to other parts of the network or the names of the computers that it has discovered on the network. The router then uses these caches to speed up the process of routing network traffic to other parts of the network or to direct the traffic to a specific computer. If these caches become corrupted with inaccurate information, they can cause the router to slow down and lose network data by directing it to the wrong computer or portion of the network.

Your router uses counters to keep track of all sorts of information, from how much traffic is sent out to a specific interface to the number of errors it has encountered. Looking at the various counters on a router is a good way to see how your router is performing. For example, if you notice that the error counter on one of your Ethernet interfaces is significantly higher than the others, you may have a problem on the network to which that interface is connected. Likewise, if you notice that the number of AppleTalk routing updates on one interface is lower than that on the others, you may have a problem with the access list permissions that are applied to that interface.

4. AppleTalk Networking

Immediate Solutions

Installing Network Monitor On Your Windows NT Server

Installing the version of Network Monitor that is bundled with Windows NT 4 on your Windows NT 4 server is a very simple procedure. Although this version is a bit crippled because it can only view network traffic going to and coming from your server, Network Monitor should be sufficient to identify many network problems. To install Network Monitor, follow these steps:

1. Select Start|Settings|Control panel. Alternatively, you can double-click on the My Computer icon located on your desktop and then double-click on the Control Panel folder located in the My Computer window.

2. Double-click on the Network icon to bring up the Network Control Panel that is shown in Figure 4.3.

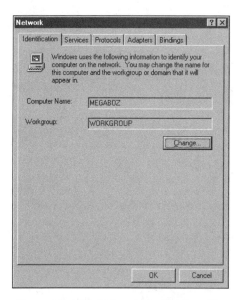

Figure 4.3   The Network Control Panel is used to configure your various network protocols.

4. AppleTalk Networking

3. Next, Click on the Services tab, shown in Figure 4.4. From the Services dialog box, you can see the different services that are installed.

4. To add the Network Monitor Tools And Agent, click the Add button.

5. Click on Network Monitor Tools And Agent (as shown in Figure 4.5) and then click on OK.

6. After you are all finished adding the Network Monitor Tools And Agent, click on OK.

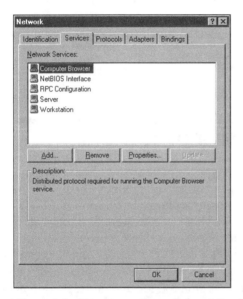

Figure 4.4   You can configure Network Services from this screen.

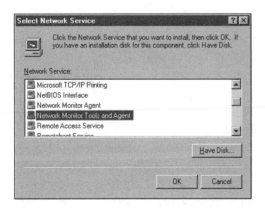

Figure 4.5   Pick Network Monitor Tools And Agent from among the options offered.

91

After you have said OK in the Select Network Service dialog box, NT will ask you for the location of the files needed to install the Network Monitoring Tools And Agent. These files are on the Windows NT Server CD-ROM that you originally used to install the server. Insert the Windows NT Server CD into your server's CD-ROM drive and click on Continue. After Windows NT has finished copying all the files needed, restart your server to finish the installation process.

NOTE: *After installing new Windows NT components, you should re-apply the current Service Pack for Windows NT so that you are using the latest versions of these components.*

Related Solutions	Found on page
Installing Services For Macintosh: The Next Steps	21

Using Network Monitor On Your Windows NT Server

As with almost any sniffer product, using Network Monitor is a very complex task worthy of its own book. Since this is not a book on using a sniffer, we will focus on some of the more basic settings that you can use in Network Monitor to help you track problems involving AppleTalk on your network. Once you have Network Monitor installed on your Windows NT server, you will find that you now have a new program item, named Network Monitor, located under the Administrative Tools submenu of the Programs menu that is located in the Start menu.

1. Start Network Monitor, which brings up the Network Monitor Capture window. This window shows you the number of packets that are being sent and received by the server that meet the criteria you have specified. Please see Figure 4.6 for an example.

2. You do not wish to look at any network traffic other than AppleTalk, so you will need to filter it all out. To do so, click on Capture|Filter, or press the F8 key.

3. The Capture Filter dialog box, shown in Figure 4.7, appears. Double-click on SAP/ETYPE= to bring up the Capture Filter SAPs And ETYPEs dialog box that we will be using to filter out all the non-AppleTalk protocols that are on the network.

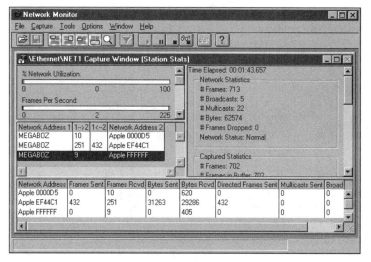

Figure 4.6   The initial Network Monitor display.

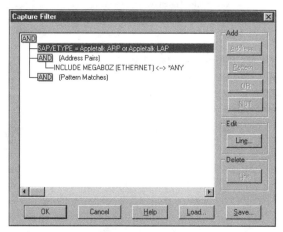

*Figure 4.7   The Capture Filter dialog box displays the protocol filters
currently in use.*

4. The Capture Filter SAPs And ETYPEs dialog box, shown
    in Figure 4.8, appears. We will be using it to filter out non-
    AppleTalk protocols that are on the nework. Click on Disable
    All to clear out all of the available protocols.

5. Then, select the two AppleTalk protocols, AppleTalk ARP,
    (Address Resolution Protocol), and AppleTalk LAP (Local Area
    Protocol), and click on Enable. Next, click on OK to close the
    Capture Filter SAPs And ETYPE dialog box.

6. Click on OK again to close the Capture Filter dialog box.

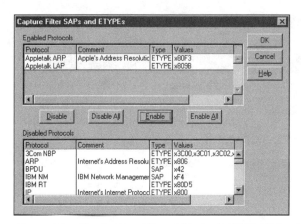

Figure 4.8   The Capture Filter SAPs And ETYPEs dialog box displays all the protocol filters currently available in Network Monitor.

Now that you have set your filters to exclude all network traffic except for AppleTalk, you are ready to start capturing network traffic that is either destined for your server or originates from your server. To do so, follow these steps:

1. Click on the Capture menu and select Start or press the F10 key. You are asked if you want to save any previously captured data. After you have either saved the data or discarded it, Network Monitor will start recording network traffic.

2. Once you have collected enough packets for you to examine, click on Capture|Stop, or press F11.

3. To examine the packets that Network Monitor has collected for you, click on Capture|Display Captured Data, or press F12. You see a summary of all the packets that you captured. This display shows the time that each packet was captured along with the source and destination for each packet as well as the protocol used by each packet that was sent or received and a brief description of what each packet is. Figure 4.9 shows an example.

To look at an individual packet in greater detail, double-click it. Doing so brings up the Capture Detail window shown in Figure 4.10. In the top frame of the window, you can see the list of packets that Network Monitor captured with the packet you are viewing highlighted. In the middle frame is a detailed breakdown of the network packet, including the Ethernet and the DDP packet information that you will want to look at in more detail when working on isolating AppleTalk related problems. In the third frame, is the hexadecimal values, or

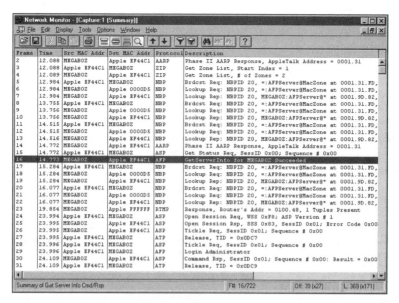

Figure 4.9   The Capture Summary shows you a list of all the packets that were captured by Network Monitor.

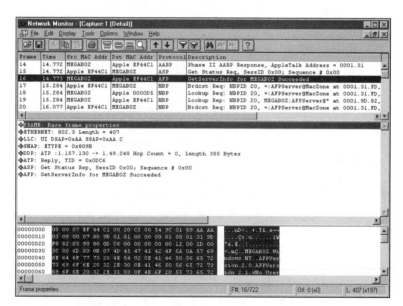

Figure 4.10   The Capture Detail windows shows you all you might want to know about a packet.

machine code, that is contained by the packet segment that you currently have selected in the middle window frame.

NOTE: *Hexadecimal or Base 16 numbers are used by computer programmers as shortcuts to define the binary numbers that are stored in each byte. Hexadecimal numbers range from 0 through F and represent one half of the 8-bit byte of memory. So, looking at a number whose value is FF, for example, you can see that FF equals 255 bytes. Looking at the hexadecimal numbers that Network Monitor displays, you can determine the values of the various bytes that make up each network packet. However Network Monitor and other tools can provide you with more readable information; you don't have to decipher the hexadecimal values.*

Reviewing How To Install Services For Macintosh

As you learned in Chapter 2, configuring a Windows NT Server to use AppleTalk is very straightforward. To install and configure AppleTalk on your Windows NT Server, all you need to do is follow the instructions on installing Services for Macintosh. The AppleTalk protocol routing component in Services for Macintosh allows Windows NT to communicate using AppleTalk as well as the tools needed to create AppleTalk zones and route AppleTalk network traffic. Consider the following steps on how to install Services for Macintosh a quick refresher course. For more detailed information, please review Chapter 2.

1. From the Services tab in the Network Control Panel, select Services For Macintosh and then click on Properties. The General tab of the Microsoft AppleTalk Protocol Properties dialog box, shown in Figure 4.11, shows you the Default Zone for the currently selected network interface.

2. Next, click on the Routing tab, shown in Figure 4.12. It displays the AppleTalk networking options that you can configure. Services for Macintosh allows you to route AppleTalk traffic between network segments as well as to configure the network numbers and zone names that are used to define each AppleTalk network.

3. Clicking on the Enable Routing checkbox activates routing and enables Windows NT to act like a very simple router. As with the more advanced Cisco router that we will discuss later in this chapter, Windows NT Server with Services for Macintosh installed allows you to direct AppleTalk traffic among various

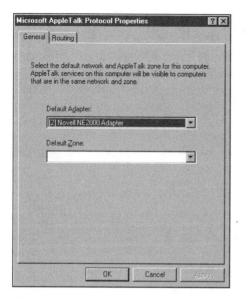

Figure 4.11   The first stage of configuring Services for Macintosh.

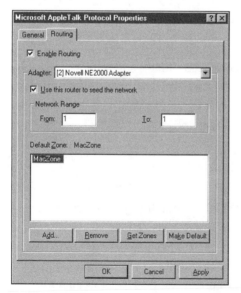

Figure 4.12   Here are your AppleTalk routing and network options.

routers. It also lets Windows NT set up the network numbers and zone names that define AppleTalk networks. If you want to have greater control over the AppleTalk traffic on your network than the simple routing control in Windows NT gives you, follow the steps in the next section.

Configuring AppleTalk On Cisco Routers

Configuring a Cisco router using Cisco's IOS is far more complex than configuring the few basic options that Services for Macintosh provides you. Unlike the process of configuring Windows NT, configuring a router using Cisco's IOS requires you to abandon the graphical interface of Windows; you must instead do most everything from a command line interface (CLI).

CLI requires that you type in each command as well as the various settings that you desire directly into the router.

NOTE: All the configuration examples in this chapter are based upon Cisco IOS version 11.2, the most current version when this book was written. The commands that you use on your router may differ slightly based upon what IOS version you are running. We suggest you consult your router installation documentation for further information.

To connect to your router, you have two options. First, you can choose to connect the serial cable to the Console or Auxiliary port on the router and then use a terminal program like ZTerm or HyperTerminal on Windows, to "talk to" the router. Alternatively, you can connect to the router remotely by using a Telnet program. To communicate with the router over your network with Telnet, simply open your Telnet application and have it connect to the IP address of the router.

NOTE: Many network administrators configure their routers to either refuse all Telnet connections or to allow connections from only a few specific network addresses. They do this to prevent unauthorized users from gaining access to the routers that control the network and then making unauthorized changes that can disrupt the network.

Once you have connected to the router, follow these steps to configure your router:

1. If required, type in a password to gain access to the router.

2. Once your access has been granted, you have only limited ability to accomplish what you want. In order to gain full control over the router, you need to switch to Enable mode. To switch the router into Enable mode, type "Cisco enable" at the router's command prompt and press Enter.

3. You are then asked for the enable password. Once you type that in, you will notice that the cursor changes to a pound sign (#) and that you have access to a greatly expanded number of commands. You can use two types of commands when configuring AppleTalk on your Cisco router: interface-related

4. AppleTalk Networking

commands and general commands. *Interface commands* are used to configure a specific network interface on the router. *General commands*, on the other hand, are used to configure the router in general.

4. To enter interface commands, you must first enter the configuration mode for that interface. To be put in configuration mode from the terminal, type "Config T" at the command prompt.

NOTE: *The other configuration modes are Memory and Network. Typing "Config M" causes the router to load configuration from memory, whereas typing "Config N" causes the router to load its configuration from a location on the network.*

---

5. Once you have entered configuration mode, select the interface that you wish to configure by typing in the name of the interface. For example, to configure the Ethernet0 interface, type "Int E0" at the config prompt. Your command prompt should then change to read Config-Int.

NOTE: *The best way to make sure that your configuration changes do not interfere with the existing settings on your router is to check them out on a test configuration before you load them on the production router. If you cannot do this, the next best solution is to make your changes to the running configuration, but do not copy them to the startup configuration. This way, if you determine that there is a problem with your configuration, you can restart the router and have it load the original configuration.*

Using Cisco IOS AppleTalk Configuration Commands

You can set a variety of interface-related configuration commands from the command prompt. When configuring your router's interfaces for AppleTalk, the following configuration commands are those you are most likely to use (items in bolded italics are the settings that you wish to use with this command):

- **appletalk access-group** *access-list-number*—This command allows you to specify an AppleTalk access list to the current interface. To remove this access list, use the **no appletalk access-group** *access-list-number* command.

- **appletalk address** *network.node*—This command configures the router to use a specific AppleTalk address.

4. AppleTalk Networking

- **appletalk cable-range** *cable-range network.node*—This command allows you to define the network numbers that are used on this interface. The effect of this command is identical to setting the network numbers in the Microsoft AppleTalk Protocol Properties dialog box. The cable range can be any number from 0 through 65,279, separated by a hyphen (-). The range of numbers must be equal to or greater than the number of networks you want on this segment of your network. The optional *network.node* switch allows you to specify the AppleTalk address that the interface uses. To disable the cable range for a specific interface, use the **no appletalk cable-range** command.

- **appletalk discovery**—This command places the selected interface into discovery mode. This mode allows the interface to "listen" to the network so that it can determine what the AppleTalk network configuration is. To disable AppleTalk discovery on a specific interface, use the **no appletalk discovery** command.

NOTE: *Setting an interface to use AppleTalk discovery requires that you have either another router or a Windows NT Server to provide network zone and cable range information.*

- **appletalk distribute-list** *access-list-number* **in/out**—This command allows you to limit the distribution of routing information based upon the configuration of the access list you have configured.

- **appletalk getzonelist-filter** *access-list-number*—This command filters the **getzonelist** command through a specified access list to limit which zones are seen. To disable the **getzonelist** filter, use the **no appletalk getzonelist-filter** access-list-number command.

- **appletalk protocol aurp**, **appletalk protocol eigrp**, or **appletalk protocol rtmp**—This command tells the router to use one of the three listed routing protocols on this interface. AppleTalk update routing protocol (AURP) is available only on tunneling interfaces. Cisco Enhanced Internetwork Gateway Routing Protocol (EIGRP) is a multi-protocol routine that can carry routing information for AppleTalk, TCP/IP, and IPX/SPX. Routing table maintenance protocol (RTMP) is the default routing protocol that AppleTalk uses to distribute AppleTalk network routes. To disable the routing protocol on this interface, use the **no appletalk protocol aurp**, **appletalk protocol eigrp**, or **appletalk protocol rtmp** command.

4. AppleTalk Networking

- **appletalk route-cache**—This command enables fast-switching mode on any supported interface. Fast-switching allows the router to handle network traffic much more rapidly than it would normally. To turn off fast switching, use the **no appletalk route-cache** command.

- **appletalk route-redistribution**—This command tells the router to convert RTMP routing information into EIGRP routing information. It allows the router to make the information it learns about network routes via RTMP available to other routers that run EIGRP. To disable AppleTalk route redistribution, use the **no appletalk route-redistribution** command.

- **appletalk routing eigrp** *router-number*—This command enables the AppleTalk EIGRP routing protocol on this interface. The *router-number* specified can be any integer from 0 through 65,535; however, it must be unique on your network. To turn off AppleTalk EIGRP routing on this interface, use the **no appletalk routing eigrp** command.

- **appletalk zone** *zone-name*—This command allows you to add an AppleTalk zone to a specific interface. To add a zone whose name contains a special character, you must specify the special character in the name by using a colon (:) followed by the hexadecimal number that equals that character's ASCII number. To delete an AppleTalk zone, use the **no appletalk zone** *zone-name* command.

Using Cisco IOS AppleTalk Administrative Commands

Other commands available in configuration mode are not bound to any specific interface. They affect all interfaces that support the options being set. The **access-list** family of commands allows you to define filters that can permit or deny network traffic, depending upon the type of traffic and its destination or origin. **access-list** commands provide you with an enormous amount of control over the network traffic that you allow on and off your network.

When using the following commands, make sure that they will not interfere with the other configuration settings that are configured on the router:

- **access-list** *access-list-number* (**permit/deny**) **additional-zones** *zones*—This command permits or denies all traffic from any zones that are not explicitly listed in the access list.

NOTE: *The* access-list-number *for AppleTalk access-list commands must be between 600 and 699.*

- **access-list** *access-list-number* (**permit/deny**) **cable-range** *cable-range*—This command lets you permit or deny AppleTalk traffic from a specified cable range on the network.

- **access-list** *access-list-number* (**permit/deny**) **includes** *(broadcast-permit/broadcast-deny) cable-range*—This command allows you to define an AppleTalk access list that overlaps any portion of a range of cable ranges or network numbers. The *broadcast-permit* and *broadcast-deny* switches allow you to permit or deny network broadcasts that meet the cable ranges or network numbers you have listed.

- **access-list** *access-list-number* (**permit/deny**) **nbp** *seq* (**type/ object/zone**) *string*—This command allows you to define permissions for specific Name Binding Protocol, NBP, type, object, or zone as defined in the string. The *seq*, or sequence number, is used to keep track of the various NBP entries in an AppleTalk access list.

- **access-list** *access-list-number* (**permit/deny**) **network** *(broadcast-permit/broadcast-deny) network-number*—This command allows you to define an access list for a specific AppleTalk network number.

- **access-list** *access-list-number* (**permit/deny**) **other-access**—This command allows you to permit or deny all traffic from any network numbers or cable ranges that are not explicitly listed in the access list.

- **access-list** *access-list-number* (**permit/deny**) **other-nbps**—This command allows you to permit or deny all traffic from any NBPs that are not explicitly listed in the access list.

- **access-list** *access-list-number* (**permit/deny**) **within** *cable-range*—This command allows you to permit or deny AppleTalk traffic from any networks within a specified range of network numbers or cable range.

- **access-list** *access-list-number* (**permit/deny**) **zone** *zone-name*—This command allows you to permit or deny AppleTalk traffic from a specified AppleTalk zone on the network.

- **appletalk event-logging**—This command tells the router to log significant network events to the system log. To turn off AppleTalk event logging, use the **no appletalk event-logging** command.

- **appletalk name-lookup-interval** *seconds*—This command sets NBP update broadcasts that it makes on all of its AppleTalk interfaces. The timing interval can be any integer from 0 on up. Cisco recommends that you choose a value between 300 seconds (5 minutes) and 1,200 seconds (20 minutes) for optimal performance. Selecting a time of 0 causes the router to flush the names cache and prevents the caching of service type data. To reset the name lookup interval to the default value, use the **no appletalk name-lookup-interval** command.

- **appletalk timers** *update-interval*, *valid-interval*, and *in-valid-interval*—This command sets the routing update timers to values different from the defaults. The *update-interval* timer (default of 10 seconds) changes the time, in seconds, between the sending of routing updates to the other routers. The *valid-interval* timer (default of 20 seconds or twice the default value of the *update-interval* timer) is the time in seconds that a router will consider a route to be valid. The *invalid-interval* timer (default of 60 seconds or three times the *valid-interval* timer) defines how long a route is kept in the routing table before it is discarded.

Using Cisco Enable Mode Commands

You can use other commands to modify or monitor your AppleTalk network settings, but you can use them only when you are in enable mode. These commands are divided into roughly two categories: those designed to allow you to clear certain caches and counters that may need to be flushed before your network will operate properly (**clear**), and those that show various network settings or information that the router has collected (**show**).

Using clear Commands

The **clear** family of commands is designed to clear out the various caches and lists that the router uses to direct AppleTalk traffic. These commands are very useful in clearing out caches or lists that contain out-of-date or incorrect information that might be preventing the router from working properly:

- **clear appletalk arp**—This command causes the AppleTalk address resolution protocol (arp) cache to be cleared of all entries. The arp cache is where the router stores information that links the AppleTalk addresses of all computers to their Ethernet addresses.

- **clear appletalk neighbor**—This command clears out all entries in the AppleTalk neighbor table.

- **clear appletalk routes**—This command clears out all of the routes listed in the route table.

NOTE: The **clear appletalk route** command is very useful when you find that your routing table has a number of inaccurate AppleTalk routes. If you think that you have inaccurate AppleTalk routes, this command is a simple way to clear them all out and generate the list fresh.

- **clear appletalk traffic**—This command resets all of the AppleTalk traffic counters on the router.

Using **show** Commands

The **show** family of commands is designed to show you the contents of the various lists that govern support of AppleTalk networking on the router. When you are diagnosing a problem or just trying to monitor the status of AppleTalk on your network, these commands can be invaluable:

- **show appletalk access-lists**—This command causes the router to display all the AppleTalk access lists that are defined on this router.

- **show appletalk adjacent-routes**—This command displays all of the routes to other routers that are either directly connected to this router or are on a segment of the network connected to a router that is directly connected to your router.

- **show appletalk arp**—This command displays all of the entries in the AppleTalk arp cache on the router. This command is very useful when you are trying to identify the network address of a specific Macintosh on the network.

- **show appletalk cache**—This command displays all of the routes in the AppleTalk fast-switching cache, which the router uses to perform rapid lookups of the routes that must be used to direct network traffic to its destination (without the fast-switching cache, the router would be forced to calculate a route for each piece of network traffic). From this list, you can look at the various AppleTalk routes that are being used to direct packets between computers.

4. AppleTalk Networking

- **show appletalk eigrp interfaces *type number*—**This command displays all the interfaces on the router that are configured for EIGRP routing. The *type* and *number* switches allow you to limit the information to a specific interface type and number.

- **show appletalk eigrp neighbors *interface*—**This command displays a list of all the router's neighbors that the EIGRP routing protocol discovers. The *interface* option allows you to limit the information returned to only the information that relates to the selected interface.

- **show appletalk globals—**This command displays all the information about and settings of the AppleTalk Internetwork and related parameters.

- **show appletalk interface *(brief) type number*—**This command displays information about all the interfaces that are configured to use AppleTalk. The *brief* switch limits the information returned to a brief summary. The *type* and *number* switches allow you to limit the information to a specific interface type and number.

- **show appletalk name-cache—**This command displays the list of services that routers and other network equipment provide as returned by NBP.

- **show appletalk nbp—**This command displays the contents of the NBP registration table.

- **show appletalk neighbors *neighbor-address*—**This command displays a list of AppleTalk routers that are directly connected to this router. The *neighbor-address* option allows you to narrow this report to a single AppleTalk neighbor.

- **show appletalk routes *type number*—**This command displays all of the static and discovered AppleTalk routes that this router knows about. The *type* and *number* switches allow you to limit the routes displayed to the ones connected to a specific interface type and number.

- **show appletalk static—**This command displays all of the static AppleTalk routes that are configured on this router. *Static routes* are routes that have been manually configured on the router rather than those that are learned from EIGRP or some other dynamic routing protocol.

- **show appletalk traffic—**This command displays all of the counters that store information about the AppleTalk traffic that enters and leaves the router.

4. AppleTalk Networking

- **show appletalk zone** *zone-name*—This command displays all of the information in the zone information table on the router. You can use the *zone-name* switch to limit the information returned to a specific zone name.

- **test appletalk**—This important command allows you to enter the test mode to help test and diagnose AppleTalk on your router.

Using Examples Of Cisco Router AppleTalk Configurations

In the following sections, we'll offer a series of configuration examples that you can use when configuring your Cisco routers for AppleTalk. These examples are deliberately generic and refer to the network layouts that we have described. By using these examples as guides, you can adapt the setup requirements for your specific installation. In each example, the exclamation point (!) is used as a remark character to help separate the lines.

TIP: When working with the Cisco IOS CLI, there are some tricks you may find useful. If you wish to see a list of commands that are available, simply type "?" and then press Enter. Likewise, if you want to see all the options available to a command like show, type "show ?" and then press Enter. If you wish to speed up entering commands when working in IOS, you can type the first few letters of a command and then press Tab. The IOS fills in the rest of the command. For example, typing "sh" and then pressing Tab causes the IOS to display show. This can be very useful when you wish to type out some of the longer commands in IOS.

Example #1

In this example you have a single AppleTalk network connected to one side of a single router.

```
Appletalk routing
!
Interface Ethernet1
AppleTalk cable-range 12-12
AppleTalk zone SouthMacLab
```

We have set up one interface on the router for this example, Ethernet1 with a distinct cable range and zone name. However, since we have not created a second AppleTalk network there is no one for this network to talk to. By creating a second AppleTalk network, as you will

4. AppleTalk Networking

see in the next example, you can route AppleTalk packets between two sections of the network.

```
AppleTalk routing
!
Interface Ethernet0
AppleTalk cable-range 10-10
AppleTalk zone NorthMacLab
!
Interface Ethernet1
AppleTalk cable-range 12-12
AppleTalk zone SouthMacLab
```

The router, in this example, is using the default AppleTalk routing protocol, RTMP, directing traffic between the two AppleTalk networks. For more complex networks, you will probably want to switch from RTMP to EIGRP to route traffic around your network.

Example #2

In this example, you have a router with AppleTalk networks on two of its Ethernet interfaces. This router is connected by another Ethernet interface to the larger network. Since you will need to provide routing information about your AppleTalk networks to the larger network, you have decided to use EIGRP.

```
AppleTalk routing eigrp 24
!
Interface Ethernet0
AppleTalk protocol eigrp
AppleTalk cable-range 10-10
AppleTalk zone NorthMacLab
!
Interface Ethernet1
AppleTalk protocol eigrp
AppleTalk cable-range 12-12
AppleTalk zone SouthMacLab
```

This configuration allows network traffic from the entire network to reach your two AppleTalk networks, and allows traffic from those networks to reach the other portions of the network. In order to limit the type of traffic that is allowed on and off your network, you can use the following commands:

```
AppleTalk routing eigrp 24
!
Interface Ethernet0
```

4. AppleTalk Networking

```
Aplletalk access-group 601
AppleTalk protocol eigrp
AppleTalk cable-range 10-10
AppleTalk zone NorthMacLab
!
Interface Ethernet1
AppleTalk access-group 601
AppleTalk protocol eigrp
AppleTalk cable-range 12-12
AppleTalk zone SouthMacLab
!
Access-list 601 permit network 10
Access-list 601 permit network 12
Access-list 601 deny other-access
```

This configuration sets up your router to allow only AppleTalk traffic from computers on AppleTalk networks 10 and 12. AppleTalk traffic from all other sources will be denied.

Example #3

The next example builds upon the earlier two by adding routing update filters, so that information about the NorthMacLab is not made available to the network and information about the SouthMacLab is not made available to computers in the NorthMacLab zone.

```
AppleTalk routing eigrp 24
!
Interface Ethernet0
AppleTalk access-group 601
AppleTalk distribute-list 602 out
AppleTalk distribute-list 603 in
AppleTalk protocol eigrp
AppleTalk cable-range 10-10
AppleTalk zone NorthMacLab
!
Interface Ethernet1
AppleTalk access-group 601
AppleTalk protocol eigrp
AppleTalk cable-range 12-12
AppleTalk zone SouthMacLab
!
Access-list 601 permit network 10
Access-list 601 permit network 12
Access-list 601 deny other-access
!
Access-list 602 deny zone NorthMacLab
```

```
Access-list 602 permit additional-zones
!
Access-list 603 deny zone SouthMacLab
Access-list 603 permit additional-zones
```

Using this configuration, the router will allow AppleTalk traffic only from the two cable ranges that you have defined on this router into the two AppleTalk networks. Additionally, information about the NorthMacLab zone is filtered out from the routing updates and any routing updates that contain information about the SouthMacLab zone from reaching the computers in the NorthMacLab zone.

Listing 4.1   A typical set of AppleTalk lists.

```
Access-list 601 permit network 10
Access-list 601 permit network 12
Access-list 601 deny other-access
!
Access-list 602 deny zone NorthMacLab
Access-list 602 permit additional-zones
!
Access-list 603 deny zone SouthMacLab
Access-list 603 permit additional-zones
```

Listing 4.2   More AppleTalk lists.

```
AppleTalk routing eigrp 24
!
Interface Ethernet0
AppleTalk access-group 601
AppleTalk distribute-list 602 out
AppleTalk distribute-list 603 in
AppleTalk protocol eigrp
AppleTalk cable-range 10-10
AppleTalk zone NorthMacLab
!
Access-list 601 permit network 10
Access-list 601 permit network 12
Access-list 601 deny other-access
!
Access-list 602 deny zone NorthMacLab
Access-list 602 permit additional-zones
!
Access-list 603 deny zone SouthMacLab
Access-list 603 permit additional-zones
```

4. AppleTalk Networking

Listing 4.3   Router 1.

```
Appletalk routing
interface tunnel 2
tunnel source e1
!Ethernet 1 is set to IP address 192.168.25.1
tunnel destination 192.168.1.1
apple cable-range 1024-1024
apple zone wormhole Tunnel
tunnel mode gre ip
```

Listing 4.4   Router 2.

```
Appletalk routing
interface tunnel 2
tunnel source e0
!Ethernet 0 is set to use IP address 192.168.1.1
tunnel destination 192.168.25.1
apple cable-range 1024-1024
apple zone wormhole Tunnel
tunnel mode gre ip
```

Using this configuration, the router allows AppleTalk traffic only from the two cable ranges that you have defined on this router into the two AppleTalk networks. Additionally, information about the NorthMacLab zone is filtered out from the routing updates and any routing updates that contain information about the SouthMacLab zone are prevented from reaching the computers in the NorthMacLab zone.

Fine-Tuning AppleTalk For Your Network

Fine-tuning of AppleTalk on your network is a complex and lengthy process. The process involves mapping out your network and then determining where AppleTalk is needed and where it is not. Once you have the network mapped out, you can start looking at the way that you want to shape the network traffic on the LAN. Finally, once you have finished shaping the network traffic the way that you want, you can look at changing the routing of packets to maximize your network's performance.

When you are starting the process of optimizing your network, follow these steps:

1. Sit down and map out your network's topology. By doing so, you are outlining where your Macintoshes are located and what servers or resources they need to talk to on the network.

2. Next, look at where AppleTalk must be allowed and where it is not needed on your network. For instance, you need it on any segment where you have Macintoshes and resources that those Macintoshes need access to; however, you do not need AppleTalk on a segment of the network that is populated with only Windows NT workstations.

Finally, you can start limiting where it is allowed. By using access lists and tunneling AppleTalk over TCP/IP, you can shape the network traffic so that only those subnets that need AppleTalk are set up to allow AppleTalk.

One very common method of preventing AppleTalk packets from getting on or off a subnet is using access lists on your routers. You can also use access lists to filter out portions of the AppleTalk or other network traffic so that just a portion of it is allowed on or off of the subnet.

When writing an access-list in Cisco's IOS, you will need to remember a few things. First, know that all AppleTalk access-lists are numbered between 600 and 699. Thus, when you look at the configuration on a Cisco router, you can readily determine which access-lists apply to AppleTalk and which do not.

Second, when planning your access-lists, remember that what is not explicitly permitted is going to be excluded by the implicit deny all that is appended to the end of each access list.

Last, you will need to remember that access-lists are interpreted from the top down. This means that if you have conflicting rules in your access-list, the one that is located closest to the beginning of the list is the one that wins. Listing 4.5 is an example of some AppleTalk access-lists.

Listing 4.5 Another example of AppleTalk lists.

```
Access-list 601 permit network 10
Access-list 601 permit network 12
Access-list 601 deny other-access
!
Access-list 602 deny zone NorthMacLab
Access-list 602 permit additional-zones
!
Access-list 603 deny zone SouthMacLab
Access-list 603 permit additional-zones
```

When you want to connect two widely separated subnets, you should look at setting up a tunnel on your network. By setting up a TCP/IP tunnel on your network, you are taking the AppleTalk packets that are located on one subnet, encapsulating them in a TCP/IP packet, and then sending them over the network to the destination subnet where they are de-encapsulated.

Although this may seem like a lot of overhead, it can actually help improve AppleTalk performance by limiting the number of subnets that your AppleTalk packets have to be routed over. Listings 4.6 and 4.7 show examples of Cisco IOS configurations that implement the tunneling of AppleTalk over TCP/IP.

Listing 4.6   Router 1.

```
interface tunnel 2
tunnel source e1
!Ethernet 1 is set to IP address 192.168.25.1
tunnel destination 192.168.1.1
apple cable-range 1024-1024
apple zone wormhole Tunnel
tunnel mode gre ip
```

Listing 4.7   Router 2.

```
interface tunnel 2
tunnel source e0
!Ethernet 0 is set to use IP address 192.168.1.1
tunnel destination 192.168.25.1
apple cable-range 1024-1024
apple zone wormhole Tunnel
tunnel mode gre ip
```

This configuration allows AppleTalk traffic from the subnet connected to the Ethernet 1 port on Router 1 to be tunneled over the rest of the network to the subnet connected to the Ethernet 0 port on Router 2. For networks that have pockets of Macintoshes on widely separated subnets, tunneling can be a very efficient way of knitting them all together.

Using access-lists and tunneling, you can shape the way that AppleTalk traffic flows over your network. In shaping the AppleTalk traffic, you can greatly improve the performance of your network by limiting AppleTalk to only where it is needed and keeping it from areas where it is not. In doing so, you can keep your network much more segregated and much more highly managed than it might otherwise be.

You can also use access-lists to limit the information that is passed around the network in the form of routing updates. By limiting the information that is passed from router to router, you can significantly change the way that AppleTalk packets flow over the network.

The problem is, of course, that by limiting the information that is passed from router to router, you can cause the network to become too rigid and fail when the network tries to reconfigure itself to cope with the failure of one of its components. Should you decide to use access-lists to limit the flow of AppleTalk information, try limiting as few things as possible. For an example of using an access-list to limit routing information, please look at the example below:

```
Access-list 601 permit network 10
Access-list 601 permit network 12
Access-list 601 deny other-access
!
Access-list 602 deny zone NorthMacLab
Access-list 602 permit additional-zones
!
Access-list 603 deny zone SouthMacLab
Access-list 603 permit additional-zones
!
AppleTalk routing eigrp 24
!
Interface Ethernet0
AppleTalk access-group 601
AppleTalk distribute-list 602 out
AppleTalk distribute-list 603 in
AppleTalk protocol eigrp
AppleTalk cable-range 10-10
AppleTalk zone NorthMacLab
```

In this example, we are blocking information about a zone called SouthMacLab from routing packets that are being received by the Ethernet0 interface. Likewise, information about the zone that is directly connected to the Ethernet0 interface, NorthMacLab, is prevented from being distributed to the other routers on the network.

Fine-Tuning AppleTalk On Your Macintosh

When attempting to limit the impact of having AppleTalk on your network, you can also change how your Macintoshes communicate with AppleTalk. By using some third-party utilities, you can significantly lessen the impact that your Macintoshes have on the network by limiting how often they request updates. Likewise, you can also help lessen any potential negative impact that your Macintoshes may have by making a few simple changes in the way that you use them.

The biggest impact that Macintoshes normally have upon the network in general is that they generate a lot of network requests for updates on the network shared volumes and other network services they are using every 10 seconds. By generating so many update requests, your Macintosh can easily fill up the network with unneeded packets and can force the Windows servers that house these shared volumes to spend an inordinate amount of their time answering requests for updates even if there have been no changes.

One obvious solution to this problem is to change the time interval that your Macintosh uses when requesting updates from the network shares and devices your Macintosh is using.

LessTalk from IPTech is a great example of such a product. Although it does not support Macintoshes running Mac OS 8 or later, it does do an excellent job of limiting the number of AppleTalk packets by changing the update interval to a user-defined value. Normally, you would set this to 300 seconds or so, thus limiting the Macintosh to asking for updates only every 5 minutes. This results in nearly a 30-fold decrease in the number of updates each Macintosh sends out over the network.

For Macintosh users running Mac OS 8 or later, you must consider changing how you work with remote volumes to reduce the number of updates that your Macintosh generates. Fortunately, the newest versions of the Mac OS incorporate versions of AppleTalk that are less "chatty" than older ones, which means the network isn't polled as often. This is one of the reasons why LessTalk was never upgraded by its publisher for the newer operating system versions.

Despite improvements in AppleTalk's performance, you may employ these other methods to fine-tune your network.

- *Simply keep the network volume closed*—This is a common trick. When you open a window in the Finder to a remote volume, your Macintosh asks the remote server every 10 seconds for an update. However, if you keep the window closed, then your Macintosh does not send out update requests to the file server.

- *Close the Chooser*—If you keep the Chooser open, your Macintosh sends out AppleTalk packets every 10 seconds as it searches for available network resources. So, by simply closing the Chooser when you are done with it (which is the usual practice anyway), you can significantly reduce the amount of AppleTalk traffic that your Macintosh generates.

Installing And Configuring DHCP

On many networks, DHCP servers are used to distribute IP addresses to the various network computers. DHCP (Dynamic Host Configuration Protocol) is a system that allows a server to distribute IP addresses from a pool of available addresses to computers that request them. You can configure both the IP address and the DHCP server to send out a variety of information regarding your network.

The DHCP server listens for IP address requests from computers on the network and when it receives such a request, it negotiates with the requesting computer. Once the negotiation is complete, the DHCP server sends the IP address and whatever information that the DHCP server has been set to deliver. When the computer has accepted the IP address from the DHCP server, the server lists the address as being in use.

To prevent all the IP addresses from being given out and never reclaimed when a computer is moved or retired, the DHCP server sets a lease time on each address that it assigns. This means that the IP address each computer gets from the DHCP server is good only for the period specified by the lease. When a computer with an IP address acquired from the DHCP wants an extension on the lease of its address, the server waits until the remaining time on the address' lease is equal to half of the original lease time before it contacts the DHCP server asking for one.

A computer that does not get a response from the DHCP server will then wait until one-quarter of the lease time is left before attempting to contact the DHCP server again. If it fails once again, it tries yet again at the one-eighths point and it continues to try until the lease actually expires. When the lease expires, the computer will release the IP address that it had received from the DHCP server and will then begin periodic attempts to obtain a new IP address.

Setting Up A DHCP Server Under Windows NT

The DHCP server that ships with Windows NT delivers IP addresses to any and all computers on the network that are set to use DHCP. In most networks, you will find that one or more Windows NT Servers are running the DHCP service so the entire network is covered. To set up and configure the DHCP server service that is included with Windows NT, follow these steps:

1. Using the procedure that we describe in Chapter 2 on how to install a new Windows NT Network Service, add the DHCP Server service.

2. Once you have rebooted the server after installing the DHCP Server service, reinstall the current Windows NT Service Pack that you are using and then reboot the server once again.

3. After the server has finished rebooting, log in to the server and then click on Start|Programs|Administrative Tools|DHCP.

4. Looking at the DHCP Manager, shown in Figure 4.13, you can see all the DHCP Servers that are available on your network. Click on Scope|Create.

5. From the Create Scope dialog box, shown in Figure 4.14, enter the beginning and ending IP addresses that you want this server to distribute to all of the computers on the network who request an address.

6. Next, enter all of the IP addresses that you do not want the DHCP server to make available.

7. Finally, set how long each IP address will be leased. Figure 4.14 shows how the DHCP scope is configured in a typical setup.

8. Next, click on OK to close the Create Scope dialog box and return to the main DHCP Manager screen.

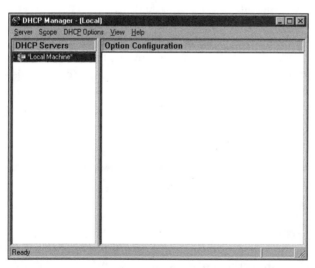

Figure 4.13   The DHCP Manager controls all aspects of a DHCP Server.

9. After you click on OK, you are asked if you wish to make this scope active. Click on Yes.

10. Next, click on DHCP_Options|Scope.

11. Look at the various options that you want to distribute informa-tion about with the IP address that the DHCP server sends out. In Figure 4.15, we have already added the DNS Server option and are about to add an option to distribute information about routers on the network.

12. Next, select each of the options and click on Value.

13. Enter the values that you want to use for each option, as shown in Figure 4.16.

14. Since this is information regarding the DNS servers available on the network, you will then want to click on the Edit Array

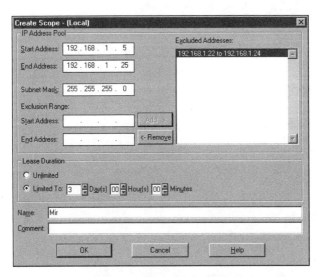

Figure 4.14   Configure your DHCP Scope by setting the various options.

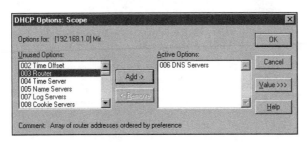

Figure 4.15   Add DHCP Options using the DHCP Options: Scope dialog box.

button and enter all of the IP addresses of the DNS servers that are you wish to distribute information about. See Figure 4.17 for a typical setup. Once you are done entering all of the DNS Servers, click on OK to close this dialog box.

15. Last, click on OK to close the IP Address Array Editor dialog box and return to the DHCP Manager.

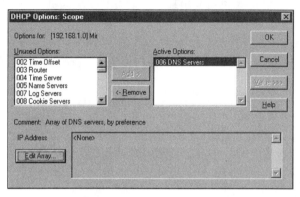

Figure 4.16   Clicking on the Value button allows you to enter settings for each option.

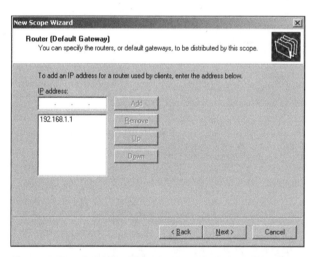

Figure 4.17   Enter the IP addresses of all the DNS servers you want to advertise.

NOTE: *Although you can configure 100 DHCP scope Options, both Windows- and Macintosh-based computers generally use only a few. The most commonly used scope options are those that distribute information about the routers or default gateways for each subnet, the DNS servers available on the network, the WINS or NetBIOS names Servers on the network, the domain name of the network and the NetBIOS node type, and a setting which determines how the Windows-based PC will search for names on the network. Macintosh OS-based computers can read information about the Default gateway, the DNS servers, and the domain name. However, most other options are not understood. Windows-based computers can read all of these common settings and more of the others; however, like the Macintosh, they do not understand all of them.*

Configuring Your Macintosh To Use DHCP

To get your Macintosh to obtain an IP address from the DHCP server, you will need to perform a few steps. You must first check to see if DHCP is available on the network segment where your Macintoshes are located. If DHCP is available, you must find out what information it is configured to distribute, along with the IP address, so that you can see if you will need to make any additional configuration changes on your Macintoshes. To start using DHCP, do the following:

1. Click on Apple|Control Panel|TCP/IP.

2. From the TCP/IP Control Panel, click on Configure|Using DHCP as shown in Figure 4.18.

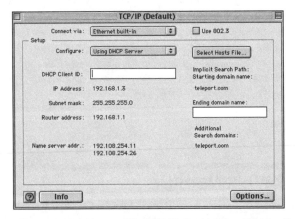

Figure 4.18   You use the TCP/IP Control Panel to configure TCP/IP on your Macintosh.

3. Click on the close box and then click on Save to save your changes.

Depending upon the information distributed by the DHCP server along with your IP address, you may have to set some of the settings manually. For example, some DHCP servers are configured to only distribute information about the WINS servers but not their DNS servers. Since Macintoshes cannot use WINS servers, you will have to manually set up the entries for the DNS servers in the TCP/IP Control Panel on each of your Macintoshes.

While the Macintosh DHCP client behaves much like the Windows DHCP client, there are some differences. For example, if your Macintosh cannot discover a DHCP server on startup, it will keep trying for about 20 seconds. If it still does not get a response, then it will choose an IP address from the non-routable IP address range 169.254.0.0 to 169.254.254.255 and set a subnet value of 255.255.0.0. Windows PCs, on the other hand, will set an address of 0.0.0.0 if they are unable to find a DHCP server before they time out.

NOTE: *When you look at the various options under the Configure menu in the TCP/IP Control Panel, you will see two options that may look a bit strange; these are BOOT Protocol (BOOTP) and Reverse Address Resolution Protocol (RARP). BOOTP is an older system of distributing IP addresses from a central server, much like DHCP. The primary difference between BOOTP and DHCP is that DHCP is able to automatically allocate IP addresses and manage them as well as distribute considerably more information with the IP address, unlike the older BOOTP. DHCP is also a considerably newer protocol and is rapidly replacing BOOTP on most networks. RARP is yet another system that allows a computer to make a request for information about its network address. RARP is different, because it sends out a broadcast containing its Ethernet address to the computers on the network where a RARP server picks up the broadcast and matches the Ethernet address against a list of IP addresses. Once it has found a match, it sends back a message telling the computer what its IP address is. One of the big downsides of RARP versus DHCP or BOOTP is that you have to have a RARP server on each subnet as the RARP broadcasts do not get routed over the network like BOOTP or DHCP packets do.*

Fine-Tuning DAVE's NetBIOS

The NetBIOS Control Panel that is part of DAVE has a variety of settings that you can use to set DAVE up for optimal performance on your network. The default settings that are established when you first install DAVE are usually fine for most networks; however, sometimes you need to make changes in order to improve network performance.

4. AppleTalk Networking

NOTE: *Before you start fine-tuning NetBIOS, you need to determine the Windows Internet Naming System (WINS), the node type, the broadcast address, and the Name Server Port that NetBIOS is using.*

To start fine-tuning the DAVE NetBIOS, follow these steps:

1. Click on the Apple menu and then select NetBIOS from the list of control panels.

2. In the NetBIOS Control Panel, see if the WINS or Dynamic Host Configuration Protocol (DHCP) checkbox, shown in Figure 4.19, is selected. If WINS is selected, check that the primary and secondary WINS servers are set to use the closest and most up-to-date WINS servers. If you are using DHCP, make sure that the DHCP server is configured to provide DAVE with the proper WINS server.

3. To see the advanced settings that you can configure, click on the Admin button to bring up the NetBIOS Administrator Options dialog box. Figure 4.20 shows all the available options.

4. Looking at the NetBIOS Administrator Options dialog box, check that the Broadcast Address and Name Server Port values are correct for your network configuration. The Broadcast Address box is usually left blank unless it has been changed from the default value. If it has been changed, make sure that you enter the new value into the Broadcast Address box.

5. Likewise, if your network is configured to use a non-standard name server port, you should change the value listed from 137 to the port number that is being used.

Figure 4.19 *The DAVE NetBIOS Control Panel is used to optimize perfor-mance on your Mac network.*

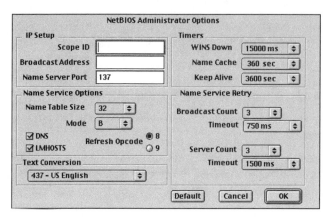

Figure 4.20   These are the options available in the NetBIOS Administrator Options dialog box.

6. Next, you need to check that the Name Service mode is set to the WINS node type that you have configured on your network. This step is very important because your workstation will not look up names efficiently if it is set to the wrong node type.

NOTE: *There are 4 NetBIOS node types that you can choose from when setting up your Names Service Options in DAVE. These node types, also frequently referred to as WINS node types, tell DAVE how it should go about matching up the NetBIOS name of a computer with its IP address. The 4 NetBIOS node types that you can choose from are as follows:*

B-Node: B-Node uses a broadcast request to all the computers on the network requesting that the computer using the NetBIOS name being searched for respond with its IP address. Broadcasts are also used by DAVE and Windows-based computers as they are started up to let the other computers on the network know their NetBIOS name. The biggest problem with using B-Node is that all these broadcasts can clog up the network, and as most routers do not forward on these broadcasts, you usually do not get an answer from other segments of your network.

P-Node: P-Node uses a directed message to the network WINS server requesting the IP address of the computer that is using a specific NetBIOS name. Computers using P-Node also are designed to contact the WINS server upon startup so that the WINS server is aware of their existence and can provide information about them to the other computers on the network. The biggest problem with P-Node is that you must know the IP addresses of the WINS servers located on your network. Additionally, if your WINS server does not have information on the computer you are trying to talk to, you will be unable to do so.

M-Node: M-Node, also known as Mixed-Node, is a combination of B-Node and P-Node. M-Node computers first send out a broadcast to the network asking for the resolution of a NetBIOS name. If they do not receive a response from their broadcast, the computer then sends a directed message to the WINS servers on the network requesting the IP address of the computer using the NetBIOS name in question.

H-Node: H-Node, or Hybrid-Node, is a combination of P-Node and B-Node. H-Node computers first send a message to the WINS servers on the Network requesting the IP address of the computer using the NetBIOS name they are trying to resolve. If the WINS servers fail to respond or do not have information regarding that NetBIOS name, then the computer trying to resolve the NetBIOS name broadcasts its NetBIOS resolution request to all the computers on the network.

On most Windows NT-based networks, you will find that the Name Service Node type is set to H-Node as this mode offers the best compromise between name resolution efficiency and network traffic.

7. You may also wish to allocate more memory for use as a name to lessen the number of times that DAVE must contact the WINS server when looking up a computer name. To do this, click on the Name Table Size menu and select a higher value.

8. If you know of computers whose names do not appear in WINS for some reason, you can add them to a file called LMHOSTS, located in your Preferences folder under the System Folder. DAVE uses this file to match up computer names with IP addresses if WINS fails to have a listing. To add a computer to the LMHOSTS file, open the file in the SimpleText application that comes with your Mac (or with any word processor, so long as you save the document in text format).

9. In SimpleText, add a line for the computer so that it looks like Listing 4.8.

Listing 4.8   Add a line for the computer as shown.

```
192.168.1.2   TestServer1   #PRE   #DOM:TestNet
192.168.1.3   TestServer2   #PRE
```

NOTE: *In the LMHOSTS file, servers are identified by their IP address, then their name. The #PRE command after a server's name tells DAVE to load the IP address and name into the name cache upon startup. The #DOM:DomainName command tells DAVE that this server is also the domain controller for the domain listed.*

In general, we do not recommend changing any of the other settings unless you are located on an extremely slow portion of the network. If that is the case, you can click on the various timer settings and select higher values than the defaults. If adjusting the settings does not help appreciably, try increasing the retry values.

Related Solution	Found on page
Configuring DAVE	36
Using DAVE To Set Up Printers For Your Mac Computers	64

4. AppleTalk Networking

Troubleshooting AppleTalk

Troubleshooting AppleTalk at the network level is more complex than diagnosing other problems you may encounter when integrating Macintosh computers into your Windows NT network. When you start to isolate a network problem, you need to determine if the problem is related to the networking hardware or if it is related to the configuration of the network itself.

Fixing The Inability To See Zones And Computers On Another Network

One of the most common problems that you may run into is not being able to see zones and computers on another network. This symptom usually results from either bad routing information on the router or access lists on the router that are blocking the network traffic.

Before continuing with your troubleshooting, you should make sure that all computers on your section of the network are having the same problem. If they are, check if computers on another network can see the zones and computers on your network. If they are visible to the rest of the network, check the access lists that are installed on the router interfaces connected to your network. To do this, log in to your router and follow these steps:

1. From the enable prompt, type "show running-config".

2. Looking at the current configuration, check the configuration settings that are applied to the interface that is connected to your network. Note the number of the access-list that is applied to the interface as well as the access-lists that are applied to AppleTalk routing.

3. Next, look at all access-lists and see if they are set to block network traffic from the other networks or zones. If they are not set in this fashion, see if the access lists that are applied to the routing updates block information about the other networks and zones.

4. If they do block that information, try removing the access list that is preventing you from seeing the remote networks and zones to see if your problem has been resolved.

5. If none of the access lists on your router block network traffic or information about the other networks and zones on your local area network (LAN), check the AppleTalk routing information table. You can examine the routing information table by typing "show appletalk routes" at the enable prompt.

6. Looking at the routes listed, see if there are routes to the remote networks and zones that you cannot see on your Macintosh. If the routes are indeed listed, clear out these routes using the **clear appletalk routes** command and then do a **show appletalk routes** again to see if the routes that are listed now are the same as those listed earlier.

7. If the routes are different, see if you can now view the remote networks and zones from your Macintosh.

8. If the routes listed did not change after you cleared out the route cache, examine the access lists that are installed on the other routers between you and the remote networks and zones to make sure that they are not blocking you.

Dealing With Seeing Only A Portion Of Network Resources

Another common problem involves seeing only a portion of the network resources on a remote network or zone. Usually, this difficulty results from the presence of an access list on either your router's network interface or on the router connected to the remote segment of the network that prevents certain NBP types from being blocked, thus rendering them invisible to computers off their network. To check for this problem, follow these steps:

1. Log in to the router using the procedure described earlier in this chapter and then type "enable" and the enable password.

2. Once you are in enable mode, type "show running-config" at the prompt and then press Enter.

3. Going through the configuration, look at the access list that is being used on the interface that connects to your AppleTalk network.

4. Check that the access list is configured to deny specific NBP types. Next, examine the list to make sure that it is not filtering out NBP types that you really want to see.

5. If the access list on your router's interface does not filter out any NBP information, you should check the router connected to the remote network or zone. More than likely, it is configured with an access list that is blocking you from seeing the NBP information needed to see the network resources you are looking for.

4. AppleTalk Networking

Fixing Sluggish Performance

Sometimes, especially on newer Macintosh models, you will find that their network performance is sluggish and that network connections frequently close unexpectedly when you are connected to the network by a Fast Ethernet network switch. This problem is commonly caused by incorrect settings on the switch port. The best way to test for this is to identify which network port on the switch your Macintosh is connected to. You usually accomplish this by looking up on a map of the network, the network port your computer is plugged into and from that, which port it is connected to on the switch. Once you have the network port information, log in to the switch and do the following:

1. Type "show interface fastethernet interface-number".

2. Look at the information returned and see if the interface is set to 100Mbps or to 10Mbps. If it is set to 10Mbps, your problem lies elsewhere. If the interface is set to 100Mbit, look to see if a large number of errors are listed.

3. If there are a large number of Ethernet errors, see if the port is configured for Full Duplex or Half Duplex.

NOTE: *Full Duplex and Half Duplex modes define the way that the Ethernet card communicates with the switch. In Full Duplex mode, the card can send information at the same time it is receiving information, making the effective amount of data being transferred equal to about 200Mbps. In Half Duplex mode, the Ethernet card must wait until the sender has finished sending data before it can send its data out. This limits the amount of data being transmitted to 100Mbps. For computers using standard 10Mbps Ethernet, the only setting that is available is half-duplex.*

---

4. If the port is configured to use Full Duplex, try changing it to Half Duplex and see if that solves your problem. Changing the configuration on a switch varies from model to model, so it is usually best to have the people responsible for maintaining the switch make the change.

4. AppleTalk Networking

Using Troubleshooting Techniques For Networks In General

When you encounter persistent networking performance bottlenecks, follow these basic steps to examine your configuration and determine the cause of the problem:

1. First, define the problem as accurately as possible. Does it occur on only one computer or does it apply to a whole group of computers on the network?

2. If this problem affects only one computer, try connecting another computer to the same network cable and see if the same symptom appears on the new computer.

3. When the problem does not occur with the other computer, take a closer look at the computer that is having the problem. Check whether the Ethernet interface on the computer that is having problems is functioning correctly. You can do this by moving the computer to another network port to see if it works there. If you have a network analyzer, such as a Network General Sniffer or Network Analyzer, which comes with Microsoft Systems Management Server (SMS), you can use it to probe the network traffic generated by the computer in question to see if it is normal.

4. If the Ethernet interface is operating properly, you need to make sure that the operating system is configured correctly to communicate with the Ethernet interface. If the Ethernet interface is not functioning correctly, you should have the computer repaired.

5. If the computer is functioning correctly, examine the network configuration that you are using on that computer. For example, double-check that the Ethernet port speed and duplex modes are set correctly and that you have set all the other network parameters to what they should be.

NOTE: *A good indicator that one of your computers has an improperly configured Ethernet interface is the number of Ethernet errors you see on the network. In a switched network, you can do this by logging in to the network switch and doing a show interface interface-type interface-number to look at the Ethernet statistics for a specific port on the switch. Thus, when a port is showing an abnormally high number of network errors, you should probably take a closer look at the computer connected to it.*

---

4. AppleTalk Networking

Examining The Network Configuration

If the problem cannot be traced to hardware, you must look at the network configuration to see if the problem lies there. To do so, follow these steps:

1. Gather information about the network your Macintoshes are connected to. In particular, get the IP address, console password, and the enable password of the router that connects your section of the network to the rest of the LAN.

2. Next, log in to the router using a Telnet program and then connecting to the router by its IP address. You can also connect to the router by going to the router directly and connecting a serial cable to the console port and then using a terminal program like ZTerm to talk to the router.

NOTE: *ZTerm is a popular shareware terminal program that is bundled with Global Village modems or available separately from popular shareware Web sites, such as Version Tracker (http://www.versiontracker.com).*

---

3. Once you have logged into the router and switched into enable mode, type "show running-config" to display the current router configuration. Examine the configuration to see if any access lists might be causing your problem. Pay particular attention to the access lists that are applied to the AppleTalk routing if you are having trouble seeing remote networks and zones.

4. If there are no problems with the configuration that is running on the router, check the AppleTalk routes in the route cache. To do this, type "show appletalk routes" and then press Enter.

5. Look at the listed routes to see if they are accurate. A good way to check if the route cache has become corrupted is to do a **clear appletalk routes** and then do another **show appletalk routes** to see if the routes listed in the route cache have changed. If they have, see if the problem has been resolved.

6. If there was no change in the routing information, expand your search outward by repeating Steps 2 through 5 on the other routers on your network, starting with the one connected to the network segment that you are having trouble seeing.

Chapter 5

Integrating Your Macintosh Into Microsoft BackOffice

In Brief

Exploring Microsoft BackOffice's Applications

Microsoft BackOffice is an interlinking set of server-based applications that offer database, electronic messaging, Internet access, and intranet capabilities for Windows-based networks. By taking advantage of the power of Microsoft BackOffice, the Macintosh users in your company can access industrial-strength databases or tie directly into the corporate email systems. Macintosh users can also reach out to the Internet or access corporate intranets to share data with other users on the network. In the following sections, we take a brief look at these applications. Later in this chapter, we'll explain how you can harness the power of Microsoft BackOffice, readily expand the capabilities of your Macs, and tap into enterprise-wide applications.

Using Microsoft SQL Server 7

Microsoft SQL Server 7 (version 7 was the current version when this book was written) gives the users on your network access to an enterprise-capable database engine. Users with other databases—such as FileMaker Pro, which comes in both Mac and Windows versions—or other applications—such as Excel or even Web servers—can access this resource. Consider SQL Server 7 a network's memory.

This version of SQL Server is the latest incarnation of Microsoft's BackOffice database server engine, capable of handling the database needs of a small company or a large enterprise. You can use SQL Server as the database to which you connect from your Macintosh when you want to expand the capabilities of FileMaker Pro to handle data or to extract data from a database using Excel.

You can also use SQL Server to deliver the database engine that allows you to create Web pages that access specific databases and make the results available to all users on your network. In short, your Macintosh clients can use SQL Server to access large amounts of data, regardless of whether the data comes from a FileMaker Pro database application or another program (such as Excel). Those clients can even use SQL Server to access a database-enabled Web page served up by IIS.

Using Microsoft Exchange 5.5

Microsoft Exchange 5.5 is the network that coordinates communication among the various parts of the network. Exchange hosts electronic mail, scheduling, and chat services. You can use this and SQL Server 7 to extend the power of Macintosh-based applications as well as to integrate your Macintosh into the enterprise communications infrastructure.

Microsoft Exchange is the email system of choice for many organizations due to its scalability and robust messaging capabilities. Unfortunately, until relatively recently, Mac users were denied access to Exchange because a native Macintosh client was unavailable. Fortunately, with the release of Service Pack 2 (SP2) for Exchange 5.5, Microsoft has provided us with a Macintosh client that provides access to most of Exchange's functionality. In fact, the only action that this client cannot perform is to directly access Exchange's calendar features.

Using Microsoft Proxy Server 2.0

Microsoft Proxy Server 2.0 is a BackOffice tool that lets you connect to the Internet and access all the various sites and other services available in it. It offers the Macintosh users on your network quick and reliable access to the World Wide Web by way of its HTTP Proxy. It also offers access to other Internet applications by way of its SOCKS Proxy. Proxy Server redirects your network traffic through a single server or group of servers and out into the Internet.

NOTE: *A Web proxy server acts as an intermediary between a user browsing the Web from a workstation and the Internet. The Web proxy intercepts the user's requests for Web pages. It then either returns a copy of the Web page it has stored in its cache of commonly viewed Web pages or contacts the remote Web server and then directs the responses back to the user's browser.*

Proxy Server 2.0 provides users with Internet connectivity as well as protection from hackers and other intruders. It has three major components:

- *The Hypertext Transport Protocol,* or *HTTP Proxy service*—This redirects users' requests for Web pages through itself. It then keeps a copy of the most commonly used Web pages in memory so that it can speed up their delivery to the users.

- *SOCKS proxy*—This is the generic proxy service that Unix- and Macintosh-based computers use to redirect requests by such programs as Internet Relay Chat or Newsgroups reader through the proxy server and out to the Internet. It provides a buffer between the user on a workstation and the Internet by intercepting and redirecting other types of Internet traffic (non-Web, for example). The primary reason for using a SOCKS proxy is that it allows the network administrator to improve network security by focusing certain types of network traffic through a single server and in certain cases a single TCP/IP port number.

- *Microsoft's Winsock proxy and Security module*—These are designed to redirect requests made by Windows-based Internet applications through the proxy server and then out into the Internet.

Using Internet Information Server (IIS)

IIS is another BackOffice tool that lets you create Web servers that serve up Web pages to the Internet or on corporate intranets. IIS, especially with Microsoft Site Server installed, delivers the same level of access to Macintosh users that it provides to Windows users. This feature allows Macintosh users to access information on Internet and Intranet servers as well as to share documents with the other users on your network through the Microsoft Posting Acceptor.

NOTE: *Microsoft Posting Acceptor is a great tool for handling document collaboration; it allows users to upload and download documents from a Web server. Posting Acceptor also acts as a version control system by recording who checked out each document and when that person checked it back in. You can also configure Posting Acceptor to keep a finite number of different revisions of each document in its database so that you can go back to earlier revisions if necessary.*

Exploring Other Utilities To Back Up The Data On Your Macintosh

Few network services are more important than the systems that back up and restore your personal and corporate data. Backing up your critical files is your sole insurance against the possibility of losing files due to drive corruption, accidental file deletion, fire, or another catastrophe.

Most modern backup systems use a central server (or servers) that goes out and searches the network for data to be backed up and then copies this data to a tape drive or other large-capacity medium. These tapes are usually stored offline so that they are safe and ready to be used. As a user on the Windows NT network, you need to make sure that your data, like that of the Windows users, is properly backed up.

NOTE: *It is also a good idea to make an extra backup of your mission-critical data and store it offsite. Doing so allows you to get up and running should your business face fire, theft, flood, or other weather-related damage that affects your primary facility.*

In the NT world, you have two options for backing up your servers. The first is to rely upon the Windows NT Backup software that is included with Windows NT. Although this is a good option if you are on an extremely limited budget, it lacks many of the features (such as being able to log on to a remote server) that are found in more-robust packages. The second option is to use a commercial backup software package such as Veritas Software's BackupExec, Computer Associates's ARCserve, or Dantz's Retrospect.

Using BackupExec And ARCserveIT

BackupExec and ARCserveIT allow you to deliver critical network functions to your Macintosh clients. You can use either program for networked backup of the files on your Macintosh workstations and servers.

BackupExec

BackupExec is the enterprise version of the backup software that comes with Windows NT. Some of its many features include the ability to read and back up Macintosh volumes on Windows NT Servers, back up data on remote servers, and then restore the data when needed. BackupExec can also handle all sorts of storage devices from a simple tape drive to a huge tape library.

The biggest upside to the current version of BackupExec, version 7.2, is that it comes with a Macintosh client that lets you directly access workstations and servers that are running the Mac OS. Thus, users on a Windows NT network that rely upon BackupExec can store their data on either their Windows NT Servers or their Macintosh workstations and servers if they wish to have it backed up.

ARCserveIT

ARCserveIT is the other major enterprise-capable backup software that you will find in use on Windows NT-based networks. ARCserveIT is similar in many ways to BackupExec in that it can back up and restore data on remote servers as well as back up Macintosh volumes located on NT Servers. ARCserveIT can also handle all sorts of backup media, making it easy for you to choose the backup medium that best suits your needs.

The big disadvantage that ARCserveIT has over BackupExec is that ARCserveIT's optional Macintosh client is a separate product that you must purchase separately. Using this client, ARCserveIT can then back up the data stored on your Macs and their AppleShare servers (instead of your having to store all of their critical data on the Windows NT Macintosh volumes).

Using Retrospect And The Retrospect Remote Windows Client

Retrospect and the Retrospect Remote Windows client allow you to back up Windows 95, 98, and NT clients to a Macintosh that is running Retrospect. Retrospect is the most widely used Macintosh OS-based backup program for both single computers and whole networks. Retrospect also has a Windows 95, 98, and NT client that can back up data from a Windows-based workstation or server on a Macintosh OS-based server. Installing the Retrospect Remote Windows client on your Windows 95/98 and NT computers and then using Retrospect to back them up is as simple as backing up your Macintosh OS clients. It allows you to service all of your Macintosh users' needs as well as those of your few Windows-based servers and workstations.

Integrating your Macintosh data into the network backup system is a simple exercise if you take some time in the beginning to understand how data is being backed up on the Windows NT servers and workstations. Once you know how the backup system is designed, you can then start setting up your Macintosh volumes and other data storage areas so that the network backup system can easily back them up.

NOTE: *The key thing to remember when setting up your backup regimen is that you do it in concert with the people who are running your other backups so that no conflicts prevent you from performing the backups.*

Exploring Other Utilities To Connect Your Macintosh To The Internet

Connecting your Macintosh to the Internet over your network can be both a simple and exceedingly complex task, depending upon how your Internet connection is configured. In most modern networks, the local area network (LAN) is protected from the wilds of the Internet by a firewall or another security system designed to keep your network traffic from getting out onto the Internet. Firewalls can be divided into two major groups: dedicated firewall products (such as Axent's Raptor and Cisco Systems's PIX firewall) or products that have firewall capabilities (such as Microsoft Proxy Server, discussed earlier in this chapter, and Tiny Software's Winroute Pro). Depending upon the type of firewall you choose, you will have several options to select from when you are connecting your Macintosh to the Internet.

NOTE: *Because of the shortage of Internet Protocol (IP) addresses available on the Internet, many companies and home users are choosing to use one of the three groups of private IP addresses that are available. Private IP addresses are those that start with 10.x.x.x, 172.16.x.x-172.31.x.x, or 192.168.x.x. They are referred to as private IP addresses because you cannot send them out on the Internet. This allows many different networks to use them without causing any conflicts. The only limitation to this process is that you must have at least one "real" IP address that the Proxy Server or Firewall can use to talk to other computers on the Internet. Both Firewalls and Proxy servers are designed to translate users' requests with private IP addresses that use the real address and back again, granting users with private IP addresses access to the Internet.*

Using Raptor And PIX Firewalls

Axent's Raptor Firewall and Cisco's PIX Firewall are devices whose sole purpose is to regulate the flow of TCP/IP network traffic to and from the Internet. Such dedicated firewalls are usually set up with the idea that less is more. In other words, the smaller the amount of TCP/IP traffic that you let through the firewall, the greater your network security will be. As such, most firewalls are configured to allow access only to the World Wide Web, FTP, and electronic mail. Depending upon the users' needs, other traffic (such as Real Audio or Internet Newsgroups) may also be allowed on the networks.

NOTE: *When you are setting up your Macs to access the Internet, it is always a good idea to talk to the people responsible for configuring the firewall to make sure that you have all the information you need to successfully configure your Macintoshes.*

Using Winroute Lite And Winroute Pro

Tools such as Winroute Lite and Winroute Pro from Tiny Software allow your Macintosh users to have full access to their Internet applications without the limitations placed upon them by Microsoft's Proxy Server 2.0. At the same time, they manage to offer a reasonable level of protection from intruders on the Internet. Winroute Pro and Winroute Lite direct all your network traffic through a single computer and provide a variety of generic proxy services. By placing these products between you and the Internet, you can restrict your Internet connection to just a few servers, thus limiting your network's exposure to the Internet.

NOTE: *Protecting yourself from hackers and others on the Internet who are trying to access your network without your permission is a major problem today. All of the tools that we describe in this section, Axent's Raptor Firewall, Cisco's PIX Firewall, and Winroute Pro, can set up filters on the network traffic that they let through, which limits your network's exposure.*

Winroute Pro and Winroute Lite seamlessly direct your Internet traffic to and from the Internet without your having to use a specific proxy server. This allows you to ignore the proxy settings and simply run Fetch, Internet Explorer, or any of your other Internet applications without having to configure them. Additionally, by making the proxy server effectively transparent to your Macintosh, Winroute Pro and Winroute Lite allow all your Macintosh Internet applications to run and function, not just those that can use a Web or SOCKS proxy.

Winroute Pro and Winroute Lite can also translate a private IP address to a real one by native address translation (NAT); users can use a private IP address on their local network and still connect to the Internet as usual. You can also use Winroute Pro to protect your network from intruders by denying specific TCP/IP ports that hackers commonly use, or to block specific applications that you don't want users to use (such as Internet Relay Chat).

For small networks, you can use Winroute Pro and Winroute Lite to distribute TCP/IP configurations to the computers on your network via their built-in Dynamic Host Configuration Protocol (DHCP) server. Using Winroute Pro, you can also limit which computers have access to the Internet and when, which is very useful when you want to limit a user's ability to use different applications and the time that he or she spends online.

NOTE: *As this book was written, Tiny Software released a major upgrade to Winroute Pro. Version 4.0 offers improvements to its already excellent packet filtering and Network Address Translation capabilities. Winroute 4.0 also offers remote administration and logging capabilities that were not available in version 3.0. For more information on Winroute Lite and Winroute Pro, visit the Tiny Software web site at http://www.tinysoftware.com.*

Immediate Solutions

Configuring SQL Server 7

Connecting to a SQL Server from FileMaker Pro 4.1 is a two-part process that involves establishing an ODBC connection between your Macintosh and the SQL Server and then a connection between the ODBC connection and your FileMaker database.

NOTE: *ODBC is software that allows your Macintosh to connect to databases on other servers. ODBC consists of the ODBC software itself and a list of connectors that are customized to deal with a specific database server.*

To configure the ODBC database connector on your Macintosh, follow these steps:

1. From the Apple menu, select Control Panels|ODBC Setup PPC.

2. In the ODBC Data Source Administrator dialog box, make sure that the User Data Source Name (DSN) tab is selected (as shown in Figure 5.1) and then click on Add to begin the process of adding a new user DSN to your Macintosh.

3. Next, select the type of database that you wish to connect to. You can choose between dBase, FoxPro, Oracle, Text-based,

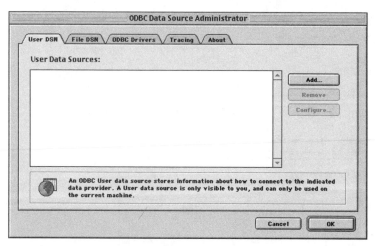

Figure 5.1   Use the ODBC Data Source Administrator to configure a user DSN.

and SQL Server databases. In this example, you should select ODBC SQL Server Driver PPC, as shown in Figure 5.2, and then click on Finish.

4. The VSI MS SQL Server dialog box, shown in Figure 5.3, now appears. In this dialog box, enter the DSN that you wish to connect to, the name of the server that hosts this database, and the TCP/IP network address of the server. You can also option-ally enter a description of the database connector that you are setting up. Before moving on, make sure that the Network Library setting is set so that SQL Server uses TCP/IP instead of Named Pipes as is the default.

5. If necessary, you can also click on Options from the VSI MS SQL Server dialog box. Doing so allows you to specify the database name you wish to log in to and the language with which you wish to talk to the database. The default language options are German, French, and U.S. English.

6. Once you have finished entering all of the configuration data, click on OK to finish creating your ODBC DSN.

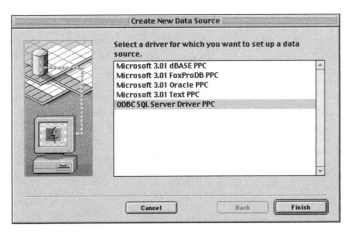

Figure 5.2   Choose the ODBC connector type on this screen.

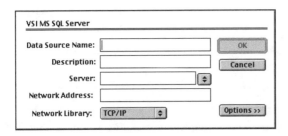

Figure 5.3   Enter the ODBC server information in this dialog box.

Configuring FileMaker Pro To Access SQL Server 7

The next step in configuring SQL Server 7 is to configure FileMaker Pro to create a connection to the ODBC connector. To establish the connection between FileMaker Pro and SQL Server via the ODBC connector, follow these steps:

1. Launch FileMaker Pro.

2. Choose File|New to create a new database.

3. Click on File|Open.

4. From the Open dialog box, click on the Show menu located at the bottom of the dialog box and then select ODBC as the file type you wish to open.

5. You see a list of ODBC connectors. From this list, select the one that you wish to access and click on OK, as shown in Figure 5.4.

6. Enter the username and password for this database and then click on OK to continue.

7. Next, you see a list of all the tables that are present in the database. Select the ones that you wish to use and then click on OK.

You are now ready to begin building your database application using data from SQL Server.

Configuring Excel To Work With SQL Server 7

Using Microsoft Excel 98, you can access databases on SQL Server 7 through an ODBC connection between your Macintosh and the Windows NT Server. Connecting your Excel spreadsheet to an SQL Server database is also a two-part process. To begin setting up your connection, you first create an ODBC DSN between your Macintosh and the SQL Server, as you did in the "Configuring SQL Server 7" sec-

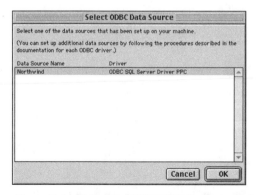

Figure 5.4   Select the ODBC DSN that you wish to use.

tion earlier in this chapter. Once you have configured the ODBC DSN, you must configure the external database options in Excel so that they point to the proper SQL database.

The first step in connecting your Microsoft Excel spreadsheet to an SQL Server database is to configure the external data source query that your spreadsheet will be using to read data from the SQL Server database. To configure your spreadsheet to access the data in a SQL Server database, follow these steps:

1. Launch Microsoft Excel.

2. Once the program is running, open the spreadsheet that you wish to connect to the database, using File|Open.

3. After you've opened your spreadsheet, click on the Data menu and then select Create New Query from the Get External Data submenu.

4. The Choose Data Source dialog box, shown in Figure 5.5, appears. Select the data source that you created when you set up your ODBC DSN in the "Configuring SQL Server 7" section earlier in this chapter and then click on OK.

5. Now, you are presented with the VSI MS SQL Server dialog box (shown in Figure 5.6). Enter the Data Source Name, a description, if you wish, and either enter the Network IP address of the server you want to connect to, or you can click the pop-up menu to the right of the Server field to select the option you need. Also, make sure the network library is set to TCP/IP.

6. In the Login section, type in the name of the database you wish to connect to, then click on the OK button.

7. In the next dialog box, you will be asked to enter the appropriate username and password that you wish to use to connect to this database. Then, click on OK.

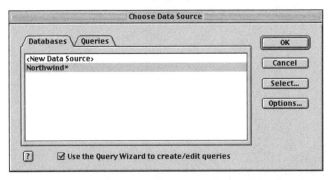

Figure 5.5   Select the ODBC connector you want from this dialog box.

Figure 5.6   Enter the requested information here.

8. You are next presented with a list of the database's fields. Select the fields that you wish to use and then click on OK to close the dialog box.

You now can set up queries and other database operations based upon the data stored on the remote SQL Server.

Once you have established your connection to the SQL Server, you can create connections to other SQL databases or to other spreadsheets. You can also set up applications in Excel that can use the data from the database in a read-only fashion (where you simply look at the data in the database) as well as interactively (where you can change and manipulate the database from your Excel spreadsheet).

NOTE: *Your ability to read or write to the database is defined by the permissions assigned the user in the SQL Server database. Depending upon her rights, she may be able to only read information from the database, or she may be able to edit its data.*

Installing And Configuring Outlook For Macintosh

Outlook for the Macintosh is available in two forms. The most common version is Outlook Express, the free email client that comes with Internet Explorer. This program comes pre-installed on all new

Macs, or you can download it directly from Microsoft's Web site (**www.microsoft.com/mac/**), which provides the download link plus additional information about Microsoft's Mac product line. The second form is Outlook, which comes with Microsoft Exchange Server 5.5 SP2. Outlook Express allows your Mac users to read their Internet mail and newsgroups; it does not allow them to connect to the Exchange servers on the network. Outlook, on the other hand, is designed strictly as an Exchange messaging client with the added functionality of a scheduling client built in.

To configure Microsoft Outlook for Macintosh, follow these steps:

1. Launch Outlook Installer and follow the instructions in the installation wizard to install Outlook for Macintosh on your computer. At the end of the installation process, you will see a Restart button on the installer screen. Click on it to continue the setup process.

2. Once Outlook is installed, you must configure it. To configure Outlook, open the Outlook Settings Control Panel and set up the connection between your Macintosh and the Exchange server that houses your mailbox.

3. In the MS Exchange Settings Properties dialog box, shown in Figure 5.7, click on Add and then select Microsoft Exchange Server from the list of available options.

4. You next see the Microsoft Exchange Server dialog box, shown in Figure 5.8. From here, enter the name of the Exchange server that houses your mailbox.

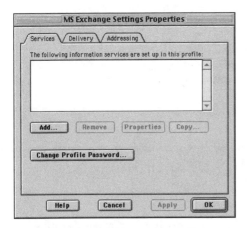

Figure 5.7   The MS Exchange Settings Properties Control Panel controls all your Exchange connection options.

*Figure 5.8   Configure all your connection options for your Exchange
server here.*

5. Next, type in your mail box's name.

6. Then, make sure that TCP/IP is selected as the proper connection type and check the startup option that you wish to use
   (Connect With The Network or Work Offline).

7. Once you have checked all your settings, click on Check Name
   to validate the connection. Doing so brings up the Enter
   Password dialog box, which asks for your account information.

8. Enter your username, the Windows NT domain that you belong
   to, and your password. Then, click on OK to proceed.

9. After you have validated the connection, click on the Advanced
   tab of the Microsoft Exchange Server dialog box to set up any
   other mailboxes that you wish to open.

10. Once you have finished configuring the Exchange server's
    properties, click on OK to close the Microsoft Exchange Server
    dialog box.

___

NOTE: *You can view only mailboxes that are located on the same server as your primary
mailbox.*

___

11. Next, click on the Delivery tab of the MS Exchange Settings
    Properties dialog box, shown in Figure 5.9, to display the
    various mail delivery options.

**5. Integrating Your
Macintosh Into
Microsoft BackOffice**

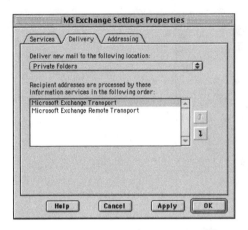

Figure 5.9   Use this dialog box to set your mail delivery options for Outlook.

12. You will now be asked for your password. Type in your password and click on Connect to continue.

13. Select the location where you wish your mail to be delivered, as indicated in Figure 5.9. Most people like to have their mail delivered to and stored on the mail server; to do this, select the Mailbox option. If you wish to have your mail stored locally on your Macintosh, select the Private Folders option.

14. To finish the setup process, click on the Addressing tab of the MS Exchange Settings Properties dialog box and select the address books that you wish to use when working in Outlook.

15. Once you have finished configuring Exchange's settings, click on OK to close the Control Panel.

You are now ready to launch, view, and test the program. To do so, follow these steps:

1. Locate the Microsoft Outlook program and launch it by double-clicking on its icon.

2. Then, you see a list of your mail folders for each mailbox located on the left and a list of all your messages in the currently selected mail folder to the right, as shown in Figure 5.10.

3. To see your calendar, click on the Calendar icon on the right-hand side of the Outlook toolbar.

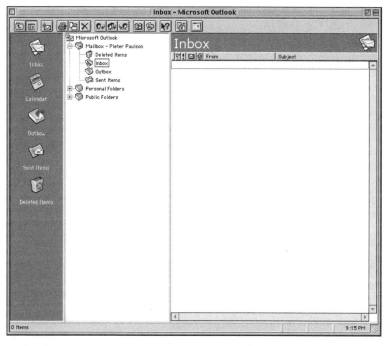

Figure 5.10   Outlook displays your waiting email in the Inbox folder.

4. If you have not already created a schedule file, Outlook prompts you to create one. Select the type of schedule file that you wish to use, or create a new one from scratch.

NOTE: *For a group of Macintosh users who wish to share access to their calendars, it is a good idea to set up a Schedule+ calendar on the Exchange server so that the Macintosh users can collaborate. If there are just a few Macintosh users or they do not wish to share their calendar, it is best to create a Local calendar file.*

---

5. From the Calendar view, you can select between the Daily view (shown in Figure 5.11), Weekly views, or Monthly views.

6. You should check your email features by sending email to another recipient and then having that person send you a message in return. Once you have checked to make sure that all of the features in Outlook are working properly, you are ready to start using it.

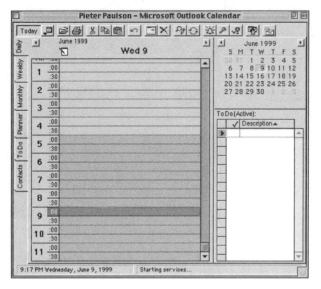

Figure 5.11   Here is your blank Outlook calendar ready to receive data.

Configuring Macintosh Applications For Use With Microsoft Proxy Server

Many Macintosh Internet applications can use Microsoft Proxy Server's Web and SOCKS proxy services. Unfortunately, not all do. Therefore, before you try to use a specific Internet application, you need to make sure that the application can access these services.

You can configure most application proxy settings through either the application itself or by changing the settings in the Configuration Manager Control Panel that comes with Microsoft's Internet Explorer or in the specific application's preferences. To set up a proxy server in the Configuration Manager Control Panel, follow these steps:

1. Click on the Apple menu and select Configuration Manager Control Panel (located under the Control Panels submenu).

2. Once you have opened Configuration Manager, you see a list of options you can configure. These range from your email settings, shown in Figure 5.12, to file download and Web browser settings.

3. Click on Proxies to bring up the Proxies page in the Configuration Manager dialog box. From this page, you can set up the proxy configurations for a variety of applications.

4. To set up your Web browser to use the Proxy Server Web proxy, as shown in Figure 5.13, click on the Enabled radio button and then click on the Protocol menu and select HTTP as the protocol you wish to proxy.

5. Next, click on the Method pop-up list and select Normal. Enter the IP address of the proxy server. Then, set the port number to

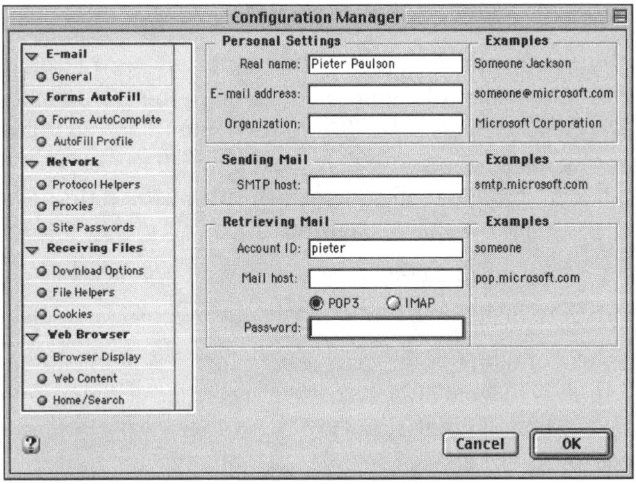

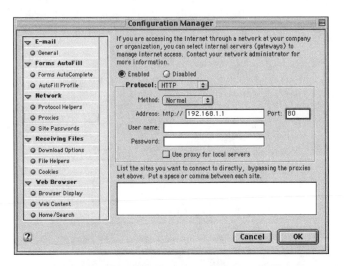

Figure 5.12   You use Configuration Manager to establish your email settings.

Figure 5.13   Use this dialog box to configure your Web browser to use the Web proxy.

either 80 (the default TCP/IP network port for Web traffic) or a special one that your company has specified (refer back to Figure 5.13 to see all these settings).

6. If you wish to set up additional proxies, select the protocol of the application that you wish to proxy and then select one like FTP. In Figure 5.14, we have selected SOCKS from the Method list, entered the IP address of the proxy server, and set the port number to 21.

7. To configure other applications to use the proxy server, select Other from the Protocol menu. Next, click on the Method menu and select SOCKS or Firewall. Then, enter the IP address of the proxy server and the port number that you wish to use. For example, Newsgroups readers use port 119 to talk to the servers that house all the newsgroups.

8. Once you have finished configuring all of your application proxies, click on OK to close Configuration Manager.

Another way to configure your proxy-aware Internet applications is to set them directly by going direct to their Preferences dialog boxes. Although the method of configuring proxy settings varies by application, the preference settings are almost always located in the applications' Preferences dialog boxes. In the next two sections, we show a few examples of how to configure the proxy settings for a couple of the more common Internet applications: Fetch 3.0.x and Internet Explorer 4.5.

5. Integrating Your Macintosh Into Microsoft BackOffice

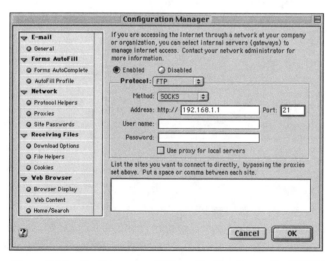

Figure 5.14   Configure your FTP application to use the SOCKS proxy.

Configuring Fetch 3.0.x For Use With The Microsoft SOCKS Proxy

Fetch is a popular Macintosh FTP client that you can use to access files from your local FTP servers or from any Internet location. It has an easy, intuitive point-and-click interface that has made it a popular choice among many users.

Fetch is free of charge for students and educational institutions. A regular user license is $25 and multiple user licenses are based on a sliding scale, depending on the number of seats. You can download your copy directly from **www.dartmouth.edu/pages/softdev/ fetch.html**.

To configure Fetch so that it can use Microsoft Proxy Server's SOCKS proxy, follow these easy steps:

1. Launch Fetch 3.0.x.

2. Once it has started and is asking to connect to a remote site, click on Cancel.

3. Next, click on Customize|Preferences.

4. Looking at the Preferences dialog box, click on the Firewall tab, shown in Figure 5.15, to switch to the proxy settings view.

5. To set Fetch to use the SOCKS proxy in Microsoft Proxy Server, click on the Use SOCKS Gateway checkbox and then enter the IP address of the proxy server (these settings should look something like what you see in Figure 5.15).

6. Once you are done, click on OK to close Fetch's Preferences dialog box.

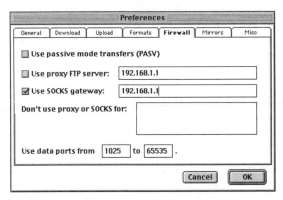

Figure 5.15   Use this screen to set up Fetch to use the SOCKS proxy.

Configuring Internet Explorer 4.5 For Use With The Microsoft Web Proxy

The popular Microsoft Internet Explorer browser comes installed on all new Macs, or you can download it directly from **www.microsoft. com/ mac/**. Setting up Microsoft Internet Explorer 4.5, as with Fetch, is a fairly simple proposition. To configure Internet Explorer, follow these steps:

1. Launch Internet Explorer.

2. Once the program is running, click on Edit|Preferences.

3. Looking at the Internet Explorer Preferences dialog box, scroll down and click on the Proxies entry under Network to switch to the proxy settings view (shown in Figure 5.16).

4. To set Internet Explorer to use the Web proxy in Microsoft Proxy Server, click on the Enabled checkbox and then select HTTP as the protocol.

5. Next, click on the Method|Normal. Then, enter the IP address of the proxy server and set the port number to 80.

6. Once you are done, click on OK to close the Internet Explorer Preferences dialog box.

NOTE: As this book was written, Microsoft was developing Internet Explorer 5.0 for the Macintosh. While Preference dialogs will change somewhat with the new version, the basic process of setting up proxies will involve essentially the same steps as outlined in this section. The biggest changes in the new version reflect the browser engine and support for the latest Web standards.

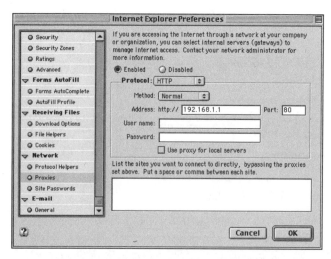

Figure 5.16   From this screen, you configure Internet Explorer 4.5 to use the Web proxy.

Configuring Winroute Pro For Macintosh Internet Applications

Configuring Winroute Pro to support a small network of Macintosh and Windows users is a fairly easy task. To set up Winroute to administer TCP/IP and establish NAT for your network, do the following:

1. To open Winroute Pro, click on Start|Program|Winroute Pro 4.0|Winroute Administration.

2. Once you have opened Winroute Administration, you will be asked to log in to Winroute Pro. Once you have entered in a valid Administrator username and password, click on OK. Once you are logged into Winroute Pro, click on Settings|Interfaces.

3. In the Interfaces/NAT dialog box, click on the network interface that is connected to the Internet and then click on the Properties button. See Figure 5.17 for additional information.

4. In the NAT dialog box, select the two checkboxes so that Winroute Pro will use the IP address provided by your ISP as the real address used in the native address translation process and to exclude this interface IP address when translating network requests.

5. Click on OK to continue.

6. Once you have finished configuring the interface, click on OK to close out this dialog box.

7. Next, click on the Settings|Advanced|Packet Filter.

8. In the Packet Filter dialog box, click on Add to add a new packet filter to Winroute. In Figure 5.18, you will see an example of how to set up a packet filter that blocks NetBIOS network traffic from coming in to your network from the Internet.

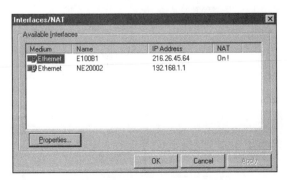

Figure 5.17   Here are the Internet Properties for Winroute Pro.

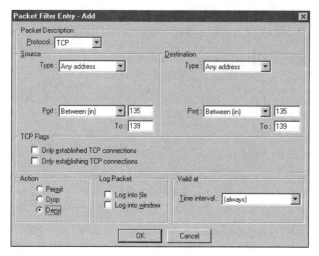

Figure 5.18   This dialog box is used to block specific network traffic from the Internet.

9. Once you have configured the settings for your incoming packet filter, you need to click on the outgoing tab and repeat the procedure to block traffic coming from your network that is undesirable.

10. When you have finished adding all of the packet filters you wish to install, click on OK. The packet filter dialog box should look like the one shown in Figure 5.19. For a list of the most common TCP/IP Port numbers, please look in the Glossary.

11. To configure the proxy portion of Winroute Pro, click on Settings|Proxy.

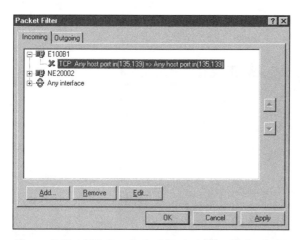

Figure 5.19   This is a typical Packet Filter dialog box configuration.

12. Once you are in the Proxy dialog box, set the proxy port to the port number you wish to use and adjust any of the other settings that you wish to change. Figure 5.20 shows a typical example of such a setup.

13. To limit the sites that users of this proxy can visit, click on the Access tab and click on Insert to add the Web sites that you wish to block, as shown in Figure 5.21. You can also specify which users and groups can view each restricted site so that teachers or parents may be allowed to view a specific group of sites, while children would be prevented from viewing those same sites.

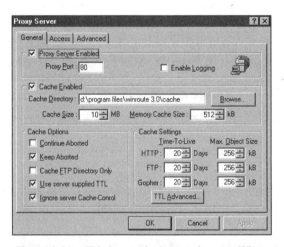

Figure 5.20   This is a typical setup for your Winroute Pro proxy dialog box.

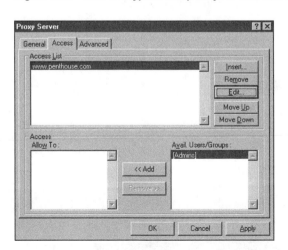

Figure 5.21   This dialog box is used to limit access to specific Web sites that may contain unacceptable content.

14. Under the Advanced tab, you will find the settings needed to connect this proxy server to another or parent proxy server, thus allowing you to build a cluster or group of proxy servers. Once you have finished configuring the proxy, click on OK

15. Next, click on Settings|DHCP to set up Winroute Pro to administer the TCP/IP configuration for your Windows and Macintosh workstations.

16. In the example shown in Figure 5.22 we have set up DHCP in Winroute Pro to lease TCP/IP addresses between 192.168.1.2 and 192.168.1.10 to all of the Windows and Macintosh workstations on the network. We have also configured it to specify the DNS or Domain Name Server, Default gateway, and Domain Name used by each computer on the network. Once you have finished configuring DHCP, click on OK to continue.

17. If you wish to set up specific users and user accounts for use in limiting the access that folks have when using the Winroute Pro proxy, click on Settings|Accounts.

18. In the Accounts dialog box, you can add users directly or you can click on the Import NT Database to import a list of all the Windows 2000 users available to this server. See Figure 5.23 for a typical example.

19. If you wish to create a group of users to control access, click on the Groups tab in the Accounts dialog box and then click on Add to create a group.

20. Then, select the group and add the users you wish to include as part of that group, as shown in Figure 5.24.

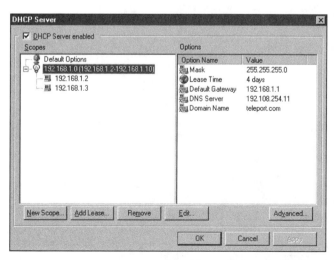

Figure 5.22   A typical DHCP setup dialog box for Winroute Pro.

5. Integrating Your Macintosh Into Microsoft BackOffice

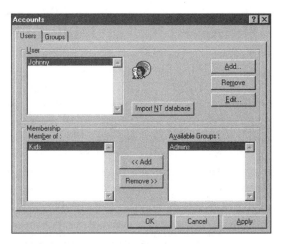

Figure 5.23   Use this dialog box to import a list of Windows 2000 users.

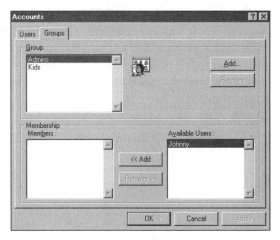

Figure 5.24   Add your users in the Groups dialog box.

21. Once you are done, click on OK to close the Accounts dialog box.

22. To close Winroute Pro, click on the Exit button in the upper right-hand corner of the window.

Once you have finished configuring Winroute Pro, you will be ready to start using it to provide your Macs with Internet access.

Related solutions:	*Found on page:*
Using Access Lists	288
Setting Up a DHCP Server Under Windows 2000	293

Protecting Your Network From The Internet

When connecting your network to the Internet, one of the first things that you need to think about is security. The Internet is a wide-open environment and unfortunately there are many individuals out there who are willing and able to attack the computers on your network. From the casual snooper interested in seeing what your network looks like to the cracker intent on stealing your company secrets, there are many different threats that you will need to protect against. This section talks about the various threats that you may face and how you can configure your Firewall or Proxy to protect you.

1. The first thing that you should think about when setting up a firewall is what type of network access you will need to allow. Will you need to allow every user to use AOL and any other Internet applications from their desks or do you intend to limit the types of Internet applications that your users can use?

2. Next, you will need to decide what network services you wish to allow your routers and servers to use when providing information to other computers. While this may be useful inside your network, you do not always want that information to be made available on the Internet.

3. Finally, you need to actually set up the applications and services that you wish to allow to and from the Internet. While we discussed how to set up filters using Winroute Pro in the previous section, the following information is easily adapted to any of the other Firewalls or Proxies available on the market.

NOTE: *To protect your Windows network from intruders on the Internet, it is important that you block TCP and UDP ports 135 through 139, as these are the ports that Windows uses to communicate between servers and workstations both for NetBIOS file access as well as for administrative purposes.*

Understanding Common Internet Applications And Their Impact

Some of the most common Internet applications that will be on your users' wish lists are described in the following bullets:

- *Email*—The most common Internet application that you will be asked to provide to your users is electronic mail. Email is the primary reason that most companies connect to the Internet. Email is a critical tool used by businesses large and small to communicate between themselves and with their customers. Email on the Internet is transferred from server to server using the Simple Mail Transport Protocol (SMTP). Mail servers on the Internet send and receive SMTP traffic using TCP port 25.

Because email is a critical service, you will most likely want to create a hole in your firewall to let it through. However, like many heavily used services, there are many different ways of attacking it. So, it is best to make sure that your firewall is configured to only allow SMTP traffic to and from the Internet to your mail server and no others. This limits the ability of any cracker to compromise your network via email.

NOTE: *As you may have heard, there are now groups of email-based computer viruses. When connecting your email system to the Internet, it is very important that you make sure that your antivirus software is kept current and that your users are well educated. Make sure that your users know they should not open email attachments from people they do not know. In addition, if they receive email attachments from known senders they didn't expect to receive, they should verify that such a file was actually sent by that person. This is in response to the uproar over such issues as the Melissa virus. Also, if possible, set your mail reader programs so that they are not capable of executing macros or scripts that may be stored in an attachment. Following a few simple steps can save you hours of lost time trying to stamp out a virus infestation.*

For users on networks that do not have their own mail servers, but rely instead on your Internet Service Provider's email servers, you will want to make sure that your firewall is set up to allow your users to access them. The most common mail reader programs use the Post Office Protocol (POP) to access the remote mail servers and pull down any mail that is stored there. Another common protocol that seems to be gaining in popularity is the Internet Message Access Protocol (IMAP). IMAP is used by a variety of programs and by Windows CE devices to access mail servers.

- *Web Access*—Next on your users wish list is undoubtedly going to be Web access, so they can spend endless hours looking for the latest news and information online. Web browsers such as Microsoft's Internet Explorer and AOL's Netscape Navigator are tools that enable users to view and interact with World Wide Web servers on the Internet. Using the Hypertext Transport Protocol, HTTP, and the secure version known as Secure HTTP, or HTTPS, web browsers can download text, graphics, and even small programs from computers located all over the world.

In general, it is best to allow your users access to the World Wide Web because online information can be immensely useful. However, a very good idea, especially in business or educational environments, is to require that all users wanting access to the World Wide Web, sign or otherwise agree to a written code of conduct that spells out what types of sites they can and cannot visit.

- *Instant Messaging*—Another service rapidly gaining popularity is instant messaging. *Instant messaging programs* such as AOL Instant Messenger, ICQ, and Microsoft's Instant Messenger allow users to hold conversations in real time over the Internet. Like email, instant messaging programs enable users to communicate quickly and efficiently with others on the Internet.

  However, instant messaging programs are not business tools per se, and businesses need to be very careful about allowing the instant messaging programs on their network. One major concern, especially with ICQ, is that many ICQ users send out viruses and other inappropriate material to unsuspecting recipients. In addition, the conversation that a user holds on the Internet is not encrypted and can be intercepted by others on the Internet. Another major concern, especially with Microsoft's Instant Messenger, is that it is not licensed for commercial use.

- *Internet-based applications*—There are also a wide variety of other Internet-based applications, such as FTP, Real Audio, Liquid Audio, and Pointcast that your users may desire access to.

  Liquid Audio and Real Audio are programs that allow you to listen to music and other audio broadcasts on the Internet. While these programs are relatively benign, both of them have been shown to consume an inordinate amount of network bandwidth. So, many network administrators have banned them from their networks. The only problem with this is that both products now are capable of using HTTP to listen to broadcasts as well as their native protocol. If you are looking to block Liquid Audio or Real Audio from your network, you will need to not only block the ports used by each program's native protocol, but also watch network utilization to spot users who are trying to get around your ban by using them with HTTP.

  Pointcast is a tool that allows users to receive customized stock quotes and news from servers located on the Internet. However, Pointcast is another tool that can be very useful, but has nonetheless been banned from many networks because it frequently consumes too much network bandwidth.

Working With Common Network Protocols And Their Ports

The following is a list of common network protocols that you will find in use on the Internet and some security suggestions for them. While this is not a complete list of all the protocols and port numbers, it does cover many of the most popular protocols that you will encounter.

- *SMTP*—SMTP uses TCP port 25 to send and receive mail. This is a well-known port and should only be made available to and from your mail server. IIS, by default, is installed with an SMTP server. Unless you are using it, you should block SMTP traffic to this SMTP server or use the custom IIS install to prevent its installation.

- *POP*—POP uses either TCP port 109, for POP version 2, or 110, for POP version 3 depending upon the version of POP server that is installed on the mail server. There is no POP version 1.

- *IMAP*—IMAP uses either TCP port 143 for IMAP version 2 mail servers or port 220 for mail servers using IMAP version 3. There is no IMAP version 1.

- *HTTP*—HTTP uses TCP and UDP port 80 to communicate with Web servers and browsers.

- *HTTPS*—HTTPS uses TCP and UDP port 443 to conduct secure communications with web servers and browsers. You will need to open this port if you want your users to access secure web sites or if you wish to create a secure web site for your clients.

- *Microsoft Instant Messenger*—Microsoft Instant Messenger uses TCP port 1863 for outgoing and gets traffic back on a random TCP port between 1024 and 65535.

- *AOL Instant Messenger*—America Online Instant Messenger and the AOL service use TCP port 5190 to send information and then expect traffic back on a random port between 1024 and 65535.

- *ICQ*—ICQ uses UDP port 4000 to send and receive data.

- *Liquid Audio*—Liquid Audio uses either TCP port 18888 for outbound and UDP port 18888 for inbound data, or TCP port 18888 for outbound data and UDP port 18888 for inbound and outbound data. The liquid audio players and server can also be configured to work using TCP port 80.

- *Real Audio*—Real Audio and Real Video use TCP ports 554 and 7070-7071 or UDP ports 6770-7170 to send and receive data from either Real Audio/Video servers or to users. Real recommends that you use UDP if possible for best performance.

5. Integrating Your Macintosh Into Microsoft BackOffice

- *NNTP*—Network News Transport Protocol, NNTP, uses TCP port 119 to send and receive information from Newsgroups servers located on the Internet.

Troubleshooting BackOffice Problems

When you are having trouble connecting your Macintosh to Microsoft BackOffice and the Internet, troubleshooting requires you to look at both your software and network configurations. In this section, we cover how to handle problems connecting to SQL Server, problems with Microsoft Exchange, and problems connecting to the Internet.

Resolving Problems When You Are Connecting To SQL Server

Setting up the ODBC connector and configuring both your Macintosh-based application and the SQL Server database can be a fairly detailed process. The first thing you need to do before starting to deploy your solution is talk to the database administrator and collect all the information you will need.

For example, to create the user DSN, you need the following information:

- The name of the server

- The name of the database

- The username and password that you use to access the database

Before proceeding to the actual troubleshooting process, you also need to make sure that the database administrator has set up the database to support your user DSN and configured everything properly.

Here are some of the common problems (and their solutions) that you will likely encounter when connecting your Macintosh OS application to a SQL Server via ODBC:

- *When creating the ODBC connector, you may encounter a problem when trying to select the server that hosts the database you wish to access*—First, check that the network library is set to use TCP/IP. If it is, try checking with the database administrator to make sure that the database is set up to be visible as a data source. If both of these are set up correctly, refer back to the "Using Troubleshooting Techniques For Networks In General" section in Chapter 4 to make sure that the Macintosh can see the server that hosts the SQL Server database.

- *You are having trouble authenticating the username and password against a remote database*—First, verify with the database administrator that you have the proper username and password. Pay special attention to the password because it frequently contains a mix of upper- and lowercase letters as well as some special characters to make the password more difficult to guess. If the username and password are still rejected, see if the database is using Windows NT to authenticate the username and password or if it is a user account that has been created inside SQL Server. If you are using Windows NT authentication, make sure that the username has the Windows NT domain added to the front of the username. For example, "Niflheim\Pieter" would be the username used instead of just "Pieter".

- *You are having trouble viewing the data after you set up your ODBC connector and have connected to the database*—First, check the database itself. Contact the database administrator to make sure that the database is set up correctly and actually contains data. Also, have the administrator verify that the user that you are trying to connect to the database has the proper rights to see the data. If the user is set up properly, check that the ODBC connector you are using properly supports your version of SQL Server.

NOTE: *Some older ODBC connectors work fine with one version of SQL Server but will fail when trying to fetch data from a newer version of SQL Server. If this is the case, make sure that you have the proper version of the ODBC connector.*

Resolving Problems When You Are Connecting To An Exchange Server

When starting to troubleshoot problems connecting Microsoft Outlook to the Exchange server, you need to retrieve a basic set of configuration information. Make sure that you know the name and IP address of the Exchange server that houses the mailbox as well as the username, password, and domain that the mailbox is configured to use. Here are some common problems (and their solutions) that you may encounter when connecting to Exchange from your Macintosh:

- *When setting up the connection to the Exchange server in the Outlook Settings Control Panel, you have trouble verifying the mailbox configuration*—This frequently happens when the Macintosh client cannot reconcile the name of the Exchange server that you have entered to its IP address on the network. In many Windows NT networks, DNS is not used to register the names of servers and their IP addresses. For non-WINS-capable operating systems, such as Macintosh OS 9, you can either enter the IP address of the Exchange server in place of the server name in the Outlook Settings Control Panel or you can edit the HOSTS file that is located in the System folder to add an entry for your Exchange server.

- *When setting up your Exchange calendar, you try to connect to a network calendar, resulting in a connection failure*—If you connect to a network calendar, make sure that a Schedule+ calendar is configured on the server you are trying to access. The Macintosh version of Outlook cannot connect to the Exchange network calendar used by Windows users, so attempting to connect to the calendar located on the Exchange server frequently results in a connection failure. To use a network calendar, make sure that a Schedule+ network calendar is configured on the server or choose to use a local calendar file. In either case, you can still retrieve all of your appointments stored on the Exchange server; you can view them in a graphical calendar format from the Schedule+ module only.

- *You cannot log in to the Exchange server to collect your email*— When this happens, you should first make sure that your username, password, and domain name are all entered correctly. If they are, check your Windows NT domain account. It is possible your account has become disabled due to too many failed login attempts, or by another system's administrator who has disabled it.

Resolving Problems When You Are Connecting To The Internet

Most problems that you encounter when connecting to the Internet from your Macintosh are related to the configuration of either your Internet application or the TCP/IP Control Panel. Before you attempt to isolate the source of your problem, make sure you have the following information:

- The IP address of the default gateway on your network subnet

- The subnet mask used on your subnet

- The IP address of the proxy server or firewall used to connect you to the Internet

- The IP address of the DNS server

- The port number of the proxy that you wish to use

5. Integrating Your Macintosh Into Microsoft BackOffice

Once you have this information, you can start troubleshooting your problem. Here are some typical problems and solutions:

- *You cannot access certain Web sites because your Web browser says that they cannot be found*—This is usually due to either a misconfigured DNS server address in the TCP/IP Control Panel on your Macintosh or on the firewall or proxy server that you are using.

  If you are configuring DNS on your Macintosh, open the TCP/IP Control Panel and double-check that you have entered the proper DNS server IP address and the proper search domain name (the name of the domain that the DNS server you are connecting to is using). For example, if you are an Earthlink.net user, the search domain should be earthlink.net. If you do not configure a DNS server on your Macintosh, talk to the network administrators about the DNS settings on the firewall and/or proxy server. Make sure that these settings as well as the search domains are set correctly. If they are not, reset them and then reboot the proxy server or firewall so that they pick up the new settings. If they are correct, contact your ISP to see if its DNS servers are configured properly.

NOTE: *DNS on the Internet is not always accurate because updates can take days to propagate through the various DNS servers that control name resolution on the Internet.*

- *Your application fails to connect when you try to use an application through a SOCKS proxy*—You should first check the proxy settings in either the Configuration Manager Control Panel or in the application's Preferences dialog box. Make sure that the IP address and port number of the SOCKS proxy are set correctly. If they are, make sure that the Macintosh can talk to the proxy server over the network. If you are using the same proxy server as your Web proxy, using a browser can be a good quick test of the proxy server. If you can reach the proxy server, make sure that the SOCKS proxy is running and properly configured.

NOTE: *Some applications—notably early editions of Fetch 3.0-3.0.3—had SOCKS support built in; however, it was not functional. If you are having trouble, make sure that your application really can use a SOCKS proxy.*

- *Your Macintosh suddenly loses its connection to the Internet after a set period of time*—This problem may occur when you are running MS Proxy Server or Winroute Pro as a firewall. It is usually due to a misconfigured port filter on the proxy server.

In cases where Proxy Server is connected to an ISP by a dial-up connection or another type of connection that relies upon DHCP to provide it with an IP address, the DHCP server sets the expiration time of the IP address lease to a fairly short period of time. This allows the server to quickly reclaim IP addresses that are no longer in use. The downside to this is that the proxy server must continually be talking to the DHCP server so that it can renew its IP address. If the port filters on the proxy server are configured to block access to User Datagram Protocol UDP ports 67 and 68, the proxy server cannot talk to the Dynamic Host Configuration Protocol DHCP server, and thus, cannot renew its IP address. This causes the server to lose its IP address—and therefore, its connection to the Internet—after a certain period of time.

To resolve this problem, reconfigure the port filter on the proxy server to allow UDP traffic on ports 67 and 68. To improve security, you might try limiting the traffic from the ISP's DHCP server; however, this is a bit risky because the ISP may move its DHCP server to another IP address without warning.

TIP: *You should always check for a misconfigured port when trying to connect to the Internet using a new application. Many applications such as Liquid Audio, ICQ, AOL, and others, use special TCP or UDP ports to communicate over the Internet. If your firewall is configured to block these ports for security purposes, you should consider opening them up so you can use your new application.*

---

5. Integrating Your Macintosh Into Microsoft BackOffice

Part II

Windows 2000

Chapter 6

Introduction To Windows 2000 And Mac OS Networking

In Brief

Remembering Things Past

Windows 2000 is the latest version of the popular Windows NT operating system. Windows NT 4 was more of an incremental upgrade of the previous versions of Windows NT, whereas Windows 2000 is almost a completely redesigned operating system. Even if you are familiar with Windows NT 4, you are likely to find Windows 2000 both familiar and strikingly different. In this chapter, we will be discussing these differences and how they impact the integration of Macintosh computers on your network.

When it came out, Windows NT 4 was seen as a big improvement over the previous version, Windows NT 3.51. NT 4 incorporated a superior user interface, improved performance, and—most important—improved stability. However, NT 4 really was not a major upgrade when it came to the overall structure of the operating system and in the tools that you used to manage it.

Windows 2000, on the other hand, is a major step forward in almost every way. Over the last few years, Microsoft has almost completely rewritten Windows NT to resolve many of the complaints it heard from users and administrators about the previous versions. When you first start using Windows 2000, you'll notice that many of the features and controls you are accustomed to using in Windows NT 4 are no longer where you are used to seeing them. Menus have changed, applications have new names, and common features seem to be either missing or located somewhere else. No doubt the situation may seem somewhat confusing at first glance; however, as you start digging through the interface, you'll find that many of the features and tools you have become used to are now grouped together or rearranged in a more logical and efficient manner. Another benefit, for example, is that you no longer have to reboot your server when you change some networking information or when you wish to enable or disable a specific network protocol. Server administrators will welcome this change because of the shortened downtime and increased convenience to users.

Understanding Changes Between Windows NT 4 And Windows 2000

As with the previous version of Windows NT, Windows 2000 can support a variety of different types of computers and operating systems all on the same network. However, the new user interface improves usability and control, and the underlying components have been rebuilt to increase performance and reliability.

Here's a brief summary of the changes and how they impact your configuration chores. You'll find more information about setting up Windows 2000 to work with your Macintosh computers in the remaining chapters of this book:

- *Server administration tools are in one application*—In Windows NT 4, when you wanted to create a new user or group or set up a new hard drive, you went to the appropriate administrative tool and performed the operation that you wanted. For example, under Windows NT 4, you created and changed users and groups in User Manager for Domains. Likewise, to create a volume and then format that volume, you used Disk Administrator. In almost every instance when configuring or administering Windows NT 4, you were forced to run a different application for every task.

  In Windows 2000, the tools needed to administer your Windows 2000 server are all consolidated into one Microsoft Management Console Snap-in called Computer Management. Computer Management combines such tools as the User Manager for Domains, Disk Administrator, Server Manager, and some portions of File Manager. From Computer Management, you can create users and groups, add new volumes and format them, and create new shares. By centralizing all of these tools into one application, Microsoft has made it far easier to administer the servers under your control.

- *All network functions are in the Network Control Panel*—In Windows NT 4, the Network Control Panel was designed with only the local area network (LAN) connection in mind. Although you could add such services as Remote Access Service (RAS), most of the services and all of the protocols were bound to specific network interfaces. This LAN-centric view forced you to go to the Dial-Up Networking folder to add new dial-up networking connections and then to jump back to the Network Control Panel when you wanted to configure the Remote Access Server

169

or other network services. As in much of Windows NT 4, this lack of centralization caused a lot of unnecessary effort when you were trying to configure all of your network settings.

In Windows 2000, all of the network functions are centralized in the Network Control Panel. This new version of the Network Control Panel combines most of the functionality of the Windows NT 4 Network Control Panel and Dial-Up Networking into one simple and easy-to-use package. When you double-click on Network Control Panel in Windows 2000, you notice right away that there are listings for all of your different network connections, both the physical LAN connections and all of your dial-up connections. By double-clicking on one of these connections, you see the current network traffic statistics for the network connection as well as the Properties and Disconnect buttons. Clicking on Properties brings up the connection's Properties dialog box, from which you can change IP addresses, add new protocols, or set up network-specific services. Clicking on the Disconnect button shuts down the network connection.

- *Computer Management hosts all shared volume tools*—Windows NT Services for Macintosh allowed Mac users to connect to shared volumes and printers on the Windows NT Server. Although Services for Macintosh did a very good job of providing Macintosh users with access to the files and printers hosted on the server, it was difficult to administer and configure because you could not use the standard tools. For example, in order to add a new shared volume for your Macintosh users, you needed to use the seldom-used File Manager to create and set permissions. Similarly, to see which users were connected and what files they had open, you had to use the MacFile Control Panel. These were definitely not the most convenient solutions to managing your Macintosh users.

  Under Windows 2000, all the tools you need to create and manage your Macintosh shared volumes are located under the Computer Management application. Based upon the Microsoft Management Console that was introduced with Internet Information Server (IIS) 4, the Computer Management Console allows you to configure File Services for Macintosh, create new shared volumes, and enable Macintosh access to them. You can also view which users are connected to each shared volume, send messages to the users connected to your server, and (if need be) disconnect them. By centralizing all of these functions into one simple-to-use application, Windows 2000 makes it much easier to administer your Macintosh shares and users.

- *You can configure File and Print services better*—In Windows NT 4, the File and Print services that supported Macintosh users were combined as part of Services for Macintosh. Although this simplified the installation of Macintosh support, it limited the flexibility of the network administrator to configure the server how he or she wanted. Additionally, by tying the AppleTalk configuration to Services for Macintosh, the administrator could configure AppleTalk on a server on a limited basis only. For example, it is impossible under Windows NT 4 to set up a server to route AppleTalk over the network without having Services for Macintosh installed.

Unlike in Windows NT 3.51 and 4, support of Macintosh and other operating systems in Windows 2000 is not segregated into a few special-purpose tools; rather, it is integrated into the primary administrative tools such as the Computer Management Console. Instead of having to go to different parts of the operating system or use a bunch of different installers, Windows 2000 allows you to add and remove parts of the operating system from a single location: the Component Installer.

In Windows 2000, File Services for Macintosh and Print Services for Macintosh are two separate Windows components that you need to install through the Windows 2000 Component Installer. Similarly, AppleTalk is now a separate protocol that you can install separately in the Properties dialog box of your network connection. By separating these functions from the older Services for Macintosh, Windows 2000 gives you much more flexibility in setting up your server. For example, you may decide that you do want a server to host Macintosh files but not Macintosh print jobs. If that is the case, all you need to do is install the AppleTalk protocol and then run the Windows 2000 Component Installer to install File Services for Macintosh. Likewise, you can just set up AppleTalk if you wish to configure your server to route AppleTalk traffic without hosting any Macintosh File or Print services.

6. Introduction To Windows 2000 And Mac OS Networking

Immediate Solutions

Configuring Your Server Using Windows NT 4 And Windows 2000

As we discussed earlier in this chapter, the tools that you use to configure your server under Windows 2000 have changed considerably from those you use in Windows NT 4.0. In this section, we will look at some specific configuration examples and how they differ between Windows NT 4 and Windows 2000.

NOTE: The steps described here are summarized to provide simple comparisons. Chapters 7–10 provide the complete procedures as they apply to a number of typical installations.

Comparing Systems: Installing AppleTalk Using Windows NT 4

To install the AppleTalk network protocol under Windows NT 4, you must install the complete Services for Macintosh by opening the Network Control Panel (as discussed in Chapter 2).

The following steps will offer quick setup for Services for Macintosh:

1. Click on Start|Settings|Control Panel. Or, double-click on the My Computer icon located on your Windows NT 4 desktop and then double-click on the Control Panel folder.

2. Double-click on the Network icon. Doing so brings up the Network Control Panel, shown in Figure 6.1.

3. Click on the Services tab, which brings up the screen shown in Figure 6.2. Look at the different services that you have installed. The services installed on this server are the standard ones that Windows NT installs.

4. To add another NT Networking Service, click on Add.

5. Select Services For Macintosh in the Select Network Service dialog box (shown in Figure 6.3) and then click on OK.

6. To add any other services, click on Add again, select the service that you desire, and then click on OK again.

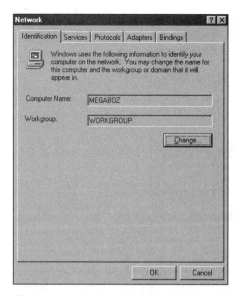

Figure 6.1   You use the Network Control Panel to configure your network protocols.

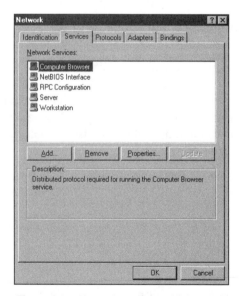

Figure 6.2   You can configure Network Services from this screen.

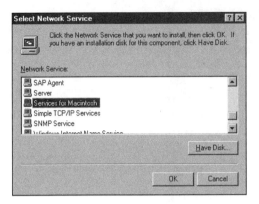

Figure 6.3   Pick Services For Macintosh from the list of available options.

7. When you are finished selecting the services you want to install, click on OK on the Select Network Service dialog box.

8. Windows NT next asks you for the Windows NT 4 Server CD-ROM so that it can load the additional components that it needs to finish the installation of Services for Macintosh.

Comparing Systems: Installing AppleTalk Using Windows 2000

To install the AppleTalk network protocol under Windows 2000, you must go into the Local Area Connection Properties dialog box for the network adapter. We will go into adding AppleTalk and the File Services for Macintosh in more depth in the next chapter. For the time being, however, here is a brief summary of how to install AppleTalk on your Windows 2000 server:

1. Click on Start|Settings|Control Panel. Or, double-click on the My Computer icon located on your Windows 2000 desktop and then double-click on the Control Panel folder.

2. Double-click on the Network And Dial-Up Connections icon. Doing so brings up the Network And Dial-up Connections window, shown in Figure 6.4. You can use this window to examine every network connection that you have set up on this computer. The most common connections are Local Area Connection (which is your connection to the local network) and Dial Connection (which is for connecting to the Internet).

6. Introduction To Windows 2000 And Mac OS Networking

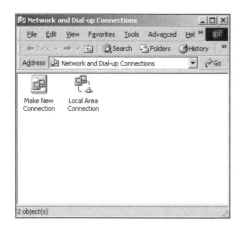

Figure 6.4   The Network And Dial-up Connections window allows you to control each of your network connections.

3. Once you have the Network And Dial-Up Connections window open, double-click on the Local Area Connection icon to open up the network preferences for your server's LAN connection.

4. The Local Area Connection Status dialog box, shown in Figure 6.5, displays information about the current network traffic in and out of the server. If you click on the Properties button in this dialog box, you can see the adapter that is currently selected and the network options and protocols that are configured for that interface. Clicking on the Disable button shuts down your network connection.

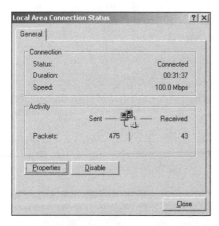

Figure 6.5   The Local Area Connection Status dialog box provides you with information on the network traffic going in and out of your server.

6. Introduction To Windows 2000 And Mac OS Networking

Follow these steps to install AppleTalk on your Windows 2000 server:

1. Click on the Properties button to bring up the Local Area Connection Properties dialog box. Look at the services that are installed. The services installed on this server are the standard ones that Windows 2000 installs.

2. To add another 2000 Network Component, click on Install.

3. Double-click on Protocols and then select AppleTalk from the list of available protocols.

4. Click on OK.

5. To add any other Network components, click on Install again, select the service that you desire, and then click on OK again.

6. You will now notice one interesting thing: no request for a reboot of your server. Eliminating this step is a key advantage of the Windows 2000 setup process.

Comparing Systems: Creating A New Macintosh Shared Volume Using Windows NT 4

To create a Macintosh shared volume under Windows NT 4, you must use File Manager to set up the volume and then specify all of your desired security settings (as fully described in Chapter 2).

To create a new Macintosh shared volume under Windows NT 4, follow these steps:

1. Start Windows NT 4 File Manager by clicking on Start|Run, typing "WINFILE.EXE", and then hitting Enter. Once File Manager has started, notice that there is a new menu item called MacFile, shown in Figure 6.6.

2. Select the folder or volume that you wish to share.

3. Then, click on Create Volume from the MacFile menu. Doing so brings up the Create Macintosh-Accessible Volume dialog box, shown in Figure 6.7. When setting up this volume, you should choose the various options that you wish to use.

4. If you want just authorized users to connect to this volume, uncheck the Guests Can Use This Volume option.

5. To limit the number of Mac users who can connect to the server at any one time, click on the Allow radio button in the User Limit box and then set the number that you wish to allow.

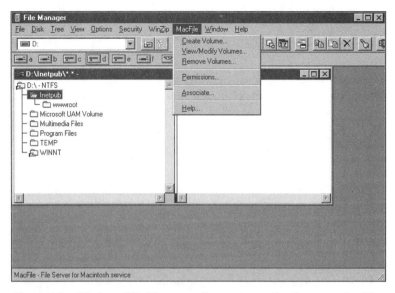

Figure 6.6   Windows File Manager offers a new option for managing Macs on your network: MacFile.

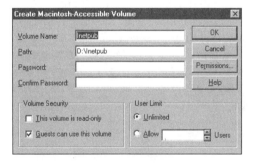

Figure 6.7   You can configure options for the selected Macintosh-Accessible volume here.

6. You can even set a special password for this file volume only. To do so, enter it in the Password text box and then retype it in the Confirm Password text box to activate it. This special password is valuable only if you want to allow guests to connect to the file volume.

7. Lastly, click on OK to close the Create Macintosh-Accessible Volume dialog box and start sharing the volume.

Comparing Systems: Creating A New Macintosh Shared Volume Using Windows 2000

Creating a new Macintosh shared volume using Windows 2000 is a considerably different process than creating one using Windows NT 4. Although we will discuss creating a new Macintosh accessible volume under Windows 2000 in greater detail in Chapter 7, we will now cover some of the steps you must perform when creating a Macintosh file share under Windows 2000. Notice the differences between this procedure and the procedure described in the previous section.

To create a new volume for your Macintosh users after you have finished installing the File Services for Macintosh, follow these steps after you have finished the installation of File Services for Macintosh:

1. Click on Start|Programs|Administrative Tools|Computer Management.

2. Right-click on the Shared Folders icon to expand it and then right-click on the Shares icon and select New Share from the shortcut menu.

3. The Create Shared Folder dialog box, shown in Figure 6.8, appears and asks you to enter the name of the folder that you wish to share along with the Share name, a description of the shared volume, and, if you are creating a Macintosh shared volume, the Macintosh shared volume name. To allow Macintosh users to connect to this volume, click on the Apple Macintosh checkbox located in the lower right-hand corner of the dialog box. Once you have selected the folder and named the shared volume, click on Next.

Figure 6.8   Select the folder or volume that you wish to share and set the share name and other options for the shared volume.

6. Introduction To Windows 2000 And Mac OS Networking

4. Next, you are asked to set the share permissions that you want, as shown in Figure 6.9. These permissions limit which users and groups can access this share over the network.

5. Once you have set the user permissions for the new shared volume, click on Finish to complete the creation of the shared volume. You will then be asked if you wish to repeat the process. Click on No.

Looking at the two examples that we have provided, you can see that it's much simpler to set up and configure a shared volume using Windows 2000 than using Windows NT 4. Notice in each example how it was easy to add new components to Windows 2000 or set up a new shared volume; you didn't have to reboot the server or use special applications to complete your tasks.

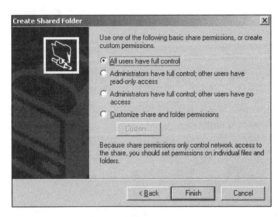

Figure 6.9   *Set the share permissions to limit which users and groups can access the share.*

Mac OS 9 Brings Enhanced New Level Of Mac Security

Starting with Mac OS 9, Apple Computer has brought Mac users greatly enhanced security tools that will help systems administrators keep tabs on network use and access.

These features, in essence, amount to the return and enhancement of the old Keychain feature that was part of Apple's PowerTalk, which first appeared in System 7.1.1 (also known as System 7 Pro). In

179

addition to standard username and password access, Apple is introducing a robust Voice Verification system, which provides a new level of system security.

In addition, Apple's Multiple Users Control Panel allows you to give each user a specific set of access privileges, which lets you restrict their use of applications, files, System Folder items and mounted disks (such as removable media).

This subject will be discussed in more detail in the next chapter.

Related solution:	*Found on page:*
Using Mac 9.0 FIle Security Options	211

Windows 2000/Macintosh OS File Sharing

In Brief

Introducing Windows 2000 File Sharing For Macintosh OS

Like Windows NT, Windows 2000 offers a rich set of resources that Mac users can use to share files with their Windows counterparts. In this chapter, we'll focus on those features that offer more opportunities for efficient file transfers between Macintosh and Windows.

Windows 2000 Server's File Services for Macintosh offers a series of related components that let Windows 2000 support Macintosh users. These tools and options allow the Mac users in your company to take advantage of many of the resources that are available to their Windows neighbors without having to resort to software emulators or special client software.

When you install File Services for Macintosh, you can create and share Macintosh files on Windows 2000 servers. Once you install and configure it (using the instructions we provide in the following pages), the Mac users on your company's LAN can use the Windows 2000 server as if it were just another AppleShare volume. You can also store applications on the server as if it were just another Mac-based server, yet you receive all the benefits that Windows 2000 offers.

In addition, by storing your Mac files on a Windows 2000 file server, the Windows users on your network can also access them. Mac users can have data backed up at a central location and restrict access to their files based upon Windows 2000's advanced file access permissions. Mac users can also run applications from the Windows 2000 server, so you no longer have to load seldom-used applications on individual workstations. This reduces support time and expense by limiting the number of workstations that your support people have to visit.

NOTE: *Your company still needs to obtain software licenses for each individual user of a program. Having a program accessible from a server is simply a matter of convenience, nothing more. Each publisher has differing requirements for multiple software licenses, so be sure to check with the appropriate publisher(s).*

---

7. Windows 2000/ Macintosh OS File Sharing

Windows 2000 also allows Mac users to limit the access that users on the network have to their files and folders. You can use these security features to specify who can modify files, and who can only read them. In addition, a log tracks file access and file modification, and lists the names of the users who access those files. The Windows 2000 File System (NTFS) and permissions features allow you to set access rights based upon a single user or a group of users.

NOTE: *Taking a clue from the Windows side of the personal computing universe, Apple's Macintosh OS 9.0 offers greatly improved system security over previous versions of the Macintosh OS. These new features, which are described later in this chapter, allow you to set up each Macintosh workstation to handle multiple users, and give each user a custom set of access privileges. Mac OS 9.0 also offers system-level file encryption.*

As with Windows NT servers, Windows 2000 servers can be used to provide Mac users with access to Windows-based printers. You'll learn more about this subject in Chapter 8.

Overall, the File Services for Macintosh feature available with Windows 2000 server offers a great solution to the problem of integrating your Macintosh and Windows workstations. It provides a common file storage area, allowing the Mac and Windows users on your network to have access to the same documents. Many programs are available in Mac and Windows versions, so having a central file resource makes it easier for users from both platforms to collaborate on individual documents. In addition, it's a lot easier to perform regular backups of your mission-critical documents than with Windows NT 4 because they are accessible from a central location.

Comparing AppleTalk Zones And Windows Workgroups

AppleTalk zones are very similar to Windows Workgroups because they group the Mac computers on your network into a single, easily accessible group. However, unlike Windows Workgroups, AppleTalk zones are assigned based on which portion of the network they are located. This means that you can select from only those zones that are on that segment of the network. On the other hand, Windows Workgroups are assigned by the person who configures the workstation. In both the AppleTalk zone and the Windows Workgroup, all the shared resources that are available on the computers belong to that zone or workgroup.

7. Windows 2000/ Macintosh OS File Sharing

Conversely, Windows 2000 domains are a type of super workgroup that can include hundreds or thousands of computers, all coordinated by a single Windows 2000 server known as a *Domain controller*. This allows for centralized user authentication and security management.

Using DAVE To Make Sharing Easy

You can use DAVE from Thursby Software Systems, Inc. to connect Macintoshes to Windows 2000-based networks. It can be a time-saver, especially if you have a smaller network and wish to make the setup process as easy as possible.

Unlike Microsoft's Services for Macintosh, DAVE lets you communicate using the NetBIOS protocol directly, allowing Macs to access file and print resources on the Windows network without making any changes to your Windows 2000 servers.

Additionally, DAVE has integrated the Windows NT Challenge Handshake Authentication Protocol (CHAP), allowing you to properly authenticate users against the Windows NT Workgroup or Domain security systems.

File and Print Services for Macintosh makes the Windows 2000 Server talk the language of the Macintosh—AppleTalk—whereas DAVE makes your Macs talk the language of Windows. With these services, Macs are not confined to communicating with servers where File and Print Services for Macintosh are installed.

DAVE can access any Windows-based files or printers shared on the network; it's not limited to Windows 2000 servers or workstations. You can even access shared files from personal computers running Windows 95, Windows 98, or even Windows for Workgroups 3.11.

NOTE: *To browse all the resources in a specific Windows 2000 Domain or Windows Workgroup, you need to specify the name of the Domain or Workgroup in the NetBIOS Control Panel.*

Using DAVE, you can log in using your normal Windows Domain or Workgroup username and password and have them authenticate properly with the Windows Domain server or the Workgroup server using the secure Microsoft CHAP authentication protocol. This protocol encrypts the conversation that occurs between your workstation and the server when it checks to see if your username and password are correct.

As a result, Windows can maintain a high degree of security and you are protected from people snooping around on your network trying to steal passwords. DAVE also allows you to access resources on the network using an alternate username and password. This feature is extremely valuable because it allows you to connect to resources that you normally don't have access to by using an account that does.

NOTE: *The best passwords are those that look like words or phrases with eight or more letters that you can remember but are deliberately misspelled. They should include both upper- and lowercase letters as well as numbers and special characters. A good example is Mac$RcOOl. If you create passwords of this sort, however, be sure to write them down and keep this copy in a safe location. You will need to refer to it later if a user forgets a password.*

The major downside to using DAVE is that you must separately install and configure it on every Mac that you wish to use to access your Windows network. Although this can be a support headache, it is usually less of an issue than using Services for Macintosh if you have only a small number of Macintoshes in your company.

Using MacLinkPlus Deluxe To Translate Windows Documents

The Mac users on your network can access Windows-based document files as easily as Mac files. But that capability doesn't count for everything. To actually run those files, you need to have a Macintosh program available that can use them. In many cases, this isn't a problem. Microsoft Office 98 For The Macintosh can easily read files created by Office 97 For Windows and older. And the Mac versions of such popular programs as Adobe Photoshop, Adobe Illustrator, and QuarkXPress translate quite well across platforms. The question gets complicated when you attempt to translate a file for which you don't have the application. Apple provides basic system-level features for file translation, such as PC Exchange, and for Mac OS 8.5 and later, File Exchange.

Whenever you translate a document, there's a good chance you may lose some critical formatting information. At minimum, font selections change, simply because Macintosh fonts and Windows fonts (even with the same name) have different metrics (width spacing values). In addition, line breaks in your document may change. Other formatting elements of your document may change as well. Fortunately, there's a

7. Windows 2000/ Macintosh OS File Sharing

solution that addresses many of these problems. It's MacLinkPlus Deluxe, a clever program from DataViz, Inc. Apple even bundled a version of the program in some of its operating system versions. The Deluxe version adds a number of useful features that make the document conversion process more convenient. They include:

- *File viewing*—If you don't have a suitable application to review translated Windows documents, MacLinkPlus Deluxe includes its own file viewing feature. This works best with picture files, which can come in many formats.

- *File decompression*—Files that are compressed in Windows-based compression software, such as Zip, can be expanded to their original form.

- *Email file viewing*—An all-too-common problem is using the files attached to email messages. MacLinkPlus Deluxe makes it possible to restore the attachments to their original form for easy viewing.

Immediate Solutions

Exploring Windows 2000 Services

Windows 2000 does not use network services in the same fashion as Windows NT 4 does. In Windows 2000, there is a group of network components as opposed to services that were added by and controlled from the Network Control Panel. Here is a list of some of these components:

- *Client Services for Microsoft Networks*—This is designed to allow you to access resources on other computers running a version of Microsoft Windows. This service is very similar to the Remote Procedure Call (RPC) service in Windows NT 4.

- *File and Printer Sharing for Microsoft Networks*—This service is designed to allow other computers to access resources on the Windows 2000 server. This feature is very similar to both the Workstation and Server services in Windows NT 4.

- *TCP/IP, IPX/SPX, and AppleTalk protocols*—These replace the separate protocols that were listed under the Protocols tab in the Network dialog box under Windows NT 4. The major difference between Windows NT 4 and Windows 2000 is that AppleTalk is now a separate protocol.

- *Network Monitor Driver*—This is used to allow Windows 2000 to examine network packets as they go through the server.

- *Gateway (and Client) Services for NetWare*—This network option is frequently installed. It allows Windows 2000 servers to talk to NetWare servers and clients.

- *Network Load Balancing service*—This is another popular network option. It spreads the network traffic out among the various network interfaces.

- *QoS Packet Scheduler*—This is designed to balance network traffic so that you maintain a specific quality of service on each network interface.

It may seem that the network components present in Windows 2000 are basically the same as those in Windows NT 4; however, most of them have been redesigned for Windows 2000's new networking

7. Windows 2000/ Macintosh OS File Sharing

architecture. Looking more closely, you can also see a much wider variety of network- and file-related services than were available in Windows NT.

Installing AppleTalk And File Services For Macintosh: The Beginning

The first step when you install AppleTalk and File Services for Macintosh is to add them to the list of Windows 2000 Network Protocols and Windows Components. These enable the Windows 2000 server to provide multi-platform support when communicating with the various computers on the network.

Follow these steps to quickly set up AppleTalk and File Services for Macintosh:

1. Click on Start|Settings|Select Control Panel. Or, double-click on the My Computer icon located on your Windows 2000 desktop and then double-click on the Control Panel folder located in the My Computer window.

2. Double-click on the Network icon. Doing so brings up the Network And Dial-Up Connections window, shown in Figure 7.1. You can examine every network connection that you have established on this computer directly from this window.

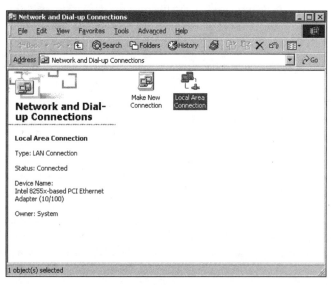

7. Windows 2000/ Macintosh OS File Sharing

Figure 7.1   The Network And Dial-Up Connections window allows you to control each of your network connections.

TIP: *A really quick way to open the Network And Dial-Up Connections window is to right-click on the Network Neighborhood icon, located on your Windows 2000 desktop. Then, select the Properties option from the drop-down menu to open the Network And Dial-Up Connections Control Panel.*

3. Once you have the Network And Dial-Up Connections window open, double-click on the Local Area Connection icon to open the network preferences for your server's LAN connection.

4. Information about current network traffic is displayed in the Local Area Connection Status dialog box, shown in Figure 7.2. This dialog box has two buttons: Properties, which allows you to configure all the networking options, and Disable, which shuts down your network connection. Click on Properties to see the adapter that is currently selected and the network options and protocols that are configured for that interface.

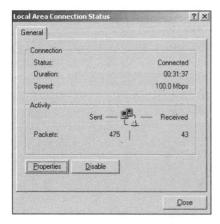

Figure 7.2   The Local Area Connection Status dialog box provides you with information on the network traffic going in and out of your server.

Installing AppleTalk And File Services For Macintosh: The Next Steps

Once you have the Network Control Panel opened, follow these steps to add AppleTalk to Windows 2000:

1. The Local Area Connection Properties dialog box is shown in Figure 7.3. The services installed on this server are the standard

7. Windows 2000/ Macintosh OS File Sharing

ones that Windows 2000 installs. To add a Windows 2000 Network Component, click on Install.

2. Double-click on Protocols in the Select Network Component Type dialog box.

3. In the Select Network Protocol dialog box, shown in Figure 7.4, select AppleTalk Protocol from the list of available protocols and then click on OK.

4. To add any other network options, click on Install, select the Network Component that you desire, and then click on OK again.

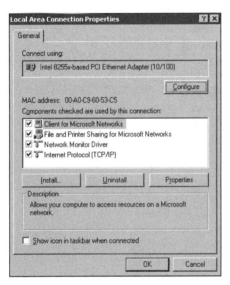

Figure 7.3   You can configure Network Options from this screen.

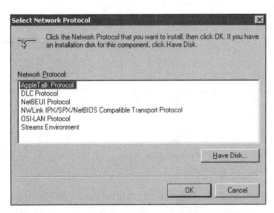

Figure 7.4   Click on AppleTalk Protocol to select it.

7. Windows 2000/
Macintosh OS File
Sharing

After you add AppleTalk to the list of available protocols, you must also add the File Services for Macintosh service to Windows 2000. To do so, follow these steps:

1. Open the Control Panel window by clicking on Start|Settings|Control Panel.

2. Next, double-click on the Add/Remove Programs icon.

3. From the Add/Remove Programs dialog box, click on the Add/Remove Windows Components option and wait for the Windows Components Wizard to start.

4. Once the Wizard has started, click on Next.

5. Look at the list of Windows components available, scroll down, and select Other Network File And Print Services, as shown in Figure 7.5.

6. Next, click on Details to see all the available options.

7. Examine the Subcomponents Of Other Network File And Print Services list, select File Services For Macintosh (as shown in Figure 7.6), and then click on OK.

8. Once you have finished adding in File Services For Macintosh, click on Next.

9. Click on Finish to complete the installation of File Services For Macintosh. Notice how you don't have to restart the computer, as you do when working with Windows NT 4 (see Chapter 2 for a description of installing the Services for Macintosh under NT 4).

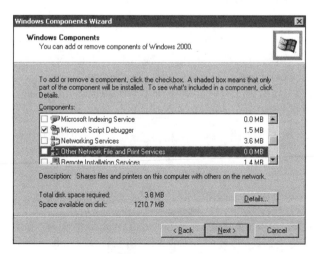

*Figure 7.5   Choose Other Network File And Print Services to locate File
Services for Macintosh.*

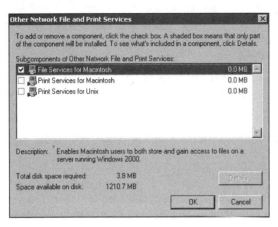

Figure 7.6   Choose File Services For Macintosh to install it.

Configuring AppleTalk Networking

After you have finished installing File Services for Macintosh, you are ready to configure it. On a network where there are already AppleTalk zones, Windows 2000 defaults to using the default zone configured for the network segment on which the server is located. To set this zone, follow these steps:

1. Open the Network and Dial-Up Connection window, double-click on the Local Area Connection icon, and then click on the Properties button to display the Local Area Connection Properties dialog box.

2. Next, select the AppleTalk protocol.

3. Lastly, click on Properties. Doing so brings up the AppleTalk Protocol Properties dialog box, shown in Figure 7.7. You can click on the list of zones available on the network and then select the one that you wish to use.

To add an AppleTalk zone to your Windows 2000 network, follow these steps:

1. Click on Start|Programs|Administrative Tools|Routing And Remote Access. Doing so brings up the Microsoft Management Console with the Routing And Remote Access snap-in, shown in Figure 7.8. For more information on configuring AppleTalk routing, please refer to the "Installing AppleTalk" section in Chapter 9.

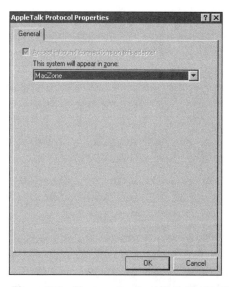

Figure 7.7   You use the AppleTalk Protocol Properties dialog box to set the AppleTalk zone in which your server resides.

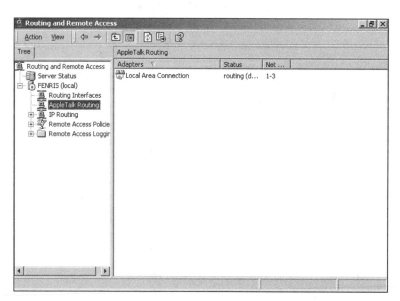

Figure 7.8   Select the routing components that you wish to configure from this setup screen.

7. Windows 2000/ Macintosh OS File Sharing

193

NOTE: *Under Windows 2000, the Routing options are available only after you have configured Routing And Remote Access. This is different from Windows NT 4.0, where AppleTalk routing options are available as soon as you install the Services for Macintosh.*

2. In the left-hand pane, click on the plus next to the server name to expand it. You will then see all the options that you can configure.

3. Again in the left-hand pane, click on AppleTalk Routing to list all the AppleTalk routers currently configured.

4. In the right-hand pane, double-click on Local Area Connection to open the Local Area Connection Properties dialog box, shown in Figure 7.9.

5. Click on Enable Seed Routing On This Network. Now, enter the appropriate value(s) in the Network Range box(es). If you have only one AppleTalk zone, enter "1" in both boxes. Otherwise, in the To column, enter a number that represents the total of the AppleTalk zones you're adding.

6. After you have entered the appropriate network numbers, click on the New Zone to enter a zone name if one is not already present.

7. Once you have finished typing in the name of your zone, click on OK. Notice that the AppleTalk zone you added is now listed in the Zones list at the bottom of the Local Area Connection Properties dialog box.

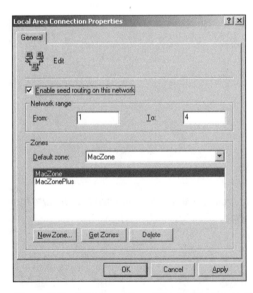

Figure 7.9   The Local Area Connection Properties dialog box allows you to specify various AppleTalk network settings.

8. To add additional AppleTalk Zones, repeat Steps 6 and 7.

9. Once you have added all the AppleTalk zones that you want, click on the zones pop-up menu and select the zone you want to be the default and then click on the Apply or OK button.

Related Solution:	See page:
Fine Tuning AppleTalk For Your Windows 2000 Network	287

Configuring AppleTalk Zones Automatically With Windows 2000

If your network already has AppleTalk zones, you can click on Get Zones in the Local Area Connection Properties dialog box and have the Windows 2000 server automatically scan for all the available AppleTalk zones. The only limitation to this process is that Windows 2000 can see only those AppleTalk zones that are available on the same network segment as the server.

NOTE: *Once you click on Get Zones, you see a warning dialog box that lets you know that all the zones that you have added will be replaced by any zones that Windows 2000 finds present on the network. If you've already manually added AppleTalk zones to your network, you may prefer to avoid using this feature.*

If you click on Get Zones and no AppleTalk zones can be found on your network, Windows 2000 informs you that it cannot find any and asks you to verify your network configuration.

Using Computer Management

Once File Services for Macintosh starts up successfully, you will notice several options have been added to the Computer Management snap-in. The Microsoft Management Console Computer Management snap-in is a new feature in Windows 2000 that consolidates almost all of the configuration tools into one central console. Using this snap-in, you can format hard drives, set up shared volumes and printers, and perform many other tasks. This snap-in may be confusing or even intimidating at first, but it will soon become very easy to use.

The Computer Management snap-in allows you to perform many network connection management tasks. Here is a list of some of them and how to accomplish each task:

- *Send a message to all the users connected to your server*—Right-click on the Shares icon, located under Shared Files, and then select All Tasks|Send Console Message. Then, enter the message that you wish to send and click on the Send button.

- *Disconnect all of the users that are currently connected to your shared volume*—Right-click on the Sessions icon under Shared Files and select Disconnect All to disconnect all of the users connected to the volume.

- *Disconnect only a single user*—Select Sessions, right-click on the specific user that you wish to disconnect, and then select Close Connection from the pop-up menu.

- *Close all of the open files on your server*—Right-click on the Open Files icon under Shared Folders and then select Close All Open Files from the pop-up menu.

- *Close a specific open file*—Select the Open Files icon, right-click on the specific file that you wish to close, and then select Close Open File.

Administering File Services For Macintosh

Windows 2000 offers a set of robust file and computer management tools that help you efficiently administer user access on your network. We will describe these tools in detail in the next few sections.

Configuring File Server For Macintosh

In the Computer manager, right-click on the shared folders and select Configure File Server For Macintosh from the pop-up menu. This allows you to configure File Server for Macintosh, as shown in Figure 7.10.

From the File Server For Macintosh Properties dialog box (shown in Figure 7.11), you can set a variety of session and security options on your Windows 2000 server. Within this dialog box, you can:

- Set the name of the server that is displayed to your Mac clients.

- Set the message, if any, that is displayed when a Mac user connects to your server.

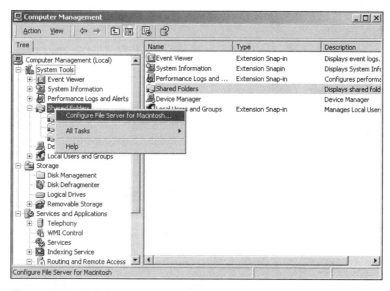

Figure 7.10   This is where you set up File Server for Macintosh.

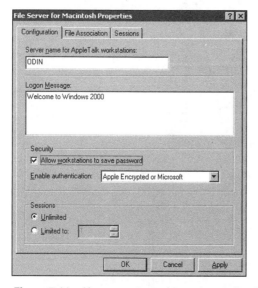

Figure 7.11   You can set session and security choices in this dialog box.

• Set the authentication options that are used when allowing a user to connect to the server.

• Limit the number of users that can connect at any one time.

File Server for Macintosh also allows you to control the mapping of file types to file extensions, view all the currently connected Macintosh

197

users, and send a message to those that have UAM installed on their Macintosh.

Associating Windows File Extensions To Macintosh Applications

The File Association tab of the File Server For Macintosh Properties dialog box, shown in Figure 7.12, is used to match up the three-letter extensions that Windows uses to tell which file belongs to which application and the file and creator types that the Mac uses to perform the same function. You can even use this feature to map file types of applications that do not exist on the Mac to applications that can read these types of files.

By default, most of the file associations you need are listed in the With Macintosh Document Creator And Type box. Windows 2000 is pre-configured with the extensions for many popular programs—such as Adobe Illustrator, Adobe PageMaker, Adobe Photoshop, QuarkXPress, and Microsoft Office—with their Mac equivalents in mind. If you have a special-purpose program that has no Mac equivalent, you can use this dialog box to choose an association of a Mac program that performs a similar function.

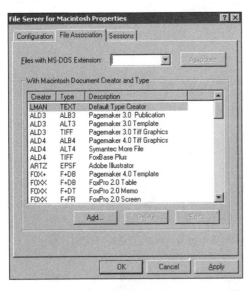

Figure 7.12   Use the File Association tab of the File Server For Macintosh Properties dialog box to match up Windows file extensions with matching Macintosh applications.

7. Windows 2000/ Macintosh OS File Sharing

Other ways to translate files are to use Apple's PC Exchange (or File Exchange for Mac OS 8.5 and later) or DataViz's MacLinkPlus Deluxe, discussed later in this chapter.

Monitoring User Sessions

Clicking on the Sessions tab of the File Server For Macintosh Properties dialog box (shown in Figure 7.13) gives you a high-level display of all of the users currently connected to your server. From this dialog box, you can see how many people are connected to your server, and you can send them messages if you want.

Creating A New Macintosh Shared Volume In Windows 2000

To create a new volume for your Macintosh users, follow these steps:

1. Right-click on the Shares icon, located under System Tools in the Computer Management program, then right-click on the Shares icon and select New Share from the shortcut menu.

2. The Folder Location screen of Create Shared Folder, shown in Figure 7.14, appears. To create a Macintosh Share, click on the checkbox labeled Apple Macintosh. Create Shared Folder then asks you to select the folder or volume that you wish to share. To enable Macintosh access, click on the Apple Macintosh

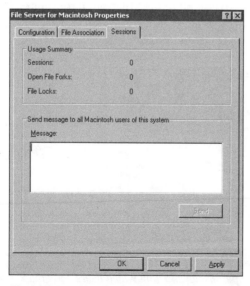

Figure 7.13   Use the Sessions tab of the File Server For Macintosh Properties dialog box to monitor user connections.

7. Windows 2000/ Macintosh OS File Sharing

Figure 7.14   Select the folder or volume that you wish to share and then enter the name it will be shared as.

checkbox. After you have selected the folder you wish to share and assigned its Windows share name and Macintosh share name, click on Next.

3. Next, the Set Permissions screen, shown in Figure 7.15, appears. It asks you to set the share permissions that you want. These permissions limit which users and groups can access this shared volume over the network.

4. Once you have finished setting up your shared volume's permissions, click on Finish to complete the creation of the share. You will now be asked if you wish to create another share, click on No, if you do not want to create another File Share.

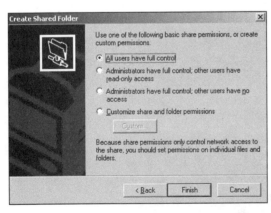

Figure 7.15   Set the share permissions to limit which users and groups can access the share.

Once you are finished, notice that the Computer Management snap-in displays two different shares, one with the Windows share name and one with the Macintosh share name. Even if these shares have the same name, Windows 2000 will still display one as a Windows share and one as a Macintosh share.

Examining And Changing A Macintosh Shared Volume

To view or modify an existing Macintosh volume on your server, simply follow these steps:

1. Click on the Shares icon, located under System Tools, in the Computer Management snap-in and then right-click on the shared volume you wish to modify. In this example, we have clicked on Book.

2. From the Book Properties dialog box (shown in Figure 7.16), you can set the number of users that can access it at any one time, a password specific for this share, and the file caching options for the share.

3. Click on the Security tab, shown in Figure 7.17, to modify the permissions that you wish to apply to this shared volume.

4. Once you have finished modifying the shared volume, click on OK.

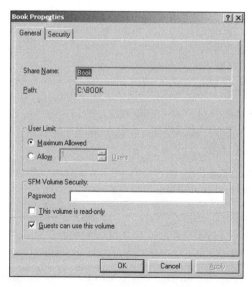

Figure 7.16   Set the properties of the selected volume from this dialog box.

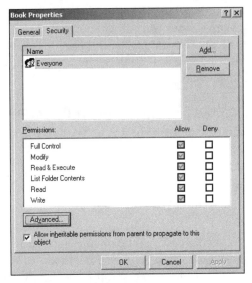

Figure 7.17   Set the permissions of the selected volume from this dialog box.

Configuring Permissions Levels For A Macintosh-Accessible Volume

You use the Macintosh View Of Directory Permissions dialog box (shown in Figure 7.18) to apply a very rudimentary set of file-access levels on the Macintosh shared volume. Unlike with a standard Windows file volume, you cannot have an unlimited number of users and groups in the Permissions list.

Mac permissions are limited to three groups. These are:

* *Owner*—The administrator(s) of the system

* *Primary Group*—The users specifically designated as having access to the Macintosh-Accessible volume

* *Everyone*—The remainder of the users on your network who can see the Macintosh-Accessible volumes

Unlike with Windows, the granularity of the file permissions is significantly reduced because you have only a limited number of access settings.

These settings allow you to permit or deny users from seeing files, seeing folders, or making changes. Additionally, you can lock the file volume so those who access the volume cannot move, rename, or delete files and folders.

7. Windows 2000/ Macintosh OS File Sharing

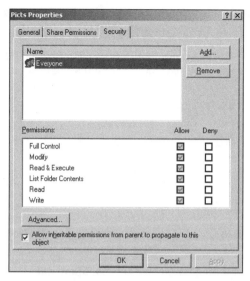

Figure 7.18   Use this dialog box to set permissions for the selected Macintosh-Accessible volume.

NOTE: *Although the permission levels that you can set for the Mac are somewhat limited, they do not affect the ones you set for your Windows users. A good idea to make administration easier is for you to create a Windows Domain group with all of your Mac users listed in it. Then, you can use this group (or special groups of just a few Mac users) to set the file permissions appropriately. For example, you might want to leave the Owner of a volume as the Administrators group and then set the Mac Users group as the Primary Group. As a result, you can deny access to the rest of the users on the network (those that fit the Everyone category), making sure that only the Administrators and Mac Users have access to the file volume.*

Deleting A Macintosh File Volume

You can easily delete a Macintosh file volume by following these steps:

1. Click on Shares, located under Shared Folders in the System Tools portion of the Computer Management snap-in and then select the share that you wish to delete.

2. Right-click on the share that you wish to delete and select Stop Sharing. Doing so causes the Windows 2000 server to delete the selected shared volume from the list of shares.

WARNING!   *Deleting the file share by using the Stop Sharing command doesn't actually cause the volume that the file share was connected to on the server to be deleted. This operation simply removes the volume from the list of resources available to Mac users. It is very important to make sure that you remove the Mac share before you actually delete the share from the server; otherwise, you can cause serious problems on the server.*

Installing DAVE On A Windows 2000 Network

Installing DAVE involves essentially the same steps as installing most Macintosh software. To begin, you use the original installation disks that come with DAVE or download the most recent version of DAVE Installer from Thursby Software Systems at **www.thursby.com**.

NOTE: *If you are unsure whether to deploy DAVE across your Macintosh network, you may want to try the time-limited demo version available at the publisher's Web site,* **www.thursby.com**. *If you do find it useful, you can purchase a copy direct from the Web site.*

To install DAVE, follow these steps.

1. Double-click on the DAVE Installer icon to start the installation process.

2. Accept the license agreement to bring up the main installer screen, shown in Figure 7.19.

3. You can choose Easy Install to install all of the DAVE components or Custom Install to install just the components you desire. These components include the DAVE client components; the DAVE Sharing, Access, and messaging components; and the NetBIOS Control Panel. Unless you have a specific reason for installing only one or two of these components, we recommend the Easy Install (default) option.

4. Click on Install to perform an Easy Install.

5. Once all of the components have been installed, restart the Macintosh.

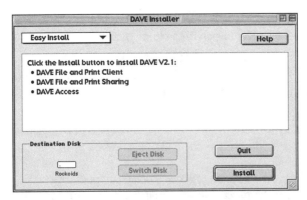

Figure 7.19   Choose your installation options from this window.

7. Windows 2000/ Macintosh OS File Sharing

Configuring DAVE For Windows 2000

After the Macintosh has finished the restart process, you are ready to configure the program to recognize your Windows 2000-based network. To configure DAVE, you must know the following:

• The NetBIOS name you wish to use for the Macintosh.

• The workgroup or domain that the Mac should be configured to use.

• Whether you will be manually configuring Windows Internet Name Service (WINS) or having your WINS configuration automatically configured for you by Dynamic Host Configuration Protocol (DHCP). WINS is a system that maps a computer's NetBIOS name to its IP addresses so that other computers can access it over the network. It is a Windows 2000 service. DHCP is a system that automatically distributes IP addresses and other network information, such as the addresses of the WINS server, to the computers on the network. DHCP is another Windows 2000 service. You'll find more information on how to set up and install DHCP in Chapter 9.

NOTE: *Although DAVE relies heavily upon WINS, Windows 2000 is designed to use Domain Name System (DNS) as its primary way to resolve a computer's IP address from its name. What this means for you is that you need to keep at least one server available for your Macintoshes running DAVE and all of your Windows 3.11, and Windows 95/98 workstations.*

Once you have this information at hand, you're ready to configure DAVE, following these steps:

1. Open the NetBIOS Control Panel (located in the Control Panel folder). The first time you use the program, you enter the name and activation key information, which brings up the screen shown in Figure 7.20.

NOTE: *Before opening the NetBIOS Control Panel, be sure you have configured the TCP/IP Control Panel to reflect the kind of network you are using, such as Ethernet built-in.*

---

2. Enter the Macintosh's NetBIOS name and the Workgroup or Domain to which you wish the Mac to belong. You can also add a description of the Macintosh in the space provided.

3. Select TCP/IP as the desired protocol.

Figure 7.20 Use this Control Panel to configure DAVE to work on your Windows NT network.

4. Depending upon your network, you may want to select the WINS and/or DHCP checkboxes. For more information on setting up DHCP on your network, please refer to the section on installing DHCP in Chapter 9. On most Windows 2000 networks, you should select only DHCP. If your DHCP server is not set to distribute WINS server information, you must select the WINS checkbox and then manually enter your primary WINS server's IP address and a secondary choice if it exists.

Related solution:	*Found on page:*
Setting Up A DHCP Server Under Windows 2000	293

Working With DAVE Under Windows 2000

The process of connecting to a Windows shared volume with DAVE is very similar to mounting an AppleShare volume with the Macintosh Chooser or Network Browser application (which first appeared in Mac OS 8.5). You can mount Windows shared volumes by using either the DAVE client under the Chooser or by using the DAVE Access application (which you can easily access via the Apple menu). To connect to a Windows shared volume using the DAVE client, follow these steps:

1. Open the Chooser and select DAVE client, which displays a screen similar to that shown in Figure 7.21.

2. Click on the name of the Windows computer that houses the shared volume that you wish to use and then click on OK.

7. Windows 2000/ Macintosh OS File Sharing

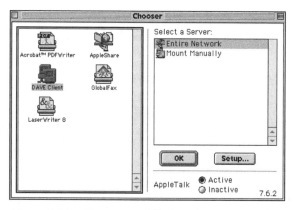

Figure 7.21   Choose your Windows-based volume from the list.

3. From the list of volumes available on the Windows-based computer, select the one that you want and click on OK. If you want to mount the shared volume on your Mac's desktop when it's restarted, select the checkbox to the right of the volume's name.

4. Enter the username and password, as required.

NOTE: *If you are trying to connect to a hidden shared volume, click on Add Share once you have selected the Windows computer on which the volume is installed and add the name of the shared volume.*

---

5. Close the Chooser.

That's all there is. Your Windows 2000 share now appears on your Mac's desktop as just another Mac volume, with files and folders readily accessible.

Using DAVE Access With Windows 2000

To use the DAVE Access tool to mount a Windows shared volume, follow these steps:

1. Launch DAVE Access from the Apple menu.

2. Click on the Mount Share icon on the DAVE Access toolbar.

3. Enter the name of the Windows computer and the shared volume that you wish to connect to. You can also enter a name that you wish to use for this volume, for easy identification.

4. Select the type of network protocol you wish to use to connect to the remote computer. Unless you must use TCP/IP, it is generally best to select NetBIOS.

The next two options allow you to disable the automatic update feature, which allows you to see changes that are made on the remote shared volume. It also lets you disable the creation of a desktop database file on that volume. Disabling the automatic update lessens the performance impact on the remote computer and the network; however, it makes it more difficult to see changes that are occurring on the share. Disabling the creation of the desktop database on the remote shared volume prevents your Mac from creating the hidden desktop files that are used to map icons to the various file types.

5. If you need to log on to the Macintosh-Accessible volume with a different username and password, select the Use Alternative Credentials checkbox.

6. Enter the username and password that you wish to use.

Accessing Windows Shared Volumes From A Macintosh

The process of connecting to a Macintosh-Accessible volume from your Macs involves the same basic steps you use when bringing up a networked disk via File Sharing:

1. Open the Chooser and click on the AppleShare icon.

2. Click on the name of the Windows computer that hosts the shared volume you wish to use and then click on OK.

3. From the list of shared volumes available on the Windows-based computer, select the one that you want and then click on OK.

4. Enter the username and password as required.

5. If you want to reconnect to the shared volume and have it mount on the desktop when you restart your Mac, select the checkbox to the right of the volume's name.

6. Close the Chooser.

NOTE: *If you're using Mac OS 8.5 or later, you may also connect to shared volumes, Macintosh- or Windows-based, using the Network Browser application. When you launch the application, which is available from the Apple menu, you'll see the listing of shared volumes that you can access. Bear in mind that when you use the Network Browser application under Mac OS 9, you will also be logged onto your ISP, if you are set up to access the Internet.*

Installing MacLinkPlus Deluxe

A convenient solution to the problem of running Windows files on a Mac for which there's no matching program is DataViz's MacLinkPlus Deluxe. The program comes with three different types of installers, depending on your purchase options. The boxed version includes either floppy disks or a CD-ROM. You may also purchase and download the installer file direct from the publisher's Web site at **www.dataviz.com**.

To install MacLinkPlus Deluxe, follow these steps:

1. Place the installer CD-ROM or floppy disk in your Mac's drive, if this applies. If you downloaded the installation software from the publisher's Web site, locate the installer application.

2. Double-click on the Installer application.

3. Enter your name and company information, and the registration number and activation key provided by the publisher.

4. Follow the prompts to continue the installation.

5. Once the installation of MacLinkPlus Deluxe is complete, restart your Macintosh.

Configuring MacLinkPlus Deluxe

Once MacLinkPlus Deluxe is installed, you may simply launch the application by double-clicking on its icon in order to translate available files. The easiest way to use the program is simply to let it do its stuff automatically, by following these steps:

1. Locate and double-click on the Windows file you wish to translate.

7. Windows 2000/ Macintosh OS File Sharing

NOTE: *If you have a number of similar programs with which to open a Windows file (such as several word processors), you should choose the one that you use most often, so you are familiar with the interface and translation problems can be dealt with quickly. In addition, use a program that performs a similar function, such as a word processor for word processing documents and an illustration program for drawings.*

---

2. You will see a Mac OS Easy Open (or File Exchange) dialog box that lists available file translation options. Choose an application from the list that includes the words "with MacLinkPlus translation". MacLinkPlus Deluxe goes to work translating the file to an appropriate Macintosh format, and then the document is opened in the selected application.

TIP: *Mac OS versions 8 and greater include a useful feature, Contextual Menus, that is basically borrowed, with some changes, from the Windows right-mouse menu feature. You can quickly call MacLinkPlus Deluxe into operation in a selected file by holding down the Control key while clicking to bring up the Contextual Menu. Then choose Send To MacLinkPlus.*

Controlling File Access With Mac OS 8.0 File Security Options

Computers running Macintosh OS 8.0 through 8.6 offer a small number of security options that they can use to limit access to shared volumes and folders. While these security options are very limited in their granularity, they are capable of protecting your files from unauthorized users. When comparing file security under Macintosh OS to Windows NTFS file security, the first thing that you will notice is that you have far fewer choices in the number of users and the types of file access that you can assign.

By selecting the icon of the folder or volume that you are sharing, and then clicking on the File menu and selecting Sharing from the Get Info sub-menu, you can see all the security settings on the shared volume or folder (see Figure 7.22). Unlike Windows NTFS file security where you can grant different access rights to a large number of users and groups, under Macintosh OS 8.x, you are only able to grant rights to the owner of the file or folder, a group of users defined on the Macintosh, or Everyone. While this is considerably more limiting than the options available to you when using Windows 2000 with NTFS, it does give you the basic tools that you need to protect your files.

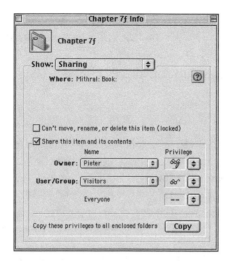

Figure 7.22   Get Info shows you the various security options that you have set.

Looking at the type of access that you can set on files using Macintosh OS 8.x, you will see that you can give users read and write access, read only access, write only access, and no access. Another limitation of Macintosh OS 8.x file security is that you are only able to set permissions on shared volumes and the folders that are on them or upon folders that you share by themselves. This means that you must build your security policy around the folders and volumes and not individual files like you can under Windows 2000 using NTFS security.

One other option is the ability to prevent users connecting to the volume or folder from moving, deleting, or renaming it. This gives you a bit more security for your files and volumes that you choose to share. To prevent folks from moving, renaming or deleting your volumes or folders, select the volume or folder and then select File|Get Info|Sharing. Looking at the Sharing portion of the Info dialog box for the folder or volume, click on the Can't Move, Rename Or Delete This Item (Locked) checkbox.

Using Mac OS 9.0 File Security Options

For Mac OS 9.0, Apple has introduced a robust set of system security tools that make it possible to provide a greater degree of control over the files and Mac volumes (including removable devices) the Mac users on your network can access and manipulate.

In this section, we'll introduce you to the new features of Mac OS 9.0. These features are expected to be continued and expanded when Apple moves towards its industrial-strength operating system, Mac OS X client (which was announced for mid-2000 release when this book went to press).

Keychain Access

Apple's Keychain feature allows you to establish a secure place for user password information. This information includes keys, passwords and certificates. You can use this feature to attach a digital signature to such things as email and files. Once the digital signature is attached, the document cannot be opened until you enter the correct user password.

Here's how you go about creating a keychain:

1. Click on the Apple menu, select Control Panel, and choose the Keychain Access Control Panel.

2. If you haven't already made a keychain, you'll see a prompt asking if you wish to make one. Click on the Create button.

NOTE: *If you've previously created a keychain, you'll want to click the Cancel button, then go to the File menu and choose the New Keychain command.*

---

3. Type in the new information for your keychain, then click on the Create button. Be sure to follow our suggestions about creating and keeping a record of the passwords you create. Your first keychain will become your default.

4. If the program you're using supports the keychain feature, you can add items to the keychain from within the program. But you should not expect to find this feature frequently, because very few Mac programs support keychains (it'll be obvious from the program's documentation or the presence of a login dialog box).

Multiple Users

You can customize the user experience for each person who works on a specific Mac. This feature gives you full control over their access to applications, files, folders, System Folder items, and mounted volumes.

Here's a brief description of how to create a custom user profile under Mac OS 9.0:

1. Click on the Apple menu, select Control Panel, and choose Multiple Users from the sub-menu. This brings up the Control Panel shown in Figure 7.23

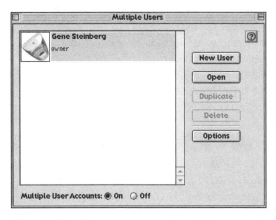

Figure 7.23   The name you entered when you set up this Mac is shown is the "owner."

2. If it's not already turned on, click the On radio button under Multiple User Accounts. If you leave it unchecked, the multiple user features will not operate.

3. To select global access features for the users on this Mac, click the Options button, which brings up the screen shown in Figure 7.24.

4. Choose your Log-in settings by checking the appropriate box.

5. If you wish to grant you or your users Voice Verification, check the Allow Alternate Password option. You'll be asked to speak your password, then repeat it for verification.

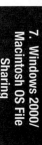

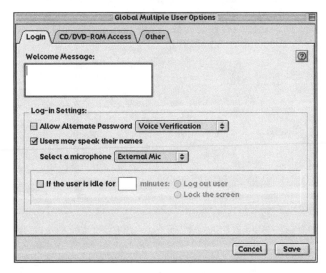

Figure 7.24   Set Log-in and other access privileges from this screen.

NOTE: *In order to use the Voice Verification feature of Mac OS 9.0, you need a Mac with a built-in mike, or one of Apple's so-called "PlainTalk" microphones, which are provided with almost every recent model (except the iBook).*

---

6. To restrict access to specific CDs and DVD-ROMs, click on the appropriate tab and mount and choose the volumes to which you wish to provide access.

7. Click on the Other button to access additional setup features, such as the ability to allow guest accounts, notification when new applications are installed, and whether or not users can select their own passwords.

8. To add users to this Macintosh, click on the New User button, which brings up the screen shown in Figure 7.25.

9. Enter a User Name and Password in the text fields.

10. Click on the icon representing the appropriate user account. Here are some of the options a Normal account gives you:

    - You can, if you wish, prevent the new users from changing their own passwords.

    - The user's ability to manage similar accounts can be restricted.

    - You can limit access by others to the user's documents.

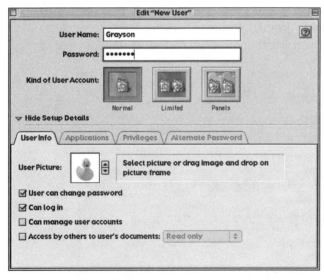

Figure 7.25   You can create a New User on this setup screen.

NOTE: *Apple provides a choice of several dozen custom pictures to be attached to a user's account. Just click the up and down arrows to pick the ones you like. You can also drag and drop small graphic files to the New User screen to provide additional choices.*

11. If you wish to restrict a user's access even further, click either the Limited or Panels icon, which will bring you to the Applications screen shown in Figure 7.26. These two account choices give you a much wider range of restrictions.

12. Once the applications to which a new user has access have been checked from the scrolling list, click on the Privileges button to control additional levels of access. See Figure 7.27 for a typical example.

13. Click on the appropriate checkboxes to select specific user privileges. Here's a brief description of what's available:

    • Access to CDs and DVD-ROMs can be restricted. The owner of the Macintosh (usually the system administrator) can provide a list of accessible disks, as explained in Step 6.

    • Access to shared folders, printers, and networked volumes can be limited.

    • You can also restrict access to Control Panels and other items in the Apple Menu.

14. Once you've made your settings for a specific user, click on the close box to activate those settings.

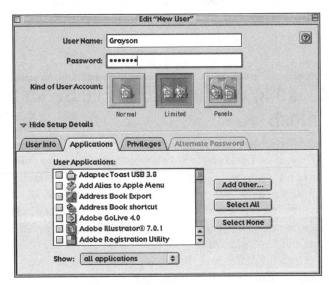

Figure 7.26   Specify which applications a user can access from the scrolling list.

7. Windows 2000/
Macintosh OS File
Sharing

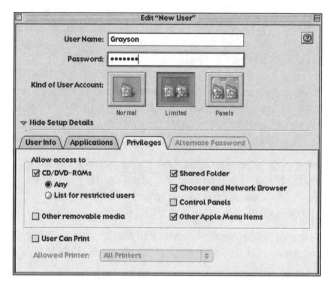

Figure 7.27   You can limit a user's access to specific features via this screen.

When you or another user finishes using that Mac, just choose Logout from the Finder desktop. If another user wishes to work on that Mac, they will have to pick their username from the list and enter (or speak) the correct password when the prompt appears.

If you choose to Restart or Shut Down the Mac, the username selection screen will appear after the Mac has completed its normal startup routine.

Troubleshooting Windows 2000 File Services For Macintosh

The process of troubleshooting File Services for Macintosh under Windows 2000 can be broken down into two major areas: problems with user authentication and problems with file access. User authentication troubles are usually the result of people forgetting their passwords or having their passwords expire without their realizing it. File access problems generally focus around problems with user access rights and the configuration of the Windows 2000 server that is running File Services for Macintosh. In the following sections, we have outlined common problems and their solutions.

7. Windows 2000/ Macintosh OS File Sharing

Dealing With Macintosh Users Who Cannot Log Into A Server

The first question you need to ask when you have a Mac user who cannot log on to a server, is "Can anyone log into this server?" If the answer is yes, you should check to see if the user can log into any other server on the network. If the user can connect to other Windows 2000 servers on the network, the problem is most likely due to the login privileges that are set on the Windows 2000 server in question.

If the user still cannot log onto the server, follow these troubleshooting suggestions for the various problems you might encounter:

- *The logon permissions are preventing the user from connecting*—You need to use the Computer Management snap-in to examine the permission levels for that specific Macintosh-Accessible volume, described earlier in this chapter.

- *The permissions might be set incorrectly*—If only those in the Everyone category can connect to this volume, be sure that permissions are set appropriately. If this is a secure server, be certain that the user in question is a member of one of the two Windows Workgroup or Domain groups that have permission to log in to the Macintosh-Accessible volume.

- *The user cannot connect to any other Windows 2000 server*—It is likely that the user has either forgotten his or her password or used the wrong password, or the password has expired.

On the other hand, if the user is certain that he or she has not forgotten or mistyped the password, follow these steps:

1. Open the Windows 2000 Computer Management snap-in.
2. Click on Systems Tools and then click on the Local Users And Groups Icon.
3. Next, click on the Users icon and then click on the user that you wish to modify from the list of users.
4. If the user has simply forgotten the password, right-click on the user and then select Set Password from the pop-up menu.
5. Then, set the password to the default used on your network and click on OK.
6. Double-click on the user and select User Must Change Password At Next Logon checkbox. Doing so forces the user to change the password the next time he or she logs on to the network.

7. Windows 2000/ Macintosh OS File Sharing

217

Another common problem that you may see occurs only when you are using Microsoft authentication for logon. If a user reports that he or she is allowed to log on only as a guest and that the Registered User radio button is grayed out, you should check to see if the user has the Microsoft UAM option installed on his or her Macintosh. If not, install the MS UAM module (following the steps described earlier in this chapter). Then, have the user restart his or her Mac.

Dealing With Macintosh Users Who Cannot See Windows 2000 Servers Or Files

When a user is having trouble with Windows 2000 servers or files, you must first determine if this is a problem seeing a specific server and its resources or if it is a problem seeing or accessing files on a Windows 2000 server. Here are some basic problems and solutions:

- *Users cannot locate a specific Windows 2000 server or its Macintosh-Accessible volumes*—See if the server is currently available. If the server is functioning properly, you need to narrow down the problem a bit more.

- *The server can be seen on the network, but certain Macintosh-Accessible volumes aren't visible*—Use Windows 2000 Computer Management snap-in to examine the shares on that server to make sure they are all currently active. Check to make sure that all the shares are currently active and that the folders on the volume are present and located where they should be. If they are not, delete the existing Macintosh-Accessible volume and re-create it following the steps described earlier in this chapter.

- *Everything looks normal, but users cannot see the file share*— Delete the Macintosh-Accessible volume from the server and re-create it. If you still have trouble, try deleting the volume again and then create it with a new name.

- *The user cannot see a specific server*—You first need to ask, "Is everyone having this problem?" If other users cannot see this server, you have to determine if this is a problem with AppleTalk or if the server is having connectivity problems. If you can see the server from a Windows-based workstation, you should go to the server and check its AppleTalk configuration. Make sure the AppleTalk zones are set correctly and then check that the Default Zone has not changed. If these settings are not correct, reset them as you prefer and restart the server.

• *The AppleTalk configuration and Default Zone are all set correctly, but the user cannot connect to Macintoshes or AppleTalk printers on other zones of the network*—Check with other members of your network team (if this applies) to make sure that they haven't made any changes to your network configuration that might cause this failure. If no network problems are blocking the server from reaching the Macs, try rebooting the server. If rebooting your server does not fix the problem, try removing and reinstalling File Services for Macintosh.

Problems with users not being able to see a file of folder on a Macintosh-accessible volume are almost always tied to the access permissions granted on the file server. The first thing you should check when a user is having problems accessing a file or folder on a Windows 2000 server is the actual file permissions you have granted on the affected volume. Make certain that these users can see the files and folders they should see and that the proper access rights are available. In particular, determine if the users are members of the appropriate groups and that they are logging on using the proper accounts. If users have multiple Windows 2000 accounts, it is very easy for them to find themselves unable to access certain files simply because they are logged in using the wrong account.

Finding Missing AppleTalk Zones

If you cannot find one or more AppleTalk zones, yet you know that these zones are present on the network, you most likely have a network-related problem. The most common cause of such a problem is a bad or poorly seated network cable. To check for this condition, follow these steps:

1. Look at the network adapter on your server to make sure that the Link light, which indicates that the network connection is live, is on.

2. If the Link light is visible, go into the Network Neighborhood window and see if you can locate any of the Windows-based computers on your network. If you can see other Windows-based computers, you may have a problem with either your Network Adapters settings or with something else on the network that is blocking the AppleTalk traffic.

**7. Windows 2000/
Macintosh OS File
Sharing**

Resolving Router Configuration Problems And Other Network Issues

A badly configured router is one of the principal causes of missing AppleTalk zones. Here are some common problems and their solutions:

- *You cannot communicate with your AppleTalk device*—Ensure that AppleTalk routing has been properly enabled to pass network traffic (packets). In addition, see if you are trying to restrict AppleTalk traffic to only one segment of your network. If you are trying to connect to an AppleTalk device on another segment of the network, you must activate AppleTalk routing on all the routers between you and the remote segment.

- *An access list on a router is blocking computers on your zone*— One way to configure routers is to block specific AppleTalk traffic by using access-lists, discussed in detail in Chapter 4. You can configure these access lists to block specific *network numbers*, the numbers used to represent a zone. Thus, if a router has an access list that blocks computers on your zone, you cannot connect to an AppleTalk device beyond that router. Try examining the configurations on the router to see how the access-list is set up. Looking at the access-list, check to see if there are rules that are expressly blocking you or if the access-list has just been written in such a way that you are getting blocked accidentally.

- *AppleTalk or File Services for Macintosh do not start properly*— Check Event Viewer, located under Start|Programs|Administrative Tools. Event Viewer has an entry in its System Log that details the problem you encountered when trying to start File Services for Macintosh. This information should help you isolate the cause of the problem.

The most common causes of failure of AppleTalk or the File Services for Macintosh to start properly include incorrectly configured network number settings, the failure of another networking service, or (more rarely), a conflict with another Windows 2000 service.

Installing The Microsoft User Authentication Module (UAM)

If you wish to use the Microsoft authentication system to allow users to securely log into your Windows 2000 Server, you need to install the Microsoft UAM into the AppleShare folder, which is located in the

7. Windows 2000/ Macintosh OS File Sharing

Extensions folder inside the Mac's System folder. To install UAM on your Mac, follow these steps:

1. Open the Chooser and click on AppleShare.

2. From the list of servers, select the Windows 2000 server and then click on OK.

3. Click on OK and select Guest Access.

4. Then, select Microsoft UAM Volume and press Enter.

5. Click on Close to close the Chooser.

6. Open the Microsoft UAM Volume and then double-click on the MS UAM Installer.

7. Restart your Macintosh.

7. Windows 2000/ Macintosh OS File Sharing

Windows 2000/Mac OS Printing

In Brief

Introduction To Cross-Platform Printer Sharing

This chapter focuses on the various features available in Windows 2000 that enable you to share network-based printer resources between Windows and Windows 2000 systems and those running the Mac OS. In addition, we will look at other options such as DAVE (from Thursby Software Systems, Inc.), which allows Macintosh users to access printers that are available to the Windows- and Windows 2000-based systems. DAVE makes it easy for your Macs to access PostScript printers that are connected to the Windows network as well as allows you to make printers that are connected to the Macintosh network available to users on the Windows network.

In this chapter, you will see both the mechanics and the realities of sharing printers among systems that are running the Mac OS, Windows, and Windows 2000. You will also see how sharing your printers among the different types of computers on your network can help you better utilize your network's printing resources. Sharing allows you to lessen the need to purchase and maintain extra output devices. In addition, by sharing one printer among multiple computers connected by a network, you can now buy larger, more powerful printers that can handle the printing needs of an entire workgroup, not just those of a single person.

Networked printers are a fairly recent development. It wasn't so long ago that if you wanted to have access to a printer, you had to install one directly on your computer, or place the file on a disk and take it directly to a computer with an attached printer. As computer networks became more common and network-aware printers started to become available, it became less important to have a printer on every computer. Today, it is not uncommon for one or more big printers to be on the network, allowing users to choose printer types and take advantage of specific options that a printer may have. In addition, such big printers use *simultaneous emulation* to handle the output from computers that are running different operating systems without a complex setup process.

NOTE: *The two most commonly used connections between a printer and workstation or server are serial and parallel. However, network connections are rapidly becoming as popular, if not more popular than serial or parallel connections. Serial connections for printers are identical to the connections you use when hooking up your computer to a modem. Serial ports send data one bit at a time. As a result, they can be fairly slow when transferring your data to a printer. Parallel ports, on the other hand, transfer a whole byte at a time and they are therefore much faster than serial connections at transferring data to the printer.*

On Windows 2000 servers, serial ports are listed as communication (COM) ports, of which two are normally available. Parallel ports are referred to as line printer (LPT) ports, and there is normally one of these on a workstation or server. When you create a network-based port, you are really creating a virtual port on the Windows 2000 server to which the printer resources can be linked. You then configure this port to use a network connection between the server and the network-based printer that you wish to control.

New in Windows 2000 is direct support for AppleTalk printers. As a result, your Windows 2000 server can directly connect to and share AppleTalk-based printers to their Windows-based clients.

NOTE: *Although Macintosh OS computers cannot access a non-PostScript printer shared by Windows 2000, you can get around that limitation. Infowave, a manufacturer of cross-platform printer solutions, makes a product that can provide a suitable alternative. Called PowerPrint for Networks, it allows Macs to access non-PostScript printers across an Ethernet network. PowerPrint for Networks includes printer drivers as well as a fast 10/100Base-T Ethernet print server and printer cable, and it is said to support over 1,600 inkjet, laser, and specialty printer models. You can get more information about this product from the publisher's Web site, **www.infowave.com**. Infowave may not be for everyone, however. If the documents you work on in your company are designed for professional printing, you will probably be better off using a PostScript printer on your network. PostScript printers provide more consistent, high-quality output for color and graphics. And the question of saving money is not a serious issue anymore. Such products may cost only a couple of hundred dollars more than their non-PostScript counterparts.*

8. Windows 2000/ Mac OS Printing

Immediate Solutions

Configuring A Printer Using Windows 2000 Server

In order to set up a printer that both your Windows-based users and those running the Macintosh OS can use, follow these steps:

1. Click on Start|Settings|Printers.

2. From the Printers window, double-click on the Add Printer icon. Doing so brings up the screen shown in Figure 8.1.

3. After the Add Printer Wizard has completed loading, click on Next.

NOTE: *All through the printer installation process, you can go back to an earlier step using the Back button (when it isn't grayed out).*

---

4. Now, choose between a printer that is connected directly to your server or one that is connected to the network via a print sharing device (such as the Hewlett-Packard JetDirect card) and one that is being shared by another workstation or server on the network. This server is the one with Services for

Figure 8.1   You can use the Add Printer Wizard program to configure your printer settings.

Macintosh installed, so you should select a printer that is locally connected to make the feature more useful.

NOTE: *Configuring Windows 2000 to use a printer that is connected locally simply means that you have specified that your server is to be in control of the printer and its associated output queue. The printer can be located across the building, on another floor, or next to the server, attached by a standard printer cable, and still be considered "locally connected."*

---

5. The Local Or Network Printer screen of the Add Printer Wizard, shown in Figure 8.2, now appears. It asks if you wish it to see if it can locate all the plug and play printers that are directly connected to the server or if you would prefer to bypass this step and manually configure your printer. For this example, select the Local printer radio button. If you choose to let Windows 2000 set up your printer connection, jump ahead to the next set of instructions. Otherwise, uncheck the Automatically Detect My Printer checkbox to go through the steps manually. When you're done, click on Next.

6. Now, on the Select the Printer Port screen (shown in Figure 8.3), you are asked to select the port to which you will connect your printer. If the printer is directly connected to the server by a serial or parallel cable, select the appropriate serial or parallel port.

7. If the printer is connected directly to the network, click on the Create A New Port radio button located towards the bottom of the dialog box. Doing so allows you to create a new port for a network printer to use.

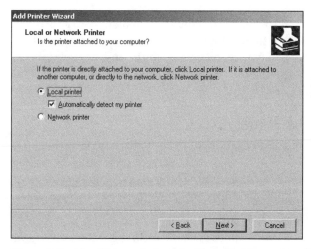

Figure 8.2   Use this screen to select how to set up your printer.

8. Windows 2000/ Mac OS Printing

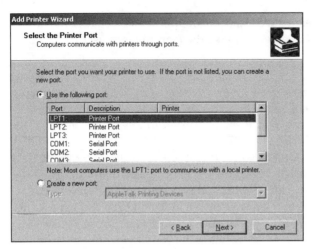

Figure 8.3   Use this screen to select the port to which your printer is connected.

NOTE: *If you select the Create A New Port radio button, you are then presented with a list of available port types: AppleTalk Printing Devices, Local Port, and Standard TCP/IP Port. Select AppleTalk from the list and click on Next. A list of all the AppleTalk zones available to the server will display. Likewise, selecting Local Port and clicking on Next asks you for the name of the port. Choosing TCP/IP causes Windows 2000 to launch the TCP/IP Printer Port Wizard that steps you through the process of setting up your TCP/IP printer. For the purposes of this example, we have chosen a printer that is directly connected to our server on LPT1.*

---

8. After you have chosen and/or configured the port to which your printer is connected, you are asked to choose the type of printer that you are connecting to the server. Computers that run the Macintosh OS are limited to using network printers that can understand Adobe PostScript (except printers using the Infowave software, discussed in the In Brief section earlier in this chapter). Therefore, you must choose a PostScript-capable printer.

Selecting The Printer

To select the make and model of printer that you are using, follow these steps:

1. Click on the printer manufacturer's name, located in the Manufacturers list on the left-hand side of the Add Printer Wizard screen, shown in Figure 8.4.

2. Then, choose the model of printer from the Printers list on the right-hand side of the screen. Then, click on Next.

8. Windows 2000/Mac OS Printing

NOTE: *If your printer's make or model number isn't displayed on the list of printers in Windows 2000, click on Have Disk and then load the printer drivers from the drivers disk(s) provided with the printer. If you do not have drivers for the printer, you may want to check the manufacturer's Web site or contact the manufacturer's technical support department for the software that you need or suggestions on choosing an alternate printer driver that may provide similar functionality.*

---

3. The Add Printer Wizard now asks you to type in the name by which this printer will be known on the network, as shown in Figure 8.5. Although you can use any name, it is generally best to select a name that reflects either the department that the printer supports or the location where it can be found. If there

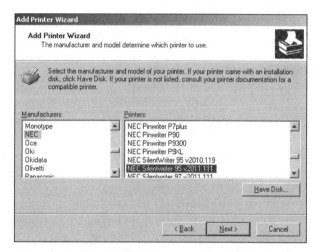

Figure 8.4   Choose the printer manufacturer from the Manufacturers list.

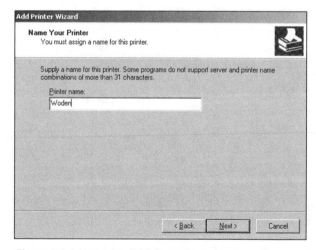

Figure 8.5   Name your printer here.

8. Windows 2000/ Mac OS Printing

is already a printer configured on this server, then you will be asked if you wish to make this new printer the Default Printer.

4. Once you have chosen the printer's name, click on Next to continue.

5. You are then asked if you want to share this printer with the other computers on the network, as shown in Figure 8.6. Click on the Share As radio button and then enter the name of the printer.

6. Now, you are asked to enter the location of the printer and some comments about it, as shown in Figure 8.7. Although this

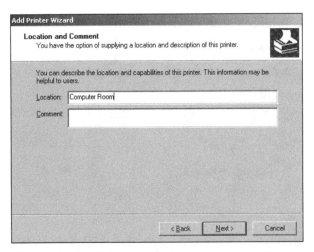

Figure 8.6   Use this screen to turn sharing on for the selected printer.

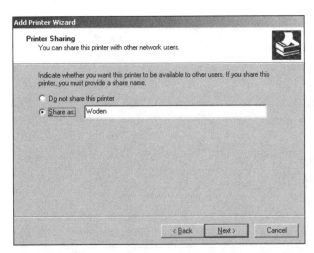

Figure 8.7   Supply a location and description of the printer here.

is a completely optional step, it is a very good idea to do it, especially if you have many printers to manage. Entering the location and comments makes it considerably easier to help locate and keep track of printer resources. When you are done, click on Next.

7. After sharing your printer, click on Next to continue the setup process.

8. Congratulations, you are nearly done with the setup process. The Print Test Page screen of the Add Printer Wizard, shown in Figure 8.8, now asks you if you want to print a test page so that you can ensure the printer is configured correctly. Click on the Yes radio button to do so.

TIP: *It is always a good idea, especially with network printers, to print a test page right after the setup process to be sure they are properly configured. Doing so avoids nasty surprises later on, when users attempt to print their documents.*

9. Once you have finished printing the test page and examined it to be sure your setup is correct, click on Next to go to the final portion of setup (see Figure 8.9). Examine all the settings listed in the Completing the Add Printer Wizard screen. If they are all set the way you want, click on Finish to complete the setup of your printer.

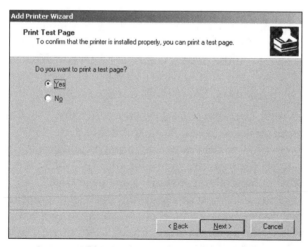

Figure 8.8   Click on the Yes radio button to print your test page.

8. Windows 2000/ Mac OS Printing

Figure 8.9   Examine all the printer settings and then click on Finish.

Solving Test Page Problems

If your network printer fails to print a test page, it's a good idea to turn the printer off and then on again, to reset the memory and controller. Depending on the type of printer, you may need to follow some additional steps to enable the test page feature. Some Hewlett-Packard network printers, for example, have different types of test pages, from configuration to font display, all accessed from the control panel display on the unit itself.

Despite being compatible with Windows, Apple laser printers do not offer a similar array of Control Panel settings, but do generate an automatic test page when the printer is turned off and on again (unless you turn off that option with a LaserWriter print program). Here are some suggestions on how to fix test-page problems:

- *You still can't get a test page from your computer after you have turned it off and on*—Go directly to the printer and use the buttons on the console to generate a test page. Although this process varies a bit from printer to printer, there is usually a button on the front panel that generates a test page when pressed. When you look at the test page, pay particular attention to the interface that is currently selected and if the printer has a network card in it, the network configuration. Check to see that the interface that is currently selected is the same one that you have selected when setting up the printer in the server. In addition, make sure that the address of the printer is the same as the one you configured on the server.

8. Windows 2000/
Mac OS Printing

- *The configuration of the printer isn't the same*—Make sure that you change it to match the settings on the server.

- *The printer is using TCP/IP and the server cannot PING (contact) the printer*—Open a command prompt on the Windows 2000 server and then type "PING XXX.XXX.XXX.XXX", where XXX.XXX.XXX.XXX is the IP address of the problem printer.

- If the printer responds properly to the PING command, double-check the network settings that you specified when you first set up the printer.

- *You do not get a response from the printer*—Check with your network group to make sure that there is a proper connection between your server and the printer.

Configuring Access Rights And Properties On Your New Printer

In order to set the properties and access permission settings on your new printer, follow these steps.

1. Right-click on the icon of the printer you wish to examine, and select Properties, as shown in Figure 8.10.

2. When you look at the General tab of the Properties page, shown in Figure 8.11, you can see the name of the printer as well as the location and comments that you entered when you initially configured it.

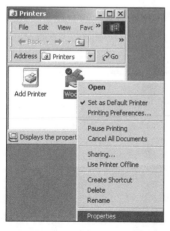

Figure 8.10   Right-clicking on a printer icon allows you to open its Properties page.

3. Next, click on the Sharing tab, shown in Figure 8.12, to look at the shared name of the printer and to determine which other printer drivers should be available for older versions of Windows and Windows NT.

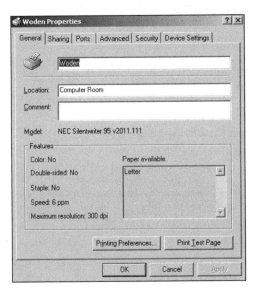

Figure 8.11   The General tab of the Properties dialog box allows you to change the name and other information for your printer.

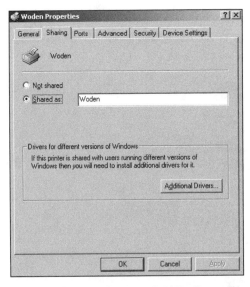

Figure 8.12   The Sharing tab of the Properties dialog box allows you to set the shared name.

8. Windows 2000/
Mac OS Printing

4. When you are done with the Sharing tab, click on the Ports tab, shown in Figure 8.13. In this tab, you can see (and, if necessary, change) the port to which the printer is connected. You can also check the Enable Printer Pooling checkbox, which allows you to configure multiple identical printers so that they look like one. This convenient process lets you set up a number of less-expensive printers that will share the print jobs, providing much greater printer throughput.

5. Clicking on the Advanced tab, shown in Figure 8.14, reveals a variety of different options that you can configure to customize your printer to your environment. For example, you can set the printer to be available only during certain times of day by clicking on the Available From radio button and setting the times that you wish the printer to be available for use. Similarly, you can set whether the printer starts printing before the file has been completely received by the spooler or if it waits to receive the entire file before starting to print.

6. When you access the Security tab of the Properties dialog box, shown in Figure 8.15, you can view all the users who currently have rights assigned on this printer and what they are.

7. If a user is having printer problems and does not have the proper rights, simply select his or her name and then choose

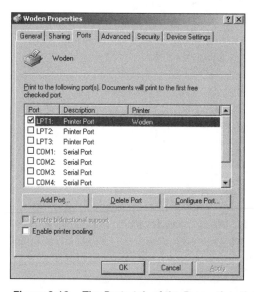

Figure 8.13   The Ports tab of the Properties dialog box allows you to see which port the printer is connected to.

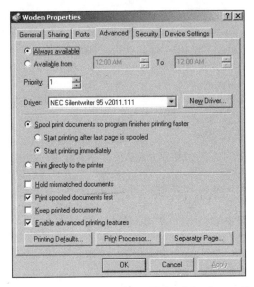

Figure 8.14   *The Advanced tab of the Properties dialog box allows you to configure a variety of printer options.*

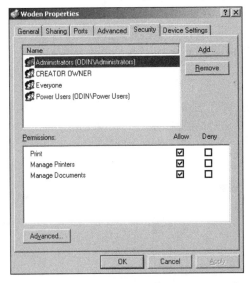

Figure 8.15   *The Security tab of the Properties dialog box allows you to examine and set a user's or group's permission levels to use this printer.*

the proper rights from the checkboxes in the frame at the bottom of the Security tab. If the user is not listed, click on Add. Doing so brings up the Select Users, Computers, Or Groups screen, shown in Figure 8.16. Select the users and groups that you wish to add to the list of those with permissions on this printer, select the permissions you wish to grant, and then click on OK.

8. Once you have ensured that permission settings are correct, click on OK to close the Select Users, Computers, Or Groups dialog box.

9. After you have configured the permissions that you want, click on the Advanced button to display the Permissions tab of the Access Control Settings dialog box, shown in Figure 8.17. This dialog box displays all the security permission levels that are configured for the printer.

10. Click on the Auditing tab if you wish to keep track of who is printing or who is trying to access printer properties. (If you don't want to use the auditing feature, click on OK to close the Properties dialog box. Skip ahead to Step 16.)

11. To set up the auditing properties on this printer, click on the Add button to select the user whose actions you wish to have logged. You can then opt to have any success or failure logged for both accounting or troubleshooting purposes.

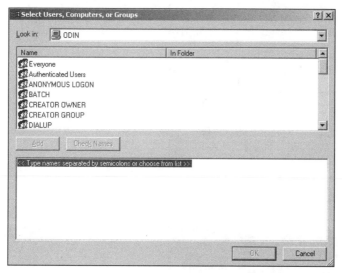

Figure 8.16   Select the users and groups you wish to add to the printer.

12. In order to establish auditing, simply enter the user or group that you wish audited and then choose which items you wish to audit, as shown in Figure 8.18.

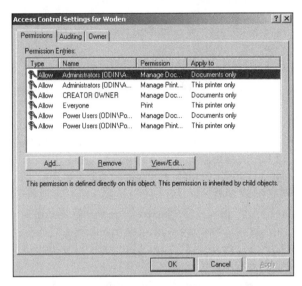

Figure 8.17   The Permissions tab of the Access Control Settings dialog box provides you with detailed permissions information.

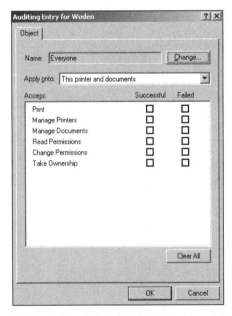

Figure 8.18   Select the items that you wish to audit.

8. Windows 2000/
Mac OS Printing

13. When you are done, click on OK to close the Auditing Entry dialog box.

14. Then, click on OK to close the Permissions tab of the Access Control Settings dialog box.

15. Once you have finished setting the security properties for your printer, click on the Device Settings tab of the Printer Properties dialog box and take a look at the different device settings currently selected for your printer. If they are all set to your specifications, click on OK to close the dialog box.

Connecting To The Printer From Your Macintosh

Once you have finished setting up the printer on your Windows 2000 server, you are ready to access and use that printer from your Macintosh computers.

To connect to and use the printer you have just set up, follow these steps:

1. Click on the Apple menu and select Chooser from the list of items.

2. When the Chooser opens, click on the LaserWriter 8 icon.

NOTE: Depending upon the version of system software installed on the Macs connected to your network, you may find different sets of printer drivers installed and displayed in the Chooser. However, for Mac OS system versions 8.5 or later, you should use the most recent version of LaserWriter 8. Although some Adobe software packages offer an alternate driver, labeled PSPrinter, it is not guaranteed to be compatible with the newest Mac operating systems.

3. Now, if your network contains more than one AppleTalk zone, then you will need to select the AppleTalk zone where the server is located. The first zone listed is the default zone that your server is configured to use.

4. Once you have selected the zone that the printer is in, select the printer from the list in the upper right-hand corner of the dialog box.

5. Next, click on Create to select the proper PostScript Printer Description (PPD) file and create a desktop printer icon.

8. Windows 2000/ Mac OS Printing

6. If you click on Auto Setup on the dialog box listing your printer setup options, your Macintosh examines the available PPD files to locate one that matches the type of printer that you have. If the correct PPD file for your printer is found, it is selected, and a desktop printing icon for the selected printer is created on your Mac's desktop.

7. Close the Chooser, and then click on OK to dismiss the message that your printer selection has been changed.

8. Repeat Steps 1 through 7 for each Macintosh with which you wish to use this printer. Once you have completed configuring all of your printers, you are ready to send your documents to that printer.

Dealing With A Missing Macintosh PPD File

The Auto Setup process is not perfect, and sometimes it fails to select the right PPD file. Another problem that you'll sometimes run into is that you may not have the right PPD installed on your Macintosh. This problem is fairly common with printers that are available in a range of similar models. In some cases, you are simply asked to choose from a list of installed printer options from a dialog box. If you are not certain what these options are, you may want to print a test page or two to make sure the printer is behaving itself. Or, you can simply check the printer's documentation to see which memory and tray options are installed.

If a PPD file for your printer cannot be found, follow these steps:

1. When the Mac can't find the suitable PPD file for your printer, you'll see a Select PPD dialog box that lists all the available PPD files. Select the one closest to your printer from the list of printers displayed.

2. Click on Select to choose the proper PPD. If the proper PPD is not present, you can click on Generic to use the basic printer driver without special options (we will discuss this option in further detail in the next section).

3. Once the printer has been created, click on the Close box to close the Chooser and then click on OK to accept the fact that your printer selection has changed.

You should now be ready to complete the configuration process on the other Macintoshes on your network.

Using Other Options To Use The Networked Printer

If your printer's correct PPD is not listed, and you cannot seem to find the proper file, you have other options to use the networked printer. Here are a couple of ways to do so and how these options may affect the printing of your documents:

- *Click on Generic option in the Select PPD dialog box*—Doing so installs a generic PPD file for the Macintosh to use when communicating to the printer. Choosing this option, however, prevents you from using any of the custom options installed in your printer. These options may include special paper formats and specialized paper trays. In addition, you won't be able to change such things as printer resolution, double-sided (duplex) printing, and screen settings. For simple letter-sized or legal-sized text documents, the Generic setting may not have a big impact. However, more complex files may well suffer. If you intend on printing large and graphically complex documents, you should probably take steps to locate and install the correct PPD file for the printer.

- *Check manufacturer or third-party resources*—Check your printer's installation disks to see if you can find the correct PPD file on them. Another good place to look is the manufacturer's Web site. Sometimes, PPD and other important driver files are available from a manufacturer's site or from its support department's site. Another useful resource is the Adobe Software Web site (**www.adobe.com/supportservice/custsupport/ LIBRARY/pdrvmac.htm**). This site contains a wide variety of PPD files for many popular and not-so-popular printer models.

NOTE: *Most printer manufacturers offer PPD files that will work on your Macintosh without explicitly referring to them as being for the Macintosh. If you have a hard time finding the printer descriptions you need, look for items labeled "PageMaker Printer Descriptions"; they usually work just fine.*

Installing A Macintosh PPD File

After you have found the correct PPD file for your printer, it's very simple to add it to the list of PPDs that are available to your Macintosh.

NOTE: *When you are configuring more than one printer for the Macs on your network to use, you need to follow the same set of setup procedures that we have described previously to configure them via Windows 2000 and then via the Macintosh Chooser.*

---

8. Windows 2000/ Mac OS Printing

Simply follow these steps:

1. Find the Printer Descriptions folder, inside the Extensions folder within your Macintosh's System folder.

2. Copy the PPD file into the Printer Descriptions folder.

3. Follow Steps 1 through 7 in the "Connecting To The Printer From Your Macintosh" section earlier in this chapter to configure your printer to use the new PPD file. Use this procedure for each Mac on your network that needs the special PPD file.

NOTE: *Once you've configured your printers and your Macintosh, you should run a test page and short text document (such as a Macintosh ReadMe file) to be sure the printer's performance is satisfactory.*

Setting Up Printers For Your Macintosh Using DAVE

As we described in Chapter 2, DAVE is a utility that lets your Windows 2000 computers work with Macs without your having to perform any special configurations or install any software on your Windows 2000 computers. Macs that have DAVE installed can connect to and use printers available on the AppleTalk network as well as the PostScript-based printers that Windows- or Windows 2000-based computers share. Having DAVE installed allows you to connect to the PostScript printer attached to a colleague's Windows workstation as well as to the big laser printer connected to the departmental server without having to perform any special configuration steps or install any special software on the Windows 2000 server.

To set up DAVE so that it can access PostScript printers on the Windows network, follow these steps:

1. Click on the Apple menu and then select Chooser from the list of items.

2. When the Chooser screen appears, click on the DAVE Client icon.

3. Log into the Windows network by typing in the correct username and password.

4. A list of all the available servers is then displayed. From the list, click on the server that hosts the printer to which you wish to connect.

NOTE: *If you are not certain which servers have shared printers and file volumes, look at the server names. All the servers that have a plus sign (+) in front of their names have resources, either file volumes or printers, that can be accessed from the network.*

---

5. After you have logged into the network, you see a list of resources being shared by the selected server. From this list, select the PostScript printer to which you want to connect, as shown in Figure 8.19.

6. Next, you see a Printer dialog box where you can select the correct PPD file for the desired printer. Select the proper PPD file for the printer. If the correct PPD file is not present, follow the steps described in the "Dealing With A Missing Macintosh PPD File" and "Installing A Macintosh PPD File" sections earlier in this chapter to make the proper PPD file available.

7. Once you have chosen the proper PPD file, DAVE displays a dialog box in which you can rename your printer. The main reason to rename the printer is that you can use a more descriptive or user-friendly name than the one selected when the printer was set up on the Windows network. This step may also be useful if you are setting up several different printers (some Mac, some Windows) with similar names.

8. After you have selected and (if needed) renamed the printer, click on OK to finish the setup process.

Related solution:	Found on page:
Installing DAVE	35
Installing DAVE On A Windows 2000 Network	204

8. Windows 2000/ Mac OS Printing

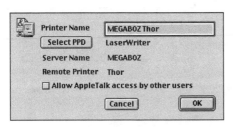

Figure 8.19   Select the desired printer from the list of the resources being shared by the server.

Working With The DAVE Printing Utility

Another very useful method for setting up a printer with DAVE is to configure the printer's attributes manually using the DAVE Print Client Control Panel. This process offers the following advantages:

• You can use a different username and password to access printers that you do not normally have permission to use.

• Setting up a printer connection using the Print Client actually installs a printer gateway on your Macintosh between the Windows network-based printer that you have connected to and the Macintoshes on your AppleTalk network. This allows them to access the printer and print to it as well as if it were actually located on a Mac's network.

To configure a printer connection using the DAVE Print Client Control Panel, follow these steps:

1. Click on the Apple menu, and choose Control Panels from the list.

2. Select the DAVE Print Client from the list of available Control Panels.

NOTE: *If the DAVE Print Client Control Panel is missing, check the list under Extensions Manager to see if the Control Panel has been disabled by mistake. If DAVE's print client has been disabled (unchecked), enable it by clicking on it so that it is highlighted; then restart your Macintosh. If the DAVE Print Client is missing, reinstall the program from the DAVE installer disks or installer application that you downloaded.*

3. Make sure that the DAVE Print Client Control Panel is running. If the DAVE Print Client is not functioning, you can turn it on by clicking on the On radio button.

NOTE: *If you get a NetBIOS error when trying to use the DAVE Print Client, check to see that the NetBIOS Control Panel is present. If it is missing, check the list under Extensions Manager to see if it was disabled by mistake. If it has been disabled (unchecked), click on it to enable it and then restart. If the NetBIOS Control Panel is present but not active, open the NetBIOS Control Panel and turn it on. The most common cause of the NetBIOS Control Panel not being active is that it does not have a legal registration code installed. Double-check to see if the NetBIOS Control Panel is registered by clicking on the NetBIOS icon in the upper left-hand corner of the NetBIOS Control Panel. If NetBIOS is missing, reinstall the program from the DAVE installer disks or installer application.*

4. Now, check the list of available DAVE Print Gateways that are currently running and see if the printer you wish to configure

has already been set up. If the printer to which you wish to connect is not shown, click on New to begin the configuration process.

5. If the printer you wish to set up already exists on the network, choose the printer in the DAVE Print Client dialog box and then click on Edit. After doing so, you see a list of the various configuration options and their current values.

6. From the DAVE Print Client dialog box, type in the name of the printer that appears on your Macintosh and on the other Macintoshes that connect to this printer through your Macintosh.

7. After you have configured and named the printer, type in the name of the server or workstation that hosts the printer you wish to use.

8. Now, type in the name of the printer to which you want to connect.

NOTE: *Allowing too many Macintosh users to access a printer on the Windows network through your Macs AppleTalk network can impair your Mac's network performance. You should consider using the Allow AppleTalk Access By Other Users option only if you have a limited number of Macintosh users who might need to have access to the networked printer. When you are faced with a larger number of Macintosh users, such as in a school computer lab or graphic arts department, you probably should use a dedicated printer gateway setup, as described in the previous section.*

---

9. You next need to choose the PPD for your printer. If the printer PPD that you selected is not the correct one, or one cannot be found, click on Select PPD in the Setup dialog box.

10. Select the proper one from the ones shown. If you cannot find the right PPD file, use the steps described in the "Dealing With A Missing Macintosh PPD File" and "Installing A Macintosh PPD File" sections earlier in this chapter to make the proper PPD file available.

11. Once you are sure that the printer is set up correctly, click on OK.

8. Windows 2000/ Mac OS Printing

WARNING! *You cannot have identical resource names on an AppleTalk zone. For example, if a printer named Sir Speedy already exists in the local zone, DAVE does not allow you to add another printer named Sir Speedy. If identical names are discovered, use the DAVE Print Client program to rename one of the printers.*

12. DAVE now asks you for the Windows 2000 domain or workgroup username that you wish to use when accessing this printer. Enter the username and password for the Domain or Workgroup to which this user belongs. Then, click on OK to activate the settings.

13. Once you have finished configuring all the settings for the selected printer, the printer name will be displayed in the DAVE Print Client Control Panel.

14. To finish, click on Close to close the DAVE Print Client.

Using DAVE To Make AppleTalk Printers Available To The Windows Network

DAVE lets Macintosh users make printers on the AppleTalk network available to computers on the Windows network. This allows Windows or Windows 2000 workstations and servers to connect to AppleTalk-only printers that would not normally be accessible to them. What's more, you can configure DAVE sharing to limit the access that you grant to these printers by choosing specific Windows 2000 domain or workgroup usernames and/or groups.

The biggest problem that you might encounter when making available the printers on your AppleTalk network is that the workload on your workstation may increase to the point where it begins to bog down.

Related solution:	*Found on page:*
Working With DAVE Under Windows 2000	206

Configuring DAVE Sharing

In order to configure DAVE sharing so that it can share AppleTalk-based printers with Windows- and Windows 2000-based computers, follow these steps:

1. Click on the Apple menu and then select Control Panels.

2. From the Control Panels sub-menu, select the DAVE Sharing Control Panel.

NOTE: *If the DAVE Sharing Control Panel is missing, check the list of files in Extensions Manager to see if the Control Panel was turned off by accident. If it has been turned off (unchecked), turn it back on and then restart your Macintosh. If DAVE Sharing isn't present in the list of files displayed in Extensions Manager, you must reinstall DAVE using the DAVE installer disks or installer application. .*

8. Windows 2000/ Mac OS Printing

3. Ensure that the File and Print Services portion of the DAVE Sharing Control Panel is activated. If the File and Print Services portion of the DAVE Sharing Control Panel is not active, click on the On radio button to start sharing.

NOTE: *When you get a NetBIOS error trying to enable DAVE sharing, check to see that the NetBIOS Control Panel is in the Control Panels folder. If it's not, check the list under Extensions Manager to see if it was turned off by accident. If it has been turned off (unchecked), turn it back on and then restart your Macintosh. If the NetBIOS Control Panel is in the Control Panels folder but not currently active, open the NetBIOS Control Panel and turn it on. The most frequent cause of the NetBIOS Control Panel not being turned on and active is that it does not have a proper registration code installed. Check to see if the NetBIOS Control Panel is registered properly by clicking on the NetBIOS icon in the upper left-hand corner of the NetBIOS Control Panel. If NetBIOS is not present in the Control Panels folder and not listed in Extensions Manager, reinstall the program from your original DAVE installer disks or installer application.*

---

4. Once sharing is enabled, click on Print to configure the printer that you are sharing with the Windows and Windows NT users.

NOTE: *You can share only one printer at a time using DAVE sharing. You must therefore configure your shared printers to maximize their efficiency. Heavily used printers such as a Tektronix Phaser color printer should be shared by either a very fast Macintosh that can share the printer without becoming too slow to be useful, or by an older Macintosh that has been set up solely as a print server. Similarly, a less-used printer could be shared by almost any of the Macintoshes on the network.*

---

5. If your Macintosh is not currently sharing any printers, click on New to begin the process of setting up the shared printer, as shown in Figure 8.20. If a printer already exists, the Add button is grayed out and the Edit button is made available.

6. Click on Edit in the DAVE Print Client Control Panel to reconfigure any of the printers currently being shared.

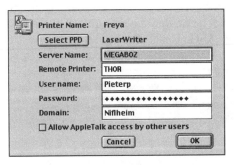

Figure 8.20   Use DAVE Sharing to add a shared Macintosh printer to your Windows network.

8. Windows 2000/ Mac OS Printing

7. To delete the shared printer, click on Remove.

8. Open the Chooser and select the zone where the printer you wish to share is located. All the zones available are listed in the lower right-hand portion of the Chooser.

9. Select the name of the printer that you want to share from the list displayed in the upper right-hand corner of the Chooser.

10. After you have chosen the proper AppleTalk zone and printer, click on OK.

11. Next, enter the share-level access settings for the printer. Although this step is optional, and depends on the level of security you want to use with your printer, it is probably a good idea to do so if you have some very expensive or sensitive printers that you do not wish everyone to use. When you are finished setting the password, if any, click on OK.

12. Once you are done configuring your printer, the Printer Resources dialog box appears. If you wish to remove the currently shared printer, click on Delete. Otherwise, click on OK to close the dialog box.

Connecting Windows To This Printer

On the Windows side, to connect to this printer, follow these steps:

1. Click on Start|Settings|Printers and then double-click on the Add Printer icon.

2. Using the Add Printer Wizard, click on Network Printer and then click on Next.

3. Then, select the printer to which you wish to connect. You can type in the name of the printer on your windows network (for example, \\servername\printername), or you can choose to use a printer on the Internet or your company's intranet, as shown in Figure 8.21. If you do not know the name of the printer, click on Next to browse the network. If you want to see all the printers available on a given server or workstation, double-click on any server or workstation whose name is preceded by a + sign.

WARNING!   *Macintoshes that are sharing a certain printer do not automatically download the proper print driver to Windows and Windows 2000 workstations as Windows 2000 Server does. As such, the Windows- and Windows 2000-based computers must have the proper print drivers loaded when they use a printer being shared from a Macintosh.*

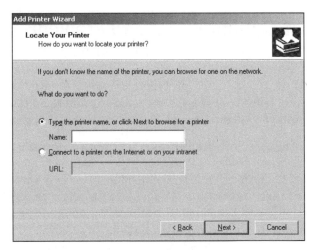

Figure 8.21 Use the Add Printer Wizard to select the network printer to which you wish to connect.

4. You should also select the proper print driver for the remote printer. If you cannot find the make and model of printer you need in the list of Windows print drivers, click on Have Disk and then load the proper drivers from either a diskette, CD-ROM or from a file that you have downloaded from the manufacturer's Web site.

5. After you have chosen the proper printer, click on Next to continue.

6. Next, the Add Printer Wizard asks if you would like to select the printer as the default. This printer is most likely not the highest-performance printer, so it is probably not the best choice to meet your normal printing needs. Click on Next to continue.

7. Once you are finished, the Add Printer Wizard informs you that the printer configuration is complete. Click on Finish to complete the process of adding a new printer connection.

After you've completed sharing your Macintosh printer, you will see its name displayed in the Connect To Printer dialog box from your Windows 2000 workstation.

8. Windows 2000/ Mac OS Printing

249

Troubleshooting Shared Printing Problems

Identifying and solving printing problems with printers shared by a Windows 2000 server or printers accessed using DAVE is a relatively straightforward procedure. Such problems break down into three general types: problems involving the network or printer and those with the user's printer configuration or the configuration of the printer.

Problems involving the network and printer hardware are usually the simplest to identify and resolve because they are usually very easy to spot. Problems with the user's printer connection on his or her workstation or the configuration of the printer are generally more difficult. In this section, we will examine both situations, along with some helpful hints on how to resolve the most common problems.

Identifying And Solving Printer Problems

When you first start trying to solve a printing problem, you need to determine if it is related to the hardware or if it is related to the software or configuration of either the user's desktop or the printer itself. You should first check to see what type of problem the user is having. If the user cannot print at all, determine which printer he or she is printing to and then follow these troubleshooting procedures (you don't have to follow them in order):

- *Is the printer visible in the Network Neighborhood window on the Windows 2000 computer*—If it is, check the printer queue on the server or workstation that controls the printer. If it's not, or a document appears to be stuck in the printer queue, examine the printer to make sure that it is not malfunctioning.

- *None of the documents from the user are visible in the queue waiting to be printed*—Check that this is not a problem on the user's workstation.

- *The printer is functioning properly, but the user still cannot print*—Check to make sure that the network connection from the user to the printer is functioning by checking the status display indicators on the printer and trying to ping it from the user's workstation. You should also check all of the printer settings from the printer console to make sure that the printer is configured and functioning properly. The printer's manual defines the various display messages and what needs to be done to fix a specific setting.

- *The printer is directly connected, but the user still cannot print*—Check the cable that connects the server or workstation

8. Windows 2000/ Mac OS Printing

to the printer to make sure that everything is plugged in securely and that the cable is in good shape.

- *You have double-checked all the printer's connections and they look good, but the user still cannot print*—Clear the print job, if there is one, from the print queue and see if that clears up your problem. You can then try sending the document to the print queue a second time. Doing so sometimes produces satisfactory results.

- *The printer still refuses to respond*—Turn the printer off and then on to see if that can clear the problem. Sometimes, just clearing a printer's memory is enough to restore good performance.

- *A print job from a Macintosh- or Windows-based workstation captures the printer and refuses to release it*—The simplest way to determine that this has happened is to try to send a print job to the printer and see if you get an error message. Getting one indicates that the printer is not responding. If that is the case, the easiest solution is to simply turn the printer off and on. This causes the network connection between the printer and the workstation to be reset. You should then try to identify which Macintosh refused to release the printer when it was done. Using an out-of-date or incompatible LaserWriter driver is often the culprit. We strongly suggest that you use the latest version of LaserWriter 8, which ships with your Macintosh system software (unless your printer manufacturer requires a special, customized driver).

Troubleshooting A PostScript-Based Printer Problem

If you are not using PowerPrint for Networks from Infowave to share printers on your Macintosh workstations, they can use only PostScript-based printers on the network. They must use either AppleTalk and Print Services for Macintosh with Windows 2000 server, or DAVE. If a user reports that he or she has connected to a printer on the network but cannot print to it, follow these steps to diagnose the problem:

1. Examine the printer to see that it is actually PostScript-based (unless you're using Infowave's software).

2. If the printer supports PostScript, look at the printer to make sure that it is functioning properly and that other users can print to it. If the printer checks out in other respects, recheck the specific user's configuration, which is where such problems usually lie.

3. If the printer in question is not a PostScript printer, inform the user that he or she cannot use this printer from a Macintosh.

8. Windows 2000/
Mac OS Printing

Troubleshooting A Printer That Has Access Rights Configured

Not all printers are available for public use. Therefore, some are configured so that only certain users can access them. If a user reports that he or she now lacks the rights to print to a printer that he or she has used in the past, follow these steps:

1. Click on Start|Settings|Printers, right-click on the printer you wish to examine, and then select Properties.

2. From the Properties dialog box, click on the Security tab to display the permissions that are currently set up on the printer.

3. In the Security tab, you can see all the users who currently have rights set on this printer and what those permissions are. If the user who is having printer problems does not have the proper rights, simply select his or her name and then set the proper rights using the checkboxes in the Select Users, Computers, or Groups screen. If the user is not listed, click on Add.

4. Choose the groups that you want to add to the list of users with access to this printer, choose the permissions you wish to give them, and then click on OK. If you wish to add specific users, do so by selecting the various users.

5. After you have checked that the permissions are configured as you wish, click on OK to close the Security tab.

Dealing With A User Who Does Not Have Access Rights

If your user does not have access rights, follow these steps:

1. Verify that he or she can access that printer, and then add the user to the list of users with permission to use the printer.

2. If the user already has the proper permission to access the shared printer, have the user drop the connection to the printer and then re-create it so that the user is forced to log into the network again. This process helps make sure that the user is logging in with the proper username and password.

3. If the user still cannot print to the specific printer, remove the entry for the user from the permission list for the printer and then re-add the user. For instructions on how to set the permissions on your printer, refer to the "Configuring Access Rights And Properties On Your New Printer" section earlier in this chapter.

Diagnosing Cross-Platform Font Problems

After network-related issues, the most typical problems with editing and printing files created on another personal computing platform concern fonts. You carefully format your document on the Windows computers on your network and then transfer them to the Macs for further editing. Once this happens, though, the document's look is apt to change.

The principal problems you can encounter with fonts include changed line break points and fonts that do not display the same as on your screen. This is a problem that's especially troublesome if you designed your document text to fit a specific amount of space, and it runs too short or too long.

Here are some suggestions on how to solve this problem:

- *Make sure your fonts on both platforms match*—Just using fonts of the same name, such as Times or Helvetica, isn't enough. Each font manufacturer may produce a different version of even the most common fonts, even if they are named the same. A key factor, font metrics (the width space values), may be different. The look or "cut" of the font may be different as well, which results in the actual size of the letterforms appearing a bit larger or smaller, even though you've selected the very same point size. For maximum compatibility, it is a good idea to purchase your fonts for both platforms from the same manufacturer. Although it is beyond the scope of this book to recommend a specific font source, Adobe fonts, for example, are an industry standard; choosing this option helps ensure the maximum level of compatibility across platforms. In addition, with its Internet Explorer browser and Office 98, Microsoft has, in recent years, offered many Mac versions of its popular Windows fonts. These fonts include Arial, Courier New, and Times New Roman.

- *Check the document carefully*—Even if you have taken measures to ensure font matching, you should still carefully proofread documents from both platforms to be sure that they look essentially the same. A key point to examine is the way lines break.

- *Check for font substitution*—When a font of the same name isn't available when you open a document on another computing platform, you may find that a similar font—or an entirely different one—has been substituted. On a Mac, for example, your document may output in Courier, a monospaced font that looks much like that used on an old typewriter.

- *Stick with the same programs on both platforms*—It is common for documents created in one application on one platform to be opened and edited in a different program on the other platform. A typical example would be taking a document built in WordPerfect Office document for Windows and opening it in Microsoft Office 98 on your Mac OS computers. The cause of this issue is that WordPerfect for the Macintosh hasn't been updated in several years, and even then it failed to match the feature-set of the Windows version. Different applications usually employ various methods to calculate the amount of space between words—or even the actual space between letters—so a careful matching of fonts may still provide unexpected surprises when you convert the document. The best advice we can offer is for you to try to use equivalent programs on both computing platforms. If this can't be done, take extra care to make sure that document conversions haven't produced an unsatisfactory result.

NOTE: *Microsoft and other software publishers routinely offer documentation about compatibility between computing platforms with native and converted documents. Consult this information, where available, to see how your documents may be affected when prepared or edited on one platform and opened and/or printed on the other. Fonts are not the only areas where disparities may occur. You may also expect that document formatting parameters, such as paragraph and table styles, will change.*

---

8. Windows 2000/ Mac OS Printing

Chapter 9

Windows 2000 And AppleTalk Networking

In Brief

Installing and configuring the AppleTalk protocol using Windows 2000 Server is both initially very simple, and yet has the potential to be exceedingly complex. We will explain this contradiction in the following pages.

The steps needed to install AppleTalk under Windows 2000 are fairly simple and very straightforward. As we walk through them in this chapter, we will talk about all of the differences between Windows NT 4 and Windows 2000 and how these changes affect the way you configure AppleTalk. We will also discuss some of the different networking options that you must set in Windows 2000 and what you need to know about your network to make sure that everything works properly.

To start off, we will review the process of installing the AppleTalk network protocol that we covered in Chapter 7. However, this time we will focus on the settings that you can change as well as look at Windows 2000 Routing and Remote Access snap-in (RRA).

Once you have finished installing and performing the initial configuration of AppleTalk, it's time to look at some of the more advanced settings. We will focus on all the differences between Windows NT 4 and Windows 2000 and how these changes affect the choices that you can make when fine-tuning.

We next start looking at the other networking services that you can use to support your Macintoshes. We will explore how you can set up the Domain Name Service (DNS), Windows Internet Service (WINS), and the Dynamic Host Configuration Protocol service (DHCP), to support your Macintosh clients.

We will also revisit the Cisco Internetwork Operating System (IOS), which we first examined in Chapter 4. We will focus on the changes that you may have to make to your Cisco routers in order to support the inclusion of Windows 2000 servers.

Finally, for those who prefer to use another tool, such as DAVE, we will discuss how you need to configure it so that it can integrate into the Windows 2000 network. Specifically, we will talk about what you need to change between the configurations you use to support Windows NT 4 and Windows 2000.

Understanding AppleTalk's Impact On The Network

The biggest challenge that most people run into when wanting to connect Macintoshes to the corporate network is the perception that AppleTalk can seriously degrade network performance. The origin of this myth, like most myths, is rooted a bit in fact and a bit in fiction. Back in the early days of personal computing, AppleTalk was designed as an easy way to network a bunch of Macintoshes on small workgroup-oriented networks. Macintoshes were designed to discover as much about their network environment as possible when they were first connected. This meant that they generated a lot of AppleTalk traffic trying to determine what resources were available on the network.

To network administrators, this traffic caused congestion and slowed the network's performance for all other computers. In addition, Macs, unlike their PC cousins, like to get regular updates from all the file servers that they are connected to. These frequent requests for updates commonly caused the servers of the day to have performance problems. Needless to say, both of these problems did not tend to make fans out of many network administrators.

However, as time passed and technology improved, many of these issues have fallen by the wayside. Modern high-speed network hubs and switches have largely resolved the issue of Macs consuming too much bandwidth on the network. Likewise, modern operating systems such as Windows NT 4 and Windows 2000 are far better at handling the update requests generated by the Macs connected to them. And yet the myth of AppleTalk's impact on the network still remains strong in the minds of many network engineers. As we move through this chapter, we will try to dispel some more of those myths. In this day and age, once you set up your Mac and Windows PCs properly, they should work together in relative harmony, despite the many differences between the two major computing platforms.

AppleTalk In-Depth

AppleTalk is a robust routable network protocol that was developed by Apple Computer in the mid-1980s to provide networking capabilities to its Macintosh family of computers. In its initial form, now known as AppleTalk Phase-1, it was limited to one network segment and 127 AppleTalk devices. While AppleTalk Phase-1 was great at supporting small workgroup networks, Apple soon realized that it needed to make some changes if it wanted to build larger networks. In 1988, Apple introduced the current version of AppleTalk that is used in all Macintoshes today—AppleTalk Phase-2. AppleTalk Phase-2 extended AppleTalk to include the concept of sub-networks as well as expanding the number of AppleTalk devices that can be present on a single network segment.

Unlike AppleTalk Phase-1, which was only able to handle one network segment, AppleTalk Phase-2 is capable of handling up to 65,298 different networks or as Apple calls them, *zones*. These zones are used to break up your AppleTalk network into a bunch of smaller networks, which may be located on the same physical segment of the network or may be located on remote network segments. By dividing the network in this way, you are now able to have more than 253 AppleTalk devices on the network. Additionally, having multiple zones allows you to break up your Macs into smaller workgroup-oriented segments that are easier to manage.

In the Open Systems Institute (OSI) model, AppleTalk is considered to be a protocol. This means that AppleTalk is defined by a specific type of network packet on the network, just like IP, the Internet Protocol, and many others. Also, like IP and other protocols, there are several different types of transport that ride on top of AppleTalk. Like TCP and UDP, the two primary transports that are used with IP, AppleTalk is the host to four major transport types. These transports, Datagram Delivery Protocol (DDP), the Printer Access Protocol (PAP), the AppleTalk Transaction Protocol (ATP), and the AppleTalk Data Stream Protocol (ADSP).

DDP and ATP are very similar to UDP—they are all *connectionless transports*. This means that there is no connection formed between the sending computer and the one receiving the DDP or ATP packets. Since no connection is formed, these transports are really designed to transfer only a small amount of data between computers. Also like UDP, DDP does not contain any error correction capability and relies instead upon what is known as "best effort delivery" of the packets. ATP on the other hand, sends an acknowledgement for every packet to ensure that all the packets arrive at the destination and in the right order.

Like TCP, PAP and ADSP are what is known as *connection-oriented transports* in that they form a connection between the sender and the receiver. Like TCP, ADSP is designed to transfer data between computers in a reliable fashion so that lost or damaged packets can easily be retransmitted preventing data loss. However, unlike TCP, ADSP utilizes DDP to handle the actual data transfer and then adds error correction and flow control capabilities to the connection. PAP likewise is a connection-oriented protocol that uses ATP to actually transport the data to the printer.

Understanding DDP Packets

DDP, the principal packet type used by AppleTalk, has two types. The first is the DDP Type 1 packet, whose structure is shown in Figure 9.1. This type of packet exchanges data among Macintoshes located on the same zone.

Here's a detailed description of the makeup of the DDP Type 1 packet:

- *Flag Byte*—These two fields are set to 01111110. This binary number is the flag that tells the Macintosh that this is an AppleTalk packet and that it should see if the destination address matches that of the Macintosh.

- *Destination Node*—This number is the AppleTalk network address of the Macintosh for which this packet is destined.

- *Source Node*—This number is the AppleTalk network address of the Macintosh that actually sent the packet.

- *Protocol Type*—This field defines the type of DDP packet that this is. For the short DDP packet described here, the value is 1.

- *Length*—This field tells the receiving Macintosh how long the packet is. This information is critical because the amount of data carried in each packet can vary.

- *Destination Socket*—This number is the AppleTalk socket on the destination Macintosh for which this packet is destined.

- *Source Socket*—This number is the AppleTalk socket on the source Macintosh that originated this packet.

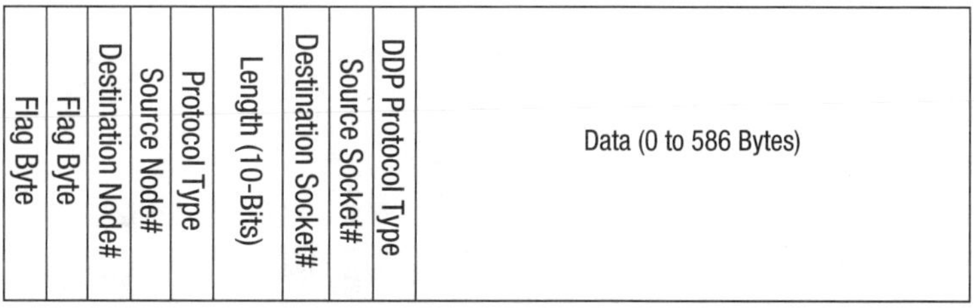

Figure 9.1   The structure of the DDP Type 1 packet.

- *DDP Protocol Type*—This field defines which DDP protocol this packet uses.

- *Data*—This field, also known as the payload of the packet, can range from 0 through 586 bytes.

The second type of DDP packet is the longer Type 2 packet, whose structure is shown in Figure 9.2. It is used for communication among Macintoshes located in different zones. These packets are longer because they must carry information about their home zone, the destination zone, and the source and destination Macintoshes.

Here's a detailed description of the makeup of the DDP Type 2 packet:

- *Flag Bytes*—These two fields are set to 01111110. This binary number is the signal that tells the Macintosh that this is an AppleTalk packet and that it should see if the destination address matches that of the Macintosh.

- *Bridge Node*—This field contains the ID of the AppleTalk bridge that this packet must use.

- *Source Node*—This number is the AppleTalk network address of the Macintosh that actually sent the packet.

- *Protocol Type*—This field defines the type of DDP packet that this is. For the long DDP packet described here, the value is 2.

- *Length*—This field tells the receiving Macintosh how long the packet is. This information is critical because the amount of data carried in each packet can vary. Also in the Length field is a 4-bit Hop Counter that is incremented by the various routers that direct the packet from network to network. This information tells the routers how many networks this packet has traversed and, if the number of routers traversed has reached 15, to discard the packet.

- *DDP Checksum*—This field is a numerical value that can be used to verify the contents of the data portion of the packet. This

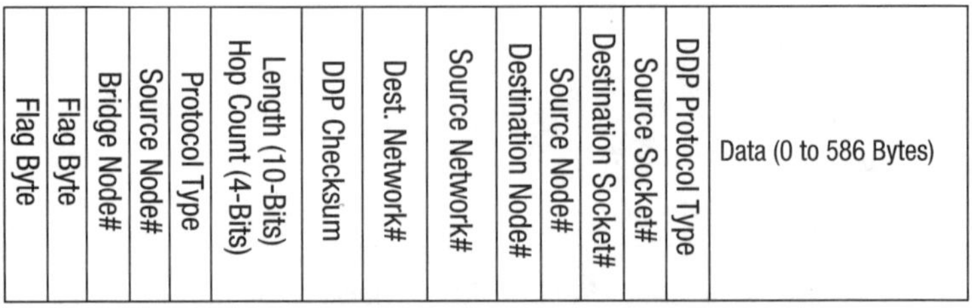

Figure 9.2   The structure of the DDP Type 2 packet.

checksum ensures that the information contained in the data portion of the packet is not corrupted during the process of being routed over the network.

- *Destination Network*—This number is the numeric identifier assigned to the zone in which the destination Macintosh resides. As with all network numbers, these are defined by the routers that seed the AppleTalk zones on the network.

- *Source Network*—This number is the numeric identifier used by the zone in which the source of this packet resides.

- *Destination Node*—This number is the AppleTalk network address of the Macintosh for which this packet is destined.

- *Source Node*—This number is the AppleTalk network address of the Macintosh that actually sent the packet.

- *Destination Socket*—This number is the AppleTalk socket on the destination Macintosh for which this packet is destined.

- *Source Socket*—This number is the AppleTalk socket on the source Macintosh that originated this packet.

- *DDP Protocol Type*—This field defines which DDP protocol this packet uses.

- *Data*—This field, also known as payload of the packet, can range from 0 through 586 bytes.

Using DHCP With Macintosh Clients

DHCP is a system that distributes and manages IP addresses on the network. The concept behind DHCP is that it is easier for a central system to distribute IP addresses to each computer along with all the other network information that they need rather than having someone go out to each computer and configure them manually. In addition, the DHCP server can reclaim IP addresses from computers that are no longer part of the network. This is done by setting a time to live value on each IP address and then recovering them if the workstation they were issued to doesn't respond in time. DHCP servers can also be configured to distribute such information to each workstation as the default gateway for each network segment, the address of the DNS servers on the network, as well as a host of other information.

On your Macintoshes running Mac OS 8.5 or later, you can configure the TCP/IP Control Panel to use DHCP to get network information. Setting all of your Macs to use DHCP is a good way to help lower your support costs and help to integrate your Macintoshes into the network. By configuring all your Macintoshes to derive all of their network configuration information from DHCP, you lower the incidence of problems due to improper configuration; it also allows you to simplify your work design by not having to set up a range of network addresses solely for your Mac users.

Learning When A Domain Is Not A Domain

The domain name that you distribute via DHCP or enter manually in the TCP/IP configuration on your Macintosh- or Windows-based PC is not the same as the Windows NT Domain that we have discussed earlier. Under TCP/IP, the domain name is the name of the Internet domain that your organization owns. For example, computers at Microsoft would have their domain name set to "Microsoft.com." Under Windows NT 4, the domain name that is used by the Windows NT domain and the Internet domain name are not related and can be completely different. In Windows 2000, however, the Active Directory that is designed to replace the existing Windows NT domain structure is designed to share the Internet domain name. Thus, workstations that are part of a Windows 2000 active directory at Microsoft would both share the name Microsoft.com.

Using DNS And WINS From Your Macintosh

The Domain Name Service, also known as DNS, and the Windows Internet Naming Service, WINS, can be used by your Macintosh to resolve the names of computers located both on your network and the Internet to their IP addresses. The only caveat to using these two services is that they are only used when your computer communicates using the TCP/IP protocol.

DNS is designed to provide you with a quick way to look up the names of workstations and servers located in an Internet domain. For instance, when you wish to visit **www.microsoft.com**, your computer checks with DNS servers on the Internet to find out the IP address of the server called www at the domain microsoft.com. If the DNS server your computer asks first has the answer, then you get the IP address back right away. Otherwise, the DNS server will contact one of the central DNS servers for the Internet to get information as to where it can get the address for **www.microsoft.com**. Your DNS server then goes to the DNS server that it learned about from one of the central DNS servers to get the correct IP address of the server.

9. Windows 2000 And
AppleTalk Networking

Once your server has learned the IP address, it then relays it back to your computer so that your browser can connect to the site. If the DNS server cannot reach any other DNS server that knows the server you are looking for, it will report that the name is not recognizable.

While DNS is great at resolving Internet domain names, it does not support the resolution of other computer naming systems like NetBIOS. To support the resolution of NetBIOS names on your network, Microsoft developed WINS. WINS allows your Macintosh using DAVE or your Windows-based PC to send out a request with the NetBIOS name of a computer that you wish to contact and to then receive the IP address of that server. However, unlike DNS, which relies upon other servers to provide the information that it does not have, each WINS server is expected to have a complete list of all the NetBIOS names and the IP addresses of every single Workstation and Server on the network. Thus, if the name of the computer that you wish to connect to is not listed in the WINS database, you will not be able to connect to it.

Caches And Counters Explained

Caches and counters are the areas where your router stores information about the network environment around it. Your router uses caches to keep lists of information that it needs to access rapidly. Routers cache information such as the routes they know of to other parts of the network or the names of the computers that they have discovered on the network. The router then uses these caches to speed up the process of routing network traffic to other parts of the network or to directing the traffic to a specific computer. If these caches become corrupted with inaccurate information, they can cause the router to slow down and lose network data by directing it to the wrong computer or portion of the network.

Your router uses counters to keep track of all sorts of information, from how much traffic it sends out to a specific interface to the number of errors that it has encountered. Looking at the various counters on a router is a good way to see how your router is performing. For example, if you notice that the error counter on one of your Ethernet interfaces is significantly higher than the others, this may indicate that there is a problem on the network to which that interface is connected. Likewise, if you notice that the number of AppleTalk routing updates on one interface is lower than that on the others, then you may have a problem with the access-list permissions that are applied to that interface.

Immediate Solutions

Installing AppleTalk

In Chapter 4, we discussed the installation and configuration of AppleTalk on a Windows NT server. In this chapter, we will review the steps covered in Chapter 4 as well as Chapter 8 as we outline the process of installing AppleTalk using Windows 2000 Server. We will also look at how this procedure evolved on the road from Windows NT to Windows 2000.

To start installing AppleTalk on a Windows 2000 Server, you will need to follow these steps:

1. Right click on the My Network Places icon and then select Properties from the Shortcut menu that is displayed. Alternatively, you can select the Control Panel from the Settings submenu under the Start menu and then double-click on the Network and Dial-up Connections Control Panel.

2. Look at the Network and Dial-up Connections Control Panel and double-click on the Local Area Connection icon to open up the network connection. Please refer to Figure 9.3.

3. When you look at the Local Area Connection Status dialog box, you can see information on how much network traffic has been sent and received by the server, as shown in Figure 9.4. Also on

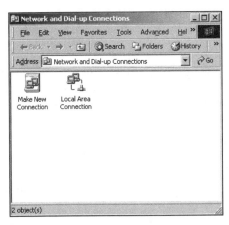

Figure 9.3   The Network and Dial-up Connections Control Panel displays all of the currently configured network connections.

9. Windows 2000 And AppleTalk Networking

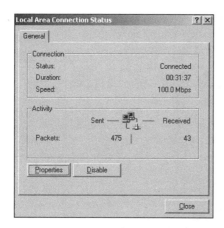

*Figure 9.4   The Local Area Connection Status dialog box displays the
network statistics for the server.*

this dialog box are two buttons, one that allows you to open up
the Properties page for your local area network and another
that allows you to disable the server's network connection.

4. From the Local Area Connection Status dialog box, click on the
   Properties button to bring up the Properties dialog box for the
   currently selected network interface.

5. The Properties dialog box lists all the network options that are
   presently installed. There is also a menu located at the top of
   the dialog box that allows you to choose which network
   adapter you are currently looking at. While many servers have
   only one network adapter, you may find yourself working on
   one that has more than one. As such, we will be discussing the
   impact that this has on your AppleTalk configuration. To add
   AppleTalk to the list of installed network components, click on
   the Install button, as shown in Figure 9.5.

*NOTE: Windows 2000 separates many of the functions that were previously assigned to the
various network services under Windows NT 4. In Windows 2000 for instance, the DHCP server
and File Services for Macintosh are now Windows 2000 components and not parts of a Network
Service as they were in Windows NT 4.0. In Windows 2000, network options are limited to
network protocols and other network specific components.*

6. From the list of network components displayed, double-click
   on the Protocol and then select AppleTalk Protocol from the
   list of available network protocols, as shown in Figure 9.6.

**9. Windows 2000 And
AppleTalk Networking**

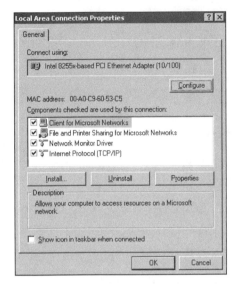

Figure 9.5   The Properties dialog box shows you all the networking components installed for the selected interface.

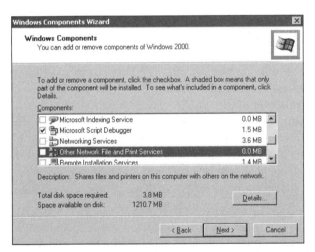

Figure 9.6   Select AppleTalk Protocol from the list of network protocols available.

7. Once you have selected the AppleTalk Protocol, click on OK to close the dialog box. Then, click on OK again to close the options dialog box.

After you have finished installing AppleTalk, the next step is to open the Windows 2000 Routing and Remote Access (RRA) snap-in for the Microsoft Management Console. The RRA snap-in is designed to give you access to the routing options available for all of the network protocols installed on the various servers. Using the RRA console, you can set up the options available under Windows 2000 to control and configure AppleTalk on your network. You will also be able to examine most of the available AppleTalk settings and change them to suit your network needs.

To finish the configuration of AppleTalk on your Windows 2000 server, complete the following steps:

1. Click on Start|Programs|Administrative Tools|Routing And Remote Access.

2. Click on the + sign located next to the name of the server that you have just installed AppleTalk on.

3. Next, double-click on the entry for the Local Area Connection located on the right hand side of the window, as shown in Figure 9.7.

4. From the Local Area Connection Properties dialog box (shown in Figure 9.8), you can configure your server to seed the AppleTalk network. To enable the seeding of the network, click on the checkbox labeled Enable Seed Routing On This Network.

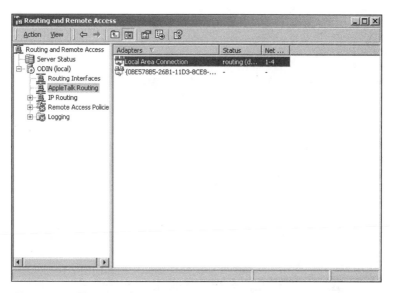

Figure 9.7   The RRA console controls all aspects of routing and network configuration.

9. Windows 2000 And AppleTalk Networking

NOTE: *When you choose to seed the AppleTalk network, you are setting up the network number and the different zones that will be made available to the Macintoshes various AppleTalk devices that are available on the network.*

NOTE: *If there are already AppleTalk zones set up on the network, you probably will not want to set up your NT server to seed the network. If you wish to add additional zones or change the names of the existing zones, then you should contact your network group and ask for its assistance in making the change. Alternatively, you can examine the different servers connected to the segment of the network that your server is connected to and see if one of them is set up to seed the network. If none of the servers on this segment of the network are set up to seed the network, then you will need to check the configuration of the network router(s) and change it to reflect the settings that you want.*

---

5. Next, you must select the network numbers that you wish to seed the network with.

NOTE: *When choosing the network numbers that you will use, you need to make sure of two things. The first is make sure that the network numbers you have selected are not in use anywhere else on the network. Once you have made sure that your network number is unique, then you need to make sure that the network numbers you have chosen as the beginning and ending numbers are far enough apart to accommodate all of the zones that you wish to set up.*

Figure 9.8   The Properties page allows you to configure AppleTalk networking options.

9. Windows 2000 And AppleTalk Networking

6. Then, you will need to set up the AppleTalk zones that you wish to use on the network. To add a new zone to your network, click on the New Zone button and then type in the name of your new zone and click on OK.

7. Repeat this process as needed to add in all the zones that you want. If you add in a zone and later need to delete it, you can do so by clicking on the zone name to highlight it and then clicking on Delete Zone.

8. Once you have completed configuring AppleTalk, click on OK to close the Properties dialog box and then close the RRA snap-in.

Once you have finished configuring AppleTalk, you should run some tests to make sure that everything is operating the way that you think that it should:

1. Go directly to one of the Mac computers on the same segment of the network as your server.

2. Open the Chooser. If you can see all of the zones that you created listed in the Chooser, then you can assume that at least this portion of your configuration is set up correctly.

3. Next, if you have a network with more than one network segment, you should go to a Macintosh on another network segment to see if it can see the zones that you created. If your network is configured to route AppleTalk between multiple network segments, all of the zones that you created ought to be visible in the Chooser of a Macintosh located on another network segment. If you have trouble seeing the zones that you created, we suggest you read the section on troubleshooting your network that is located at the end of this chapter.

Related solutions:	Found on page:
Fine-Tuning AppleTalk On Your Macintosh	113
Installing AppleTalk And File Services For Macintosh: The Beginning	188

Using A Sniffer On Your Network

A *sniffer* is a piece of software or hardware that allows you to examine network traffic in detail. When you run a sniffer, you can look at individual network packets and see what values are present in each portion of the packet. You can also use it to provide information on how many packets are on the network and which computers are generating them. Using this information, you can develop a better understanding of how the AppleTalk traffic is flowing on your network and which computers or other devices are generating it (which is why we went into so much detail in the previous section).

For Windows NT 4 and Windows 2000 users, a slightly crippled sniffer called Network Monitor is bundled with the OS. This version of Network Monitor can read network traffic only to and from the Windows NT- or Windows 2000-based computer on which it is running. Despite this annoying limitation, Network Monitor does do a good job of letting you look at the AppleTalk traffic that is going to and coming from the server you have configured to support Macintosh clients.

For those of you who have Microsoft's Systems Management Server 1 or 2, you can install the full version of Network Monitor. This version of Network Monitor can listen to all the traffic on the network, not just that destined for the server or workstation on which it is running. You can therefore set up a workstation with Network Monitor on it and have it record all the traffic on the network for a certain period of time. You can then go back and review the packets that Network Monitor collected to look for problems on your network and to help trace them right back to the computer or other device that might be causing them. As you can see, knowing what raw stuff a packet is made of can be very useful when you need to get down to the nitty-gritty of how network performance is suffering.

Installing Network Monitor On Your Windows 2000 Server

As with Windows NT 4, the version of Network Monitor that ships with Windows 2000 is limited to seeing only those packets that originate from, or are destined for, the server or workstation on which you install it. To install Network Monitor for Windows 2000, follow these steps:

1. Open the Control Panels window by clicking on Start|Settings|Control Panels.

2. Next, double-click on Add/Remove Programs.

3. In the Add/Remove Programs window, click on Add/Remove Windows Components and then wait for the Windows Components Wizard to start.

4. Click on Next to continue.

5. Look at the list of available Windows components, scroll down, and then select Management And Monitoring Tools, as shown in Figure 9.9.

6. Then, click on Details to see all of the available options.

7. Look at the list of Management And Monitoring Tools, select Network Monitor Tools (as shown in Figure 9.10), and then click on OK.

8. Then, click on Next.

9. Click on Finish to complete the installation of Network Monitor on your server.

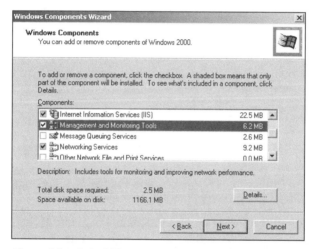

Figure 9.9   Select Management And Monitoring Tools from the list of available Windows 2000 components.

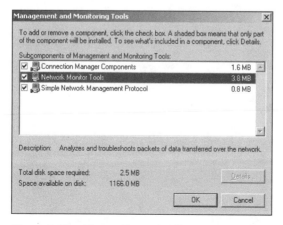

Figure 9.10   Choose Network Monitor Tools from the list of available management tools.

Using Network Monitor On Your Windows 2000 Server

As with almost any sniffer product, using Network Monitor is a very complex task worthy of its own book. Our goal here, though, is to focus on some of the more basic settings that you can use in Network Monitor to help you track down problems involving AppleTalk on your network.

NOTE: *After you've installed Network Monitor on your Windows NT or Windows 2000 server, a new program item is located under Start|Programs|Administrative Tools.*

To get a feel for how to run Network Monitor on your network, follow these steps, which are for a typical network installation:

1. Start Network Monitor, which brings up the Network Monitor window, shown in Figure 9.11. This window shows you how many packets that meet the criteria you have specified are being sent and received by the server.

2. You don't want to look at any network traffic other than AppleTalk, so you need to filter it all out. To do so, click on Capture|Filter, or press F8.

3. The Capture Filter dialog box, shown in Figure 9.12, appears. Double-click on the SAP/ETYPE = line.

4. The Capture Filter SAPs And ETYPEs dialog box, shown in Figure 9.13, appears. We will be using it to filter out all the

9. Windows 2000 And AppleTalk Networking

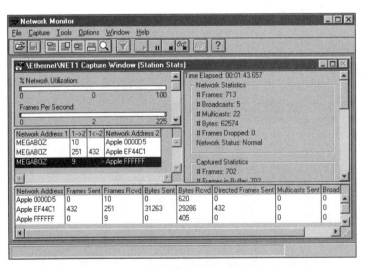

Figure 9.11   Here is the initial Network Monitor display.

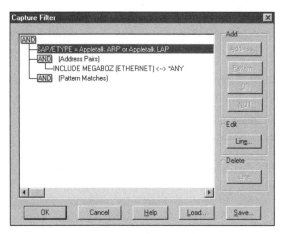

Figure 9.12 The Capture Filter dialog box displays the protocol filters currently in use.

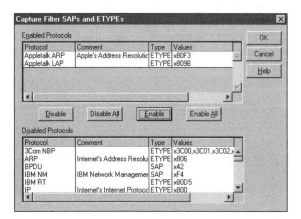

Figure 9.13 The Capture Filter SAPs And ETYPEs dialog box displays all the protocol filters currently available in Network Monitor.

non-AppleTalk protocols that are on the network. Click on Disable All to clear out all the available protocols.

5. Then, select the two AppleTalk protocols, AppleTalk ARP (Address Resolution Protocol) and AppleTalk LAP (Local Area Protocol) and then click on Enable.

6. Next, click on OK to close the Capture Filter SAPs And ETYPEs dialog box.

7. Click on OK again to close the Capture Filter dialog box.

Now that you have set your filters to exclude all network traffic except for AppleTalk, you are ready to start capturing network traffic

9. Windows 2000 And AppleTalk Networking

that is either destined for your server or originates from your server. To do so, follow these steps:

1. Click on the Capture menu and select Start, or press F10.

2. Once you have collected enough packets to examine, click on Capture|Stop, or press F11.

3. To examine the packets that Network Monitor has collected for you, click on Capture|Display Captured Data, or press F12. You see a summary of all the packets that you captured. This display shows the time that each packet was captured, the source and destination for each packet, the protocol used by each packet that was sent or received, and a brief description of what each packet is. Figure 9.14 shows an example.

4. To look at an individual packet in greater detail, double-click on it. Doing so brings up the Network Monitor window, shown in Figure 9.15. In the top frame of the window, you can see the list of packets that Network Monitor captured, with the packet you are viewing highlighted. In the middle frame is a detailed breakdown of the network packet, including the Ethernet and the DDP packet information.

NOTE: *You should look at the information in the middle frame in more detail when working on isolating AppleTalk-related problems.*

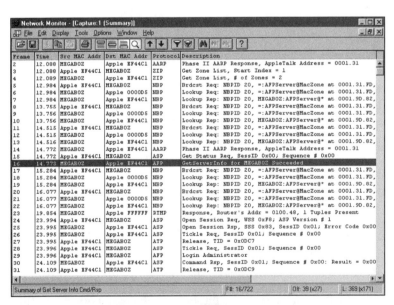

Figure 9.14   The Capture Summary dialog box shows you a list of all the packets that Network Monitor captured.

9. Windows 2000 And AppleTalk Networking

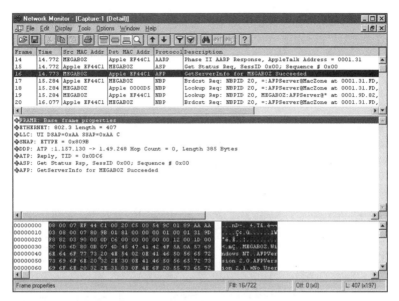

Figure 9.15 The Network Monitor window shows all you might want to know (and more) about a packet.

In the third frame are the hexadecimal values, or machine code, that is contained by the packet segment that you currently have selected in the middle frame.

NOTE: *Hexadecimal, or Base 16, numbers are used by computer programmers as shortcuts to define the binary numbers that are stored in each byte. Hexadecimal numbers range from 0 through F and represent one-half of the 8-bit byte of memory. Looking at a number whose value is FF, for example, you can see that FF equals 255 bytes. Looking at the hexadecimal numbers that Network Monitor displays, you can determine the values of the various bytes that make up each network packet. However, Network Monitor and other tools can provide you with more readable information, so you generally don't have to attempt to decipher the hexadecimal values.*

Setting Up Your Cisco Routers For AppleTalk

Setting up a Cisco router running Cisco's Internetwork Operating System is a vastly different procedure than that which you went through when setting up AppleTalk under Windows 2000 and then configuring it using the Routing and Remote Access manager. Configuring a Cisco router also demands that you leave the nice safe world of the Windows 2000 graphical interface and return to the world of the command-line interface.

Unlike the graphical interface that you used on the Macintosh or Windows, the command-line interface or CLI demands that you type in each command and all of the options for that command every time that you wish to use it. There are no buttons or icons to double click, just words to type into the CLI.

NOTE: *All the configuration examples are based upon Cisco IOS version 11.2, the standard release available when this book was written. All the commands that we describe should be present in some form when using any version of IOS later than 11.2 that includes support for AppleTalk.*

To access your router, you can use a serial cable connected to the Console port or Auxiliary port on the router, and then use a terminal program like ZTerm or Reflections or HyperTerminal on Windows, to access the routers command-line interface to the router. Alternatively, you can use Telnet to connect to and access the router remotely to talk to the router over your LAN. To connect to the router using Telnet, simply start Telnet and then use it to connect to the IP address or the DNS name of the router.

Getting To Know Your Router

Before you start working with your router, you must know the IP address of the router, the console password, and the secret password that puts the router into enable mode. The IP address that the router uses is defined in the configuration that you have installed in the router. To view the current configuration running on the router, follow these steps:

1. Connect the router, type "enable" and then enter the secret password to switch into enable mode.

2. Once you see the **#** cursor (which tells you that you are in the enable mode), type "show running-config" to see the configuration that is currently in use. The running configuration is customized for each router, as determined by the type of router, the version of Cisco IOS that it is running, and the types of network interfaces installed.

NOTE: *For more information regarding your router's current configuration, contact the people who installed and maintain your routers. For security purposes, many network administrators set up their routers to either deny all Telnet connections or to allow connections from only a few specific workstations. This restrictive type of configuration prevents unauthorized users from gaining access to the routers that control the network.*

After you have connected to the router from your workstation, follow these steps:

1. If required, type in the password to gain access to the router.

2. Once you have access to the router, you have only limited ability to accomplish what you want. To get full control over the router, you must turn on the router's Enable mode. To do so, type the following at the router's command prompt:

```
Cisco> enable <Return>
```

3. You are then asked for the enable password. Once you type in the proper password, the cursor changes to # and you have access to a greatly expanded number of commands.

NOTE: *In Cisco IOS, there are two types of commands that you can use to configure AppleTalk on your Cisco router: interface-related commands and general router commands. Interface commands are those used to configure specific network interfaces on the router. General commands, on the other hand, are used to configure such things as routing options and other general router options.*

---

4. To enter interface commands, you must first enter the configuration mode for that interface. To enter configuration mode from the terminal, type "Config T" at the command prompt.

NOTE: *This puts you in configuration mode from the terminal. The other configuration modes are Memory and Network. Typing "Config M" causes the router to load configuration from memory, whereas typing "Config N" causes the router to load its configuration from a location on the network.*

---

5. Once you have entered configuration mode, select the interface that you wish to configure by typing in the name of the interface. For example, to configure the Ethernet0 interface, type "Int E0" at the config prompt. Your command prompt should then change to read "Config-Int".

Cisco Interface Configuration Commands

You can set a variety of interface-related configuration commands from the command prompt. When configuring your routers' interfaces for AppleTalk, these are the configuration commands that you are most likely to use and a description of the functions that they perform:

- **appletalk access-group** *access-list-number*—The purpose of this command is to allow you to specify an AppleTalk access list to the current interface. To remove this access list, use the **no appletalk access-group** *access-list-number* command.

- **appletalk address** *network*.**node**—This command configures the router to use a specific AppleTalk address.

- **appletalk cable-range** *cable-range network.node*—This command allows you to define the network numbers that will be used on this interface. This command is identical in behavior to setting the network numbers in the Services For Macintosh dialog box. The cable range can be any number from 0 through 65,279, separated by a hyphen (-). The range of numbers must be equal to or greater than the number of networks you want on this segment of your network. The optional *network.node* switch allows you to specify the AppleTalk address that the interface uses. To disable the cable-range for a specific interface, use the **no appletalk cable-range** command.

- **appletalk discovery**—This command places the selected interface into discovery mode. This mode allows the interface to "listen" to the network so that it can determine what the AppleTalk network configuration is. To disable AppleTalk discovery on a specific interface, use the **no appletalk discovery** command.

NOTE: *Setting an interface to use AppleTalk discovery requires that you have either another router or a Windows NT server provide network zone and cable range information.*

- **appletalk distribute-list** *access-list-number* **in/out**—This command allows you to limit the distribution of routing information based upon the configuration of the access-list that you have configured.

- **appletalk getzonelist-filter** *access-list-number*—The purpose of this command is to filter the **getzonelist** command through a specified access-list to limit which zones are seen. To disable the getzonelist filter, use the **no appletalk getzonelist-filter** command.

- **appletalk protocol aurp, eigrp, or rtmp**—This command tells the router to use one of the three listed routing protocols on this interface. AppleTalk update routing protocol (AURP) is only available on tunneling interfaces. Cisco's Enhanced Internetwork Gateway Routing Protocol (EIGRP) is a multi-protocol routine that can carry routing information for AppleTalk, TCP/IP, and IPX/SPX. Routing Table Maintenance Protocol (RTMP) is the default routing protocol used by AppleTalk to distribute

AppleTalk network routes. To disable the routing protocol on this interface, use the command **no appletalk protocol aurp, eigrp, or rtmp**.

- **appletalk route-cache**—This command enables fast-switching mode on any supported interface. Fast-switching allows the router to handle network traffic much faster than it would normally. If you wish to turn off fast-switching, use the **no appletalk route-cache** command.

- **appletalk route-redistribution:** This command tells the router to convert RTMP routing information into EIGRP routing information. The purpose of this command is to allow the router to make available the information it learns about network routes via RTMP to other routers running EIGRP. To disable AppleTalk route-redistribution, use the **no appletalk route-redistribution** command.

- **appletalk routing eigrp** *router-number*—This command enables the AppleTalk EIGRP routing protocol on this interface. The router-number specified can be any integer from 0 to 65,535; however, it must be unique on your network. To turn off AppleTalk EIGRP routing on this interface, use the **no appletalk routing** command.

- **appletalk zone** *zone-name*—This command allows you to add an AppleTalk zone to a specific interface. To add a zone whose name contains a special character, you must specify it in the name by using a : followed by the hexadecimal number that equals that character's ASCII number. To delete an AppleTalk zone, use the **no appletalk zone** *zone-name* command.

Testing Your Configuration

The best way to make sure that your configuration changes do not interfere with the existing settings on your router is to test them out on a test configuration before you load them on the production router. If you cannot do this, the next best solution is to make your changes to the running configuration, but do not copy them to the startup configuration. This way if you determine that there is a problem with your configuration, you can restart the router and have it load the original configuration.

Using Cisco Interface Commands

Other commands available in configuration mode are not bound to any specific interface. They affect all interfaces that support the options being set. The **access-list** family of commands allows you to define filters that can permit or deny network traffic, depending upon the type of traffic and its destination or origin. Access-lists provide you with an enormous amount of control over the network traffic that you allow on and off of your network. When selecting these options, you need to make sure that they will not interfere with the other configuration settings that are configured on the router.

NOTE: *The access-list-number for AppleTalk access-lists must be between 600 and 699.*

- **access-list** *access-list-number* **(permit/deny) additional-zones**—The purpose of this command is to permit or deny all traffic from any zones that are not explicitly listed in the access-list.

- **access-list** *access-list-number* **(permit/deny) cable-range**—This command enables you to allow or deny AppleTalk traffic from a specified cable range on the network.

- **access-list** *access-list-number* **(permit/deny) includes (broadcast-permit/broadcast-deny)**—The purpose of this command is to allow you to define an AppleTalk access-list that overlaps any portion of a range of cable ranges or network numbers. The broadcast-permit and broadcast deny switches allow you to permit or deny network broadcasts that are meet the cable ranges or network numbers you have listed.

- **access-list** *access-list-number* **(permit/deny) nbp** *seq* **(type/object/zone)** *string*—The Name Binding Protocol, NBP, allows you to define permissions for specific NBP type, object or zone as defined in the string. The *seq*, or sequence number, is used to keep track of the various NBP entries in an AppleTalk access-list.

- **access-list** *access-list-number* **(permit/deny) network (broadcast-permit/broadcast-deny)L**—This command allows you to define an access-list for a specific AppleTalk network number.

- **access-list** *access-list-number* **(permit/deny) other-access**—The purpose of this command is to permit or deny all traffic from any network numbers or cable-ranges that are not explicitly listed in the access-list.

- **access-list** *access-list-number* **(permit/deny) other-nbps**—The purpose of this command is to permit or deny all traffic from any NBPs that are not explicitly listed in the access-list.

- **access-list** *access-list-number* (permit/deny) **within** *cable-range*—This command allows you to allow or deny AppleTalk traffic from any networks within a specified range of network numbers or cable range.

- **access-list** *access-list-number* (permit/deny) **zone** *zone-name*—This command allows you to allow or deny AppleTalk traffic from a specified AppleTalk zone on the network.

- **appletalk event-logging**—This command tells the router to log significant network events to the system log. To turn off AppleTalk event logging, use the **no appletalk event-logging** command.

- **appletalk name-lookup-interval** *seconds*—The purpose of this command is to set the Name Binding Protocol update broadcasts that it makes on all of its AppleTalk interfaces. The timing interval can be any integer from 0 on up. For optimal performance, Cisco recommends that you choose a value between 300 seconds (5 minutes) and 1200 seconds (20 minutes). Selecting a time of 0 causes the router to flush the names cache and prevents the caching of service type data. To reset the name lookup interval to the default value, use the **no appletalk name-lookup-interval** command.

- **appletalk timers** *update-interval, valid-interval,* and *invalid-interval*—This command is used to set the routing update timers to a value different from the default ones. The *update-interval* timer changes the time, in seconds, between the sending of routing updates to the other routers. The default value for this timer is 10 seconds. The *valid-interval* timer is time in seconds that a router will consider a route to be valid. The default value for the *valid-interval* is 20 seconds or twice the default value of the *update-interval*. The *invalid-interval* timer defines how long a route is kept in the routing table before it is discarded. The default value for this timer is 60 seconds or three times the *valid-interval* timer.

Cisco Enable Mode Commands

Other commands that you can use to modify or monitor your AppleTalk network settings can only be used when you are in the Enable mode. These commands are designed to allow you to see various settings on the AppleTalk network as well as to clear certain caches and counters that may need to be flushed before your network will operate properly. These commands can be divided roughly into those which Clear caches or lists and those that Show various network settings or information that the router has collected.

The **clear** family of commands are designed to clear out the various caches and lists that the router uses to direct AppleTalk traffic. These commands are very useful in clearing out caches or lists that contain out-of-date or incorrect information that might be preventing the router from working properly:

- **clear appletalk arp**—This command causes the AppleTalk address resolution protocol, arp, cache to be cleared of all entries. The arp cache is where the router stores information linking the AppleTalk addresses of each computer to their Ethernet addresses.

- **clear appletalk neighbor**—The purpose of this command is to clear out all entries in the AppleTalk neighbor table.

- **clear appletalk route**—This command allows you to clear out all of the routes listed in the route table.

NOTE: *The **clear AppleTalk route** command is very useful when you find that your routing table has a number of inaccurate AppleTalk routes. If you think that you have inaccurate AppleTalk routes, this command is a simple way to clear them all out and generate the list fresh.*

- **clear appletalk traffic**—This command resets all of the AppleTalk traffic counters on the router.

The **show** family of commands is designed to show you the contents of the various lists and caches that are used to support AppleTalk networking on the router. When diagnosing a problem or just trying to monitor the status of AppleTalk on your network, these commands can be invaluable:

- **show appletalk access-lists**—This command causes the router to display all the AppleTalk access lists that are defined on this router.

- **show appletalk adjacent-routes**—This command displays all of the routes to other routers that are directly connected to this router or are one network hop away.

- **show appletalk arp**—The purpose of this command is to display all of the entries in the AppleTalk address resolution protocol cache on the router. This command is very useful when trying to identify the network address of a specific Macintosh on the network.

- **show appletalk cache**—This command displays all of the routes in the AppleTalk fast-switching cache. The fast-switching cache is used by the router to perform rapid lookups of the routes that should be used to direct network traffic to its destination. Without the fast switching cache, the router would be forced to calculate a route for each piece of network traffic. From this list you can look at the various AppleTalk routes that are being used to direct packets between computers.

- **show appletalk eigrp interfaces** *type number*—The purpose of this command is to display all the interfaces on the router that are configured for EIGRP routing. The type and number switches allow you to limit the information to a specific interface type and number.

- **show appletalk eigrp neighbors** *interface*—This command displays a list of all the router's neighbors that are discovered by the EIGRP routing protocol. The interface option allows you to limit the information returned to that related to the selected interface.

- **show appletalk globals**—The purpose of this command is to display all the information about and settings of the AppleTalk Internetwork and related parameters.

- **show appletalk interface (brief)** *type number*—This command displays information about all the interfaces that are configured to use AppleTalk. The brief switch limits the information returned to a brief summary. The type and number switches allow you to limit the information to a specific interface type and number.

- **show appletalk name-cache**—The purpose of this command is to display the list of services provided by routers and other network equipment as returned by the network binding protocol, or NBP.

- **show appletalk nbp**—This command displays the contents of the network binding protocol, nbp, registration table.

- **show appletalk neighbors** *neighbor-address*—The purpose of this command is to display a list of AppleTalk routers that are directly connected to this router. The *neighbor-address* option allows you to narrow this report to a single AppleTalk neighbor.

9. Windows 2000 And AppleTalk Networking

- **show appletalk routes *type number*—**This command displays all of the static and discovered AppleTalk routes that this router knows about. The *type* and *number* switches allow you to limit the routes displayed to the ones connected to a specific interface type and number.

- **show appletalk static—**The purpose of this command is to display all of the static AppleTalk routes that are configured on this router. Static routes are the ones that have been manually configured on the router rather than those which are learned from EIGRP or some other dynamic routing protocol.

- **show appletalk traffic—**This command displays all of the counters that store information about the AppleTalk traffic that enters and leaves the router.

- **show appletalk zone *zone-name*—**The purpose of this command is to display all of the information in the zone information table on the router. The zone-name switch can be used to limit the information returned to a specific zone name.

One other important command is **test appletalk**. This command allows you to enter the test mode to help test and diagnose AppleTalk on your router.

Appletalk Configuration Examples

In the following section, we offer a series of configuration examples that you can use when configuring your Cisco routers for AppleTalk. These examples are by necessity generic and refer to the network diagrams that we have provided to help illustrate each example. In each example, the ! character is used as a remark character to help separate the lines in these examples.

Example #1

In this example you have two AppleTalk networks connected to either side of a single router.

```
Interface Ethernet0
AppleTalk cable-range 10-10
AppleTalk zone NorthMacLab
!
Interface Ethernet1
AppleTalk cable-range 12-12
AppleTalk zone SouthMacLab
```

We have set up two interfaces on the router for this example, Ethernet0 and Ethernet1 each with a distinct cable range and zone name. However, since we have not enabled AppleTalk routing yet, these two networks are effectively cut off from each other. By turning on AppleTalk routing, as you will see in the next example, you can communicate between the two sections of the network.

```
AppleTalk routing
!
Interface Ethernet0
AppleTalk cable-range 10-10
AppleTalk zone NorthMacLab
!
Interface Ethernet1
AppleTalk cable-range 12-12
AppleTalk zone SouthMacLab
```

The router, in this example, is using the default AppleTalk routing protocol, RTMP, directing traffic between the two AppleTalk networks. For more complex networks, you will probably want to switch from RTMP to EIGRP to route traffic around your network.

Example #2

In this example, you have a router with AppleTalk networks on two of its Ethernet interfaces. This router is connected by another Ethernet interface to the larger network. Since you will need to provide routing information about your AppleTalk networks to the larger network, you have decided to use EIGRP.

```
AppleTalk routing eigrp 24
!
Interface Ethernet0
AppleTalk protocol eigrp
AppleTalk cable-range 10-10
AppleTalk zone NorthMacLab
!
Interface Ethernet1
AppleTalk protocol eigrp
AppleTalk cable-range 12-12
AppleTalk zone SouthMacLab
```

This configuration allows network traffic from the entire network to reach your two AppleTalk networks, and allows traffic from those networks to reach the other portions of the network. In order to limit the type of traffic that is allowed on your network and off your network, you can use the following commands:

```
Access-list 601 permit network 10
Access-list 601 permit network 12
Access-list 601 deny other-access
!
AppleTalk routing eigrp 24
!
Interface Ethernet0
Aplletalk access-group 601
AppleTalk protocol eigrp
AppleTalk cable-range 10-10
AppleTalk zone NorthMacLab
!
Interface Ethernet1
AppleTalk access-group 601
AppleTalk protocol eigrp
AppleTalk cable-range 12-12
AppleTalk zone SouthMacLab
```

This configuration sets up your router to allow only AppleTalk traffic from computers on AppleTalk networks 10 and 12. AppleTalk traffic from all other sources will be denied.

Example #3

The next example builds upon the earlier two by adding routing update filters, so that information about the NorthMacLab is not made available to the network and information about the SouthMacLab is not made available to computers in the NorthMacLab zone.

```
Access-list 601 permit network 10
Access-list 601 permit network 12
Access-list 601 deny other-access
!
Access-list 602 deny zone NorthMacLab
Access-list 602 permit additional-zones
!
Access-list 603 deny zone SouthMacLab
Access-list 603 permit additional-zones
!
AppleTalk routing eigrp 24
!
Interface Ethernet0
AppleTalk access-group 601
```

9. Windows 2000 And
AppleTalk Networking

```
AppleTalk distribute-list 602 out
AppleTalk distribute-list 603 in
AppleTalk protocol eigrp
AppleTalk cable-range 10-10
AppleTalk zone NorthMacLab
!
Interface Ethernet1
AppleTalk access-group 601
AppleTalk protocol eigrp
AppleTalk cable-range 12-12
AppleTalk zone SouthMacLab
```

Using this configuration, the router will allow AppleTalk traffic only from the two cable ranges that you have defined on this router into the two AppleTalk networks. Additionally, information about the NorthMacLab zone is filtered out from the routing updates and any routing updates that contain information about the SouthMacLab zone from reaching the computers in the NorthMacLab zone.

Fine-Tuning AppleTalk For Your Windows 2000 Network

As you learned in the first part of this book, fine-tuning AppleTalk on your network is a complex and lengthy process that involves mapping out your network and then determining where you do and don't need AppleTalk. After you have mapped out the network, you can start looking at how you want to shape the network traffic on the LAN. Finally, you can look at changing the routing of packets to maximize your network's performance.

When you are starting the process of optimizing your network, follow these steps:

1. Sit down and map out your network's topology. By doing so, you are outlining where your Macintoshes are located and what servers or resources they need to talk to on the network.

2. Next, look at where AppleTalk must be allowed and where you do not need it on your network. For instance, you need it on any segment where you have Macintoshes and resources that those Macintoshes need access to. You do not need it on a segment of the network that is populated with only Windows NT or Windows 2000 workstations.

3. Finally, you can start limiting where AppleTalk is allowed. By using access lists and tunneling AppleTalk over Transmission Control Protocol/Internet Protocol (TCP/IP), you can shape the network traffic so that only those subnets that need AppleTalk are set up to allow it. Doing so allows you to greatly improve the performance of your network by limiting AppleTalk to only where it is needed. You can therefore keep your network much more segregated and much more highly managed than it might otherwise be. We will go into more detail about access lists and tunnels in the next sections.

Using Access Lists

One very common method of preventing AppleTalk packets from getting on or off a subnet is using access lists on your routers. You can also use them to filter out portions of AppleTalk or other network traffic so that just a portion of it is allowed on or off the subnet.

When writing an access list in Cisco's Internetwork Operating System (IOS), you need to remember a few things. First, know that all AppleTalk access lists are numbered between 600 and 699. Thus, when you look at the configuration on a Cisco router, you can readily determine which access lists apply to AppleTalk and which do not.

Secondly, when planning your access lists, remember that what is not explicitly permitted is going to be excluded by the implicit deny all that is appended to the end of each access list. Lastly, remember that access lists are interpreted from the top down. This means that if you have conflicting rules in your access list, the one located closest to the beginning of the list is the one that wins. Listing 9.1 is an example of a typical set of AppleTalk access lists.

Listing 9.1   This is the author's rendition of a typical set of AppleTalk access lists.

```
Access-list 601 permit network 10
Access-list 601 permit network 12
Access-list 601 deny other-access
!
Access-list 602 deny zone NorthMacLab
Access-list 602 permit additional-zones
!
Access-list 603 deny zone SouthMacLab
Access-list 603 permit additional-zones
```

You can also use access lists to limit the information that is passed around the network in the form of routing updates. By limiting the information that is passed from router to router, you can significantly change how AppleTalk packets flow over the network.

The problem is, of course, that by limiting the information that is passed from router to router, you can end up in a situation where the network becomes too rigid and fails when the network tries to reconfigure itself to cope with the failure of one of its components. If you decide to use access lists to limit the flow of AppleTalk information, try limiting as few things as possible. Listing 9.2 shows how you can use an access list to limit routing information.

Listing 9.2   This listing demonstrates how an access list is used to limit routing information.

```
Access-list 601 permit network 10
Access-list 601 permit network 12
Access-list 601 deny other-access
!
Access-list 602 deny zone NorthMacLab
Access-list 602 permit additional-zones
!
Access-list 603 deny zone SouthMacLab
Access-list 603 permit additional-zones
!
AppleTalk routing eigrp 24
!
Interface Ethernet0
AppleTalk access-group 601
AppleTalk distribute-list 602 out
AppleTalk distribute-list 603 in
AppleTalk protocol eigrp
AppleTalk cable-range 10-10
AppleTalk zone NorthMacLab
```

In this example, we are blocking information about a zone called SouthMacLab from routing packets that are being received by the Ethernet0 interface. Likewise, information about the zone that is directly connected to the Ethernet0 interface, NorthMacLab, is prevented from being distributed to the other routers on the network.

Using Tunnels

When you want to connect two widely separated subnets, you should look at setting up a tunnel on your network. By setting up a TCP/IP tunnel on your network, you are taking the AppleTalk packets that are located on one subnet, encapsulating them in a TCP/IP packet, and then sending them over the network to the destination subnet where they are de-encapsulated.

Although this may seem like a lot of overhead, it can actually help improve AppleTalk performance by limiting how many subnets your AppleTalk packets have to be routed over. Listings 9.3 and 9.4 show examples of Cisco IOS configurations that implement the tunneling of AppleTalk over TCP/IP.

Listing 9.3   Router 1.

```
interface tunnel 2
tunnel source e1
!Ethernet 1 is set to IP address 192.168.25.1
tunnel destination 192.168.1.1
apple cable-range 1024-1024
apple zone wormhole Tunnel
tunnel mode gre ip
```

Listing 9.4   Router 2.

```
interface tunnel 2
tunnel source e0
!Ethernet 0 is set to use IP address 192.168.1.1
tunnel destination 192.168.25.1
apple cable-range 1024-1024
apple zone wormhole Tunnel
tunnel mode gre ip
```

This configuration allows AppleTalk traffic from the subnet connected to the Ethernet 1 port on Router 1 to be tunneled over the rest of the network to the subnet connected to the Ethernet 0 port on Router 2. For networks that have pockets of Macintoshes on widely separated subnets, tunneling can be a very efficient way of knitting them all together. And, just as important, tunneling can sometimes prevent AppleTalk from causing performance slowdowns to the rest of your network.

Changing How Your Macintoshes Communicate With AppleTalk

The other approach you can take when attempting to limit the impact of having AppleTalk on your network is to change how your Macintoshes communicate with AppleTalk. By using some third-party utilities, you can significantly lessen the impact that your Macintoshes have on the network by limiting how often they request updates. Likewise, you can help lessen any negative impact that your Macintoshes may have by making a few simple changes in how you use them.

The biggest impact that Macintoshes normally have upon the network in general is that they generate a lot of network requests for updates on the network shared volumes and other network services that they are using every 10 seconds. By generating so many update requests, your Macintosh can easily fill up the network with unneeded packets and can force the Windows servers that house these shared volumes to spend an inordinate amount of their time answering requests for updates even if there have been no changes.

One obvious solution to this problem is to change the time interval that your Macintosh uses when requesting updates from the network shares and devices that your Macintosh is using. LessTalk from IPTech is a great example of a product that does just that. Although it does not support Macintoshes running Mac OS 8 or later, it does an excellent job of limiting the number of AppleTalk packets by changing the update interval to a user-defined value. Normally, you would set this to 300 seconds or so, limiting the Macintosh to asking for updates only every five minutes. This results in nearly a 30-fold decrease in how many updates each Macintosh sends out over the network.

For Macintosh users running Mac OS 8 or later, you must look at changing how you work with remote volumes to reduce the number of updates that your Macintosh generates. Fortunately, the newest versions of the Mac OS incorporate versions of AppleTalk that are less "chatty" than older ones, which means that the network isn't polled as often. This is one of the reasons why LessTalk's publisher never upgraded it for the newer OS versions.

Despite improvements in AppleTalk's performance, you may employ other methods to fine-tune your network:

- *Simply keep the network volume closed*—This is a common trick. When you open a window in the Finder to a remote volume, your Macintosh asks the remote server every 10 seconds for an update. However, if you keep the window closed, your Macintosh does not send out update requests to the file server.

- *Close the Chooser*—If you keep the Chooser open, your Macintosh sends out AppleTalk packets every 10 seconds or so, trying to discover all the network resources that are available. So, by simply closing the Chooser when you are done with it (which is the usual practice anyway), you can significantly reduce the amount of AppleTalk traffic your Macintosh generates.

Learning How DHCP Works With Your Macs

DHCP servers are commonly used on many networks to distribute IP addresses to the various network computers. DHCP is a system that allows a server to distribute IP addresses from a pool of available addresses to computers that request them. You can configure both the IP address and the DHCP server to send out a variety of useful information about your network. DHCP is used on many networks to help automate the distribution of information regarding the TCP/IP networking configuration used on the network. As with many network services, you need to be aware how the Macintosh looks at the information it receives from the DHCP server.

The DHCP server listens for requests for an IP address from computers on the network, and when it receives a request for one, it negotiates with the requesting computer. Once the negotiation is complete, the DHCP server sends the IP address and whatever information the DHCP server has been set to deliver. When the computer has accepted the IP address from the DHCP server, the server lists the address as being in use. This process, of course, takes place behind the scenes in the blink of an eye.

To prevent all the IP addresses from being given out and never reclaimed when a computer is moved or retired, the DHCP server sets a lease time on each address it assigns. This means that the IP address each computer gets from the DHCP server is good for only the period specified by the lease. When a computer with an IP address acquired from the DHCP server wants an extension on the lease of its address, it waits until the remaining time on the address' lease is equal to half of the original lease time before it contacts the DHCP server asking for one.

A computer that does not get a response from the DHCP server waits until only one-quarter of the lease time is left before attempting to contact the DHCP server again. If it still fails, it tries yet again at the one-eighth point and then again until the lease actually expires. Once the lease expires, the computer releases the IP address that it received from the DHCP server and begins periodic attempts to obtain a new IP address.

Setting Up A DHCP Server Under Windows 2000

Like Windows NT, Windows 2000 comes with a DHCP server available as an option. Windows 2000 is designed with TCP/IP as the principal networking protocol, so you can expect to find several Windows 2000 servers on your network configured to act as DHCP servers. To configure your Windows 2000 server to act as a DHCP server, follow these steps:

1. First, following the steps in Chapter 6, add the DHCP Server component from the list of network services.

2. Once you have finished installing the DHCP server on your Windows 2000 server, click on Start|Programs|Administrative Tools|Computer Manager.

3. Looking at Computer Manager, click on the Services And Applications icon and then select the DHCP icon.

4. To configure the DHCP server, click on Action|New Scope, or right-click on the DHCP icon and then choose New Scope from the pop-up menu. The Add A Scope screen of Computer Manager, shown in Figure 9.16, appears.

5. Windows 2000 next starts the New Scope Wizard, which walks you through the process of creating a new DHCP scope.

6. After the New Scope Wizard has started, you are asked to enter the IP addresses that you wish the server to distribute to all the

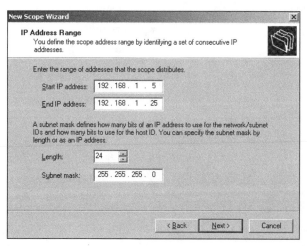

Figure 9.16   Computer Manager allows you to configure your DHCP server.

computers on the network that request IP addresses from the DHCP server. Figure 9.17 shows a typical setup. Then, click on Next.

7. Next, as shown in Figure 9.18, enter the IP addresses that you wish to exclude from the pool of addresses you have told the DHCP server to distribute. Then, click on Next.

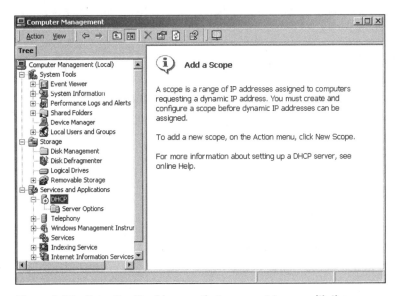

Figure 9.17   Enter the IP addresses that you want to use with the DHCP server.

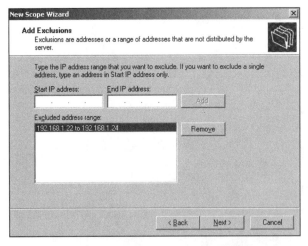

Figure 9.18   Use the New Scope Wizard to add all of the IP addresses that you wish to exclude from the scope.

8. You are next asked to set for how long each address will be leased, as shown in Figure 9.19. After you have set the lease time, click on Next.

9. Next, the New Scope Wizard asks if you want to configure some of the most common DHCP options that are distributed with the IP address. To configure these options, click on the Yes radio button and then click on Next.

10. You are now asked to enter the address (or addresses) of the router(s) or default gateway(s) that are on your network, see Figure 9.20. This information will be distributed, along with the

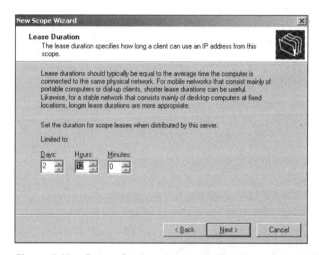

Figure 9.19   Determine how long each IP address is to be leased.

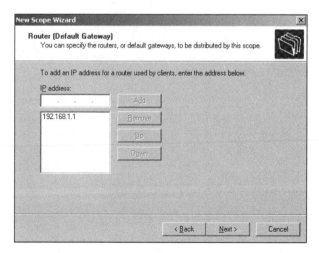

Figure 9.20   Set the IP address(es) of the routers and default gateways that you wish to distribute.

9. Windows 2000 And AppleTalk Networking

IP address, to each computer that requests an IP address from the DHCP server. Then, click on Next to continue.

11. The New Scope Wizard then asks you to enter the name of your domain and all of the addresses for the DNS servers that you wish to distribute. When you have entered all the DNS servers' IP addresses, click on Next. Figure 9.21 shows this setup.

12. After asking for information on the DNS servers, the New Scope Wizard requests that you enter information about the WINS servers on the network. Enter the IP address of the WINS servers that you wish the DHCP server to distribute, as shown in Figure 9.22, and then click on Next.

13. Next, Windows 2000 asks if you wish to make your new scope active. Click on the Yes radio button and then click on Next.

14. Now, click on Finish to close the New Scope Wizard. You can now add additional scope options.

15. To add a new scope option, click on the scope you wish to modify and then click on the Scope Options folder icon, located in the right-hand window.

16. Then, click on Action|Configure Options.

17. Looking at the Scope Options dialog box, shown in Figure 9.23, click on the checkbox next to the item that you wish to add. Then, enter the values that you want to set for the option.

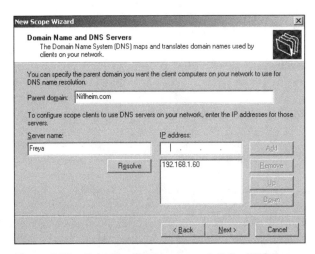

Figure 9.21   Enter the IP addresses of all the DNS servers you wish to make available.

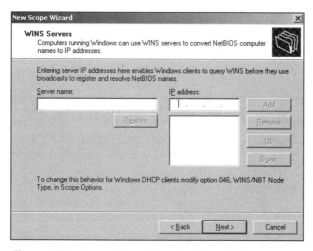

Figure 9.22   Enter information about the WINS servers on your network.

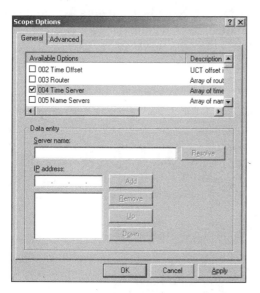

Figure 9.23   Enter the values for the specific option you want.

NOTE: *Although you can configure nearly 100 DHCP scope options, both Windows- and Macintosh-based computers generally use only a few. The most commonly used scope options are those that distribute information about the routers or default gateways for each subnet, the DNS servers available on the network, the WINS or NetBIOS name servers on the network, the domain name of the network, and the NetBIOS node type. Macintosh OS-based computers can read information about the default gateway, the DNS servers, and the domain name. However, most other options are not understood. Windows-based computers can read all of these common settings and more of the others; however, like the Macintosh, they do not understand all of them.*

When you have finished configuring the DHCP server on your Windows 2000 server, you are ready to start using it.

Configuring Your Macintosh To Use DHCP

To get your Macintosh to obtain an IP address from the DHCP server, you need to perform a few simple steps. You must first find out from your network administrator if DHCP is available on the network segment where your Macintosh is located. If it is, you must find out what information it is configured to distribute, along with the IP address, so you can see if you need to make any additional configuration changes on your Macintosh. To start using DHCP, follow these steps:

1. Click on Apple|Control Panels|TCP/IP.

2. The TCP/IP (Default) dialog box, shown in Figure 9.24, appears. Click on the Configure pop-up menu and then select Using DHCP Server from the list of options.

3. Click on the close box and then click on OK to save your changes.

Depending upon the information distributed by the DHCP server, along with your IP address, you may have to set some of the settings manually. For example, some DHCP servers are configured to distribute only information about the Windows Internet Name Service (WINS) servers but not their Domain Name System (DNS) servers. Macintoshes cannot use WINS servers, so you have to manually set

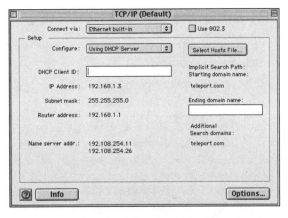

Figure 9.24   Use the TCP/IP (Default) dialog box to configure TCP/IP on your Macintosh.

9. Windows 2000 And AppleTalk Networking

up the entries for the DNS servers in the TCP/IP (Default) dialog box on each of your Macintoshes.

Although the Macintosh DHCP client behaves much like the Windows DHCP client, there are some differences. For example, if your Macintosh cannot discover a DHCP server on startup, it keeps trying for about 20 seconds. If it still does not get a response, it chooses an IP address from the non-routable IP address range 169.254.0.0 through 169.254.254.255 and sets a subnet value of 255.255.0.0. Windows PCs, on the other hand, set an address of 0.0.0.0 if they cannot find a DHCP server before they time out.

Comparing DHCP To BOOTP And RARP

When you look at the various options under the Configure menu in the Mac's TCP/IP Control Panel, you see two options that may look a bit strange: BOOTP and RARP. BOOTP, much like DHCP, is an old system of distributing IP addresses from a central server. The primary difference between BOOTP and DHCP is that DHCP can automatically allocate IP addresses and manage them. DHCP can also distribute considerably more information with the IP address than BOOTP. In addition, DHCP is a considerably newer protocol and is rapidly replacing BOOTP on most networks.

RARP is yet another system that allows a computer to make a request for information about its network address. RARP is different than DHCP or BOOTP, however, because it sends out a broadcast that contains its Ethernet address to the computers on the network, where a RARP server picks up the broadcast and matches the Ethernet address against a list of IP addresses. Once it has found a match, it sends back a message telling the computer what its IP address is. One of the big downsides of RARP versus DHCP or BOOTP is that you have to have an RARP server on each subnet because the RARP broadcasts do not get routed over the network like BOOTP or DHCP packets do.

Tuning NetBIOS With DAVE

The NetBIOS Control Panel, which gets installed when you install DAVE (discussed in Chapter 2), has several settings that you can change to tune its performance. DAVE's default settings are normally good enough for most networks. However, if you aren't satisfied with the performance you're getting, you may wish to configure NetBIOS differently to see if the changes have a beneficial effect.

Before you start making changes to the NetBIOS settings, the first thing to do is gather information about your network. Specifically, if you are using DHCP, you need to know if the DHCP server distributes WINS and DNS information, along with each IP address.

You must also know what NetBIOS node type is being used on the network. The *node type* defines how the computer searches for the IP address that is associated with a specific NetBIOS name. To configure the DAVE NetBIOS Control Panel, follow these steps:

1. Click on Apple|Control Panels|NetBIOS.

2. In the NetBIOS Control Panel, shown in Figure 9.25, look to see if the WINS and/or DHCP checkboxes have been checked. If your DHCP server is set to deliver information about the WINS servers on the network, make sure that the WINS checkbox is not selected. If you need to manually set the WINS server addresses, click on the WINS checkbox and then enter the IP addresses of the primary and secondary WINS servers.

3. To configure the more advanced options available to you in the NetBIOS Control Panel, click on Admin. Doing so opens the NetBIOS Administrator Options dialog box.

4. When you look at the values set in the NetBIOS Administrator Options dialog box, check that all the values are set to those that you use on your network. This is particularly important if you use non-standard values for the Broadcast Address. To

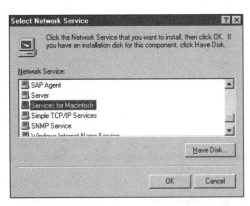

Figure 9.25   You configure WINS information from DAVE's NetBIOS Control Panel.

9. Windows 2000 And AppleTalk Networking

change the Broadcast Address that NetBIOS uses, enter the value that is used on your network. If your network uses the default Broadcast Address, leave the space provided blank.

5. Next, check to see that the Name Server Port is set to the value that you normally use on your network. On most Windows-based networks, this is port 137. However, double-check this because some networks may use a different port setting.

6. Next, see if the NetBIOS node type is set to the correct one. Setting NetBIOS to use the wrong node type can result in unwanted network traffic and sometimes in name resolution problems. If you do not know the proper node type for your network, contact your network administrator for assistance.

7. If you wish to improve the ability of your Macintosh to resolve NetBIOS names, you may want to allocate additional memory to the Name Table Size. The default is 32; however, you can choose to lower it to 16 or raise it to 64, 128, or 256 using the drop down menu.

8. If you wish to use certain computers on your network but their NetBIOS names are not listed in either the DNS or WINS database, you can add them to a file on your Macintosh. DAVE uses the LMHOSTS file that you create on your Macintosh to match NetBIOS names to the appropriate IP address, as does WINS. To create a computer in the LMHOSTS file, edit the file with SimpleText or some other text editor.

9. Using SimpleText, create a new entry for the computer by adding a line after the last entry in the LMHOSTS file. Here is an example of what these entries should look like:

```
192.168.1.2  TestServer1  #PRE  #DOM:TestNet
192.168.1.3  TestServer2  #PRE
```

NOTE: *In the LMHOSTS file, computers are listed first by their IP address, then their NetBIOS name. The **#PRE** command after their name tells DAVE to load the IP address and NetBIOS name into the NetBIOS name cache during startup. The **#DOM: DomainName** command informs DAVE that the computer is a Domain controller for the domain listed.*

TIP: *In general, you should think long and hard before you change any of the default settings in the NetBIOS Administrator Options dialog box. It is far too easy to actually degrade the performance of your Macintosh on the network by changing how NetBIOS functions. If you do decide to go ahead and make changes anyway, it is a good idea to make note of your previous settings in case things do not work out quite as you plan.*

Related Solution:	Found on page:
Configuring DAVE For Windows 2000	205

Troubleshooting

Trying to identify and resolve AppleTalk problems on the network level is much more complex than diagnosing some of the other problems you might encounter when adding Macintoshes to your network. To start the process of isolating an AppleTalk network problem, you must first determine if this problem is due to the hardware or if it can be traced back to the network configuration itself.

A common problem that you may well encounter when setting up your AppleTalk network is the inability to see zones and AppleTalk enable devices located on another segment of the network. This problem is frequently caused by either inaccurate routes propagated around the network or by poorly-planned access-lists installed on various network routers. To isolate the source of the problem, you should first make sure that every Macintosh on this segment of the network is experiencing the same problem. If all of the Macintoshes are unable to see remote zones and devices, you should check to see if the Macintoshes on a different network are able to see the zones and devices on your network. If the Macs on the remote network can see the zones and devices on your segment of the network, then you will need to check the AppleTalk access-lists that are set up on the routers which are connected to your segment of the network.

To check the AppleTalk access lists that are set up on your router(s), connect to your router and perform the following steps:

1. From the enable prompt, type "show running-config".

2. Examine the current configuration to see what AppleTalk access-lists are applied to the network interface that is connected to your network. Check the access list number that is assigned to the interface as well as the access-list that is applied to the AppleTalk routing configuration.

3. Once you have determined the access-lists bound to the network interface, look at the access lists and check to see if they are set to block network traffic from the other networks or zones. Should these access lists not block AppleTalk traffic, you will need to check the access lists that are set in the

AppleTalk routing configuration to see if they block routing updates from the other networks and zones.

4. Should the access lists block AppleTalk traffic or routing information from other networks or zones, you should try changing the access list blocking you from talking with the remote network and then check the network again to see if your problem has been resolved.

5. If all of the access lists are set up correctly on your router and yet something continues to block network traffic or information about the other segments of your network, you will need to examine the AppleTalk routing information table. You can look at the AppleTalk routing information table by typing "show appletalk routes" at the enable prompt.

6. Look at all the routes listed to the remote networks and zones that you are not able to see. Should there be some routes listed, clear them out using the **clear appletalk routes** command. Once that is complete, do a **show appletalk routes** again to see if the routes that were present the first time now are the same as are listed now.

7. If the routes do not match, you should immediately check to see if you the zones and devices on the remote segment of the network are now visible.

8. If the routes listed do not change after clearing out the route cache, you will need to examine the access lists that are configured on all the other routers that are located between you and the remote network whose zones and devices you wish to examine.

Another problem that you may encounter occurs when you are only able to see a portion of the network resources on a different segment of the network. This problem is normally caused by an access-list that is configured on either your router's network interface or the network interface on the remote network segments router, which causes certain Name Binding Protocol types to be blocked, thus rendering them invisible to computers on other network segments. To identify if this is the problem, you must do the following:

1. Connect to the router using the procedure described earlier in this chapter and then type "enable" and the enable password.

2. Once you are in enable mode, type "show running-config" at the prompt and hit return.

3. Look at the router's configuration and examine the access lists that are being used on the interface that connects to your segment of the network.

4. Check the access list to make sure that it is not configured to deny specific NBP types. If it is, then you will need to look at the access-list to make sure that it is not filtering out NBP types that you really want.

5. If the access lists on your router are not configured to filter out any NBP information, then you must check the configuration on the router connected to the remote network. Connect to that router and then check its configuration to make sure that its access-lists are not blocking you from seeing the NBP information you need to see the network resources on this network.

With some newer Macintoshes, you may discover that the network performance seems sluggish and that network connections are terminated unexpectedly when you are connected to the network by a fast Ethernet switch. The cause of this problem frequently is the incorrect settings on the switch port that the Mac is connected to.

To determine if this indeed is the case, you should identify which port your Macintosh is connected to. The simplest way to do this is usually to look up in a master network map the network port that you are using and from there, determine which port on the switch your network port is connected to. Once you have identified the network port you are connected to, you will need to connect to the switch and do the following:

1. After you have logged into the switch, type "show interface fastethernet *interface-number*".

2. Look at the information returned and see if the interface is set to 100Mbit or to 10Mbit. If it is set to 10Mbit, your problem lies elsewhere. If the interface is set to 100Mbit, look to see if there are a large number of errors listed.

3. If there are a large number of Ethernet errors, check to see if the port is configured for Full Duplex or Half Duplex.

NOTE: *Full and Half duplex modes define the way that the Ethernet card communicates with the switch. In Full Duplex mode, the card can send information at the same time it is receiving information, thus making the effective amount of data being transferred equal to about 200Mbits/ a second. In Half Duplex mode, the Ethernet card must wait until the sender has quit sending data before it can send its data out. This limits the amount of data being transmitted to 100Mbits a second.*

---

9. Windows 2000 And AppleTalk Networking

4. If the port is configured to use Full Duplex, try changing it to Half Duplex and see if that solves your problem. Since changing the configuration on a switch varies from model to model, it is usually best to have the people responsible for maintaining the switch make the change.

Additional Network Troubleshooting Techniques

You will want to try the following steps to diagnose various network-related problems:

1. The first thing that you should do when trying to diagnose any network problem is to define the problem as accurately as possible. Does the problem occur on only one computer or does it occur on a whole group of computers on the network?

2. If this problem affects only one computer, then you should try connecting another computer to the same network cable and see if the same symptom appears on the new computer.

3. If the problem does not occur with the other computer, then you should take a closer look at the computer that is having the problem. The first thing that you should check is whether the Ethernet interface on the computer having a problem is functioning correctly. You can do this by moving the computer to another network port to see if it works there. If you have a network analyzer, such as a Network General Sniffer or the Network Analyzer that comes with Microsoft Systems Management Server, SMS, you can use that to examine the network traffic generated by the computer in question to see if they are normal.

4. If the Ethernet interface is operating properly, you need to make sure that the operating system is configured correctly to communicate with the Ethernet interface. If the Ethernet interface is not functioning correctly, then you will need to have the computer repaired.

5. If the computer is functioning correctly, you should examine the network configuration that you are using on that computer. For example, double-check to make sure that the Ethernet port speed and duplex modes are set correctly and that you have set all the other network parameters to what they should be.

NOTE: *A good indication that one of your computers has an improperly configured Ethernet interface is the number of Ethernet errors on the network. In a switched network, you can see this by logging into the network switch and doing a **show interface** interface-type interface-number to look at the Ethernet statistics for a specific port on the switch. Thus, when a port is showing a high number of network errors, you should probably take a closer look at the computer connected to it.*

9. Windows 2000 And AppleTalk Networking

6. If the network problem cannot be traced to a hardware problem, then you must look at the network configuration to see if the problem lies there.

7. The first step that you should do is to gather information about the network your Macintoshes are connected to. In particular, get the IP address, console password, and the enable password of the router that connects your section of the network to the rest of the LAN.

8. Next, log into the router using a Telnet program and then connecting to the router by its IP address. You can also connect to the router by going to the router directly and connecting a serial cable to the console port and then using a terminal program like ZTerm to talk to the router.

9. Once you have logged into the router and switched into enable mode, type "show running-config" to display the current router configuration. Examine the configuration to see if there are any access lists that might be causing the problems that you are seeing. Pay particular attention to the access lists that are applied to the AppleTalk routing if you are having trouble seeing remote networks and zones.

10. If there are no problems with the configuration running on the router, then you should check the AppleTalk routes that are in the route cache. To do this, type "show appletalk routes" and then press Return.

11. Examine the routes that are listed to see if they are accurate. A good way to check if the route cache has become corrupted is to do a **clear appletalk routes** and then do another **show appletalk routes** to see if the routes listed in the route cache have changed. If they have, check to see if the problem has been resolved.

12. If there was no change in the routing information, then you will need to expand your search outward by repeating Steps 8–11 on the other routers on your network, starting with the one connected to the network segment that you are having trouble seeing.

Chapter 10

Using Microsoft BackOffice With Macintosh Applications

In Brief

Much like a huge Swiss army knife, Microsoft BackOffice can take advantage of Windows 2000 to provide services to both Macintosh and Windows users. This chapter will focus on the tools and services of Microsoft BackOffice, from tapping into the power of email by connecting to a Microsoft Exchange server to using Microsoft Proxy server to provide your Macintosh clients with access to the Internet.

In this chapter, we will discuss how you can connect to and use Microsoft Exchange server, SQL Server, and Microsoft Proxy Server to provide you with email, database support, and access to the Internet. In addition, we will look at how you can use other cross-platform tools to provide email, database, and Internet access.

Exploring Microsoft BackOffice

The Microsoft BackOffice suite of products is a group of Windows 2000 server-based applications that offer databases, electronic messaging, Internet access and Web servers for Windows-based networks.

The following is a brief overview of the various BackOffice components:

- *Microsoft SQL Server 7.0*—The latest incarnation of Microsoft's SQL Server. SQL Server 7 is designed to offer users a high-speed and robust database server that is capable of a variety of database tasks. From storing and displaying satellite images of Earth to keeping track of your accounting data, SQL Server can be used to handle a wide variety of your database needs.

- *Microsoft Exchange Server 5.5*—Along with the soon-to-be-released (as of the time this book was written) Exchange 2000, this application provides both Macintosh and Windows users with email, chat, and scheduling capabilities. As the electronic messaging core of Microsoft BackOffice, Exchange can be configured to direct electronic mail based upon predefined workflow rules so that you can automate a variety of mundane tasks as well as send mail to and from the Internet or other email systems.

- *Microsoft Proxy Server 2.0*—As the gateway between your network and the Internet, Microsoft Proxy server is designed to provide a secure way for your Macintosh and Windows users to connect to the Internet and, to a lesser degree, a firewall that can protect your network from hackers on the Internet. Microsoft Proxy server contains a variety of different proxy servers, only two of which can be used by Macintosh-based clients. The Winsock proxy is designed to allow Windows-based PCs to use the proxy server to handle requests from their Internet applications, such as ICQ and newsgroup readers like Outlook Express. The SOCKS proxy does much the same for Macintosh-based applications that can use it.

SOCKS, which was originally developed for UNIX computers, is a way of directing an application's network traffic through a proxy server. For Macintosh applications that are capable of using it, the SOCKS proxy allows you to set up your SOCKS-capable, Internet-based applications to use the proxy server when connecting to the Internet. The Web proxy is designed to redirect requests for Web pages through the proxy server. Microsoft Proxy server is also capable of acting as a caching proxy, by storing copies of the Web pages that are retrieved and then sending them back to the next user who requests them without having to go back to the original Web site. This can speed up Web viewing quite a bit. There is a downside, though. Sometimes, you run the risk of displaying out-of-date Web pages.

- *IIS*—The Microsoft Internet Information Server is a high-performance Web server that can handle everything from a small internal Web site or Intranet, to a large Internet-based e-commerce site. Add-ons such as Microsoft Site Server and Site Server Commerce Edition extend the capabilities available to IIS with such features as an enhanced search engine, as well as adding completely new features such as document management. Site Server Commerce Edition also gives you all the tools needed to set up a Web-based store. The new document management tools in Site Server allow you to check in and check out documents as well as track all of the changes that have been made to the document. If you are running the Commerce edition of Site Server, you will also have all the tools you need to build a great e-commerce site on the Web. Commerce edition includes all the scripts and templates needed to build up a Web-based electronic store.

- *Critical network functions applications*—Using such tools as Veritas Software's Backup Exec and Computer Associates International's ARCServeIT, you can back up data located on all your Windows 2000 servers and Workstations, and if you are using either the ARCServeIT or Backup Exec Macintosh clients, your Macintosh workstations as well. If you are primarily a Macintosh shop and want to back up the few Windows-based computers on your network, you should consider Retrospect from Dantz Development. Retrospect's Windows clients allow you to back up all your Windows-based computers over the network.

- *QuickMail*—For people who find that Exchange is too complicated or has features that aren't really needed, there is a useful alternative. QuickMail from CE Software offers you a great cross-platform email solution. QuickMail can handle your inter-company and Internet mail, and it also can direct your mail, based upon rules (procedures) that you set up to help automate the workflow. QuickMail also contains a robust directory server that keeps all of your contact information.

- *Winroute Lite and Winroute Pro*—When it comes to accessing the Internet on a budget, few tools can beat Winroute Lite and Winroute Pro from Tiny Software. Winroute Lite offers a nice, basic solution to connecting your Macintosh and Windows PCs to the Internet quickly and easily. Winroute Pro also offers a quick and painless way to connect your Windows and Macintosh clients to the Internet, as well as a firewall and other features designed to help protect your network from hackers and other folks on the Internet.

Backing Up Your Data Over The Network

Backing up your data is perhaps the single most important thing that you can do. You will want to make sure your valuable data is safely stored so that it can be restored in case of disaster; this is critical when running either a home office or a business. Backing up your data will protect against losing a file from a hard disk failure or the accidental deletion of a critical file. You will also be able to restore previous versions of a file that you have been working on. It's a real time-saver, in the event you discover that you deleted some element of the file that you really needed. Such situations are not uncommon in production environments, especially when deadlines approach.

In most Windows 2000-based networks, backups are performed by a centrally located server to which several large storage devices, such as tape libraries, are attached. Such a server is designed to communicate with the other servers and workstations on the network and then to back up all of the data stored on them. By doing so, you now have a copy that can be safely stored offsite, ready for use in case disaster strikes.

Macintosh users, like their Windows counterparts, need to make sure that their data is safely backed up on a regular basis.

NOTE: *Backups are only useful if the media they are on survives. Therefore, you should consider storing your backups at a safe, offsite location (perhaps even a bank vault) on a regular basis. That way you can be assured your data will survive whatever disaster might strike your network.*

Using Windows 2000, you have a couple of options that you can utilize when trying to back up your data. The first and least expensive option, from a software standpoint, is the Microsoft Windows Backup software that comes bundled with Windows 2000. While this is a good choice if you are on a budget (or have a small network), the program lacks a lot of the sophisticated features found in other backup applications and it can only connect to and back up data on other servers that they make available in shares.

While there are a large number of backup applications for Windows 2000 currently available on the market, two applications can easily be called the market leaders: Backup Exec from Veritas Software and ARCServeIT for NT from Software Associates.

* *Veritas Software's Backup Exec*—This is the commercial version of the backup software that comes bundled with Windows 2000. Compared to the bundled edition, Backup Exec has a much greater number of features that you can take advantage of when using it to back up the data on your Windows 2000 network, whether it is located on Windows 2000 Macintosh volumes or on a standard Windows 2000 volume.

When using Backup Exec, you can choose between a wide variety of backup media on which to store the data that you are backing up. From a Zip drive to a huge tape library containing hundreds of tapes, Backup Exec can handle nearly all of them. From a Macintosh standpoint, however, Backup Exec has one major advantage—the client that it uses to access Macintosh servers and workstations directly is free. This means that Macintosh users do not have to pay for the ability to back up their data with Backup Exec as you do with ARCserveIT.

• *Computer Associates International's ARCserveIT*—Like Backup Exec, ARCserveIT is capable of reaching out and backing up data on Windows-based servers and workstations via the network. ARCserveIT is also capable of utilizing a wide variety of storage devices upon which to store your data. ARCserveIT's major disadvantage for Macintosh users is that Computer Associates International charges for the Macintosh-based client for ARCserveIT that allows Macintoshes with the client installed to be backed up over the network by Windows 2000 servers running ARCserveIT. This means that you have to pay extra for the benefit of protecting the data your Macintosh users store on both their workstations and on the Windows 2000 Macintosh volumes that they use.

On networks where Macintoshes are the primary platform and you only have a few Windows-based computers, you should consider another solution—Retrospect from Dantz Development. Using Dantz's Windows backup agent, you can back up data located on Windows-based computers using your Macintosh-based server or workstation.

The Retrospect Windows client makes the process of backing up the data on your Windows-based computers just as simple as backing up your Macintosh clients. All you need to do is select it in Retrospect's simple interface, same as any other server workstation.

Making sure your Macintosh data is properly backed up on a regular basis is normally a very simple exercise. The key thing that you need to do is look at the type and amount of data that you are backing up and what type of backup schedule you wish to establish. Once you have finished looking at these two issues, you will then want to actually set up the various backup jobs.

NOTE: *When setting up your backup process, it is critically important that you contact the administrators in your company who are in charge of the server backups so that you can make sure that all of your backups do not conflict with any of their backups.*

Setting Up Private IP Addresses

Due to the limited number of IP addresses that are available for use on the Internet, many companies and users are taking advantage of the three groups of private IP addresses that have been set aside for use on internal networks. These three IP ranges, 10.x.x.x, 172.16.x.x-172.31.x.x, and 192.168.x.x are what are known as *non-routable IP addresses*. What that means is that any network traffic that has a network address that is within those three ranges will not be sent to the Internet. Thus, users that are using these private addresses on their network find that they must convert the addresses used by their workstations to an IP address that can be sent out onto the Internet, by using native address translation or by running all Internet traffic through a proxy server that has a valid IP address. Products like Winroute Lite and Winroute Pro switch all of the IP addresses on your network traffic from using the non-routable or private IP address to using an IP address that is capable of being sent out over the Internet. The other option is to have a proxy server, like Microsoft Proxy Server 2.0, handle all of your Internet requests for you using its valid IP address to send and receive information from the Internet.

10. Using Microsoft BackOffice With Macintosh Applications

Immediate Solutions

Understanding SQL Server 7's Capabilities

SQL Server version 7 is the current version of Microsoft SQL Server as of the time this book was written. SQL Server forms one of the cornerstones in Microsoft BackOffice and is designed to provide database services for all the components in the BackOffice family. As such, you can use SQL server to provide database services for everything from Microsoft Excel and the Internet Information Server, IIS, to FileMaker Pro.

Using SQL server, you can create a connection between the database and the Web pages that you are serving up, by using IIS to build exciting Web-based applications. Likewise, you can create applications based on such programs as Microsoft Excel and FileMaker Pro that reference data located in the SQL Server. These applications can be designed to provide an easy to use front end that allows users to look at and—if you wish—to modify the data that is stored in the SQL Server.

Configuring The ODBC Connector To SQL Server 7

To begin using Microsoft SQL Server 7 from your Macintosh Applications, you must first create a connection between the SQL Server database and your Macintosh. Setting up this connection is pretty simple, but it does require that you know the following about your SQL Server:

- *Data Source Name (DSN) that you plan on connecting to*—The DSN is the name that you give a specific database connection, which you have previously configured on the SQL Server.

- *ODBC (Open Database Connector)*—This is the software that allows you to connect to the SQL Server database from your Macintosh.

To set up an ODBC database connection between your Macintosh and the SQL Server database you wish to use, just follow these steps:

1. Select the ODBC Setup PPC Control Panel, located in the Control Panels folder, which you can access via the Apple Menu.

2. From the ODBC Data Source Administrator, make sure that you are looking at the User DSN tab. If you bring up a different function, click on the User DSN tab to bring that component of the Control Panel to the front. Once you are looking at the USER DSN tab box, click on Add. See Figure 10.1 for an example of a typical setup.

3. From the Create a New Data Source dialog box, select the type of database server that you are connecting to. From the database types listed, select the entry for ODBC SQL Server Driver PPC and then click on the Finish button. Take a look at Figure 10.2 for an example.

4. The next screen will display the VSI MS SQL Server dialog box. From here, enter the Data Source Name that you wish to connect to.

5. You will also need to enter in the name of the server that hosts the database as well as the IP address of the server. If you wish, you can also add in a brief description of the database in the space provided. The result is shown in Figure 10.3.

6. Should you need to log in to the database with a specific username and password or set the connector to use a non-English character set, you will also need to click on the Options button.

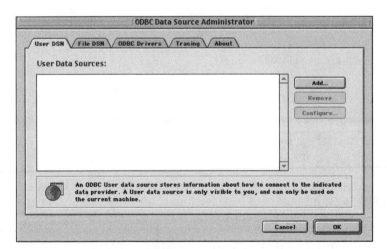

Figure 10.1   To create and edit ODBC connectors, use the ODBC Data Source Administrator.

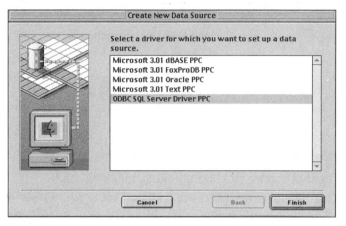

Figure 10.2 Choose the Data Source type that you wish to connect to with ODBC.

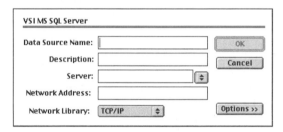

Figure 10.3 Enter all of the Server information that you need to finish the ODBC connection.

After you have entered in all of the configuration information that you need to finish configuring the DSN, click on OK to complete the creation of the DSN.

Connecting To SQL Server 7 From FileMaker Pro

After you have finished setting up the ODBC connector between the SQL Server database and your Macintosh, it is now time to put it to use.

In this example we will be using FileMaker Pro 4.1 to connect to the ODBC connector that we have created and then view the database that was set up on the SQL Server. For the purposes of this example, we are using the Northwind example database that comes with SQL Server 7.0. To configure FileMaker Pro to connect to the SQL Server, please perform the following steps:

1. Start FileMaker Pro.

2. From the File menu, select New to open a new database.

3. Once you have created a new database, click on the File drop-down list and select Open.

4. Looking at the Open dialog box, click on the Show menu that is located towards the bottom of the dialog box and choose ODBC as the file type.

5. Now, you will be presented with a complete list of all the ODBC connectors that are currently available on this Macintosh. See Figure 10.4 for an example.

6. If needed, enter the username and password that are required for access to this database.

7. Now, you will be shown a list of all the tables that are present in the Northwind database. From here, you can select the tables you wish to connect to using FileMaker. Select the tables that you wish to use and then click on OK to begin using them.

Now, you are ready to start designing your FileMaker database application using the data from the Northwind database.

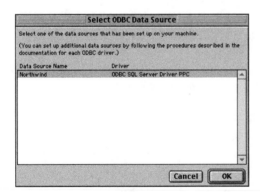

Figure 10.4   Choose the ODBC DSN you wish to use from this list.

Using SQL Server 7 With Microsoft Excel 98

As with FileMaker Pro, you can use Microsoft Excel 98 to connect to and manipulate databases that are stored on the SQL Server. This allows you to build applications using Microsoft Excel that will provide a nice and highly graphical front end to the database being stored on the SQL Server. Setting up Excel to connect to the databases stored on the SQL Server requires that you first set up an ODBC DSN to the SQL Server database as we did earlier in this chapter. Once you have configured the ODBC DSN, you will need to follow these steps to create the connection between Excel and the database.

After making sure that you have a valid ODBC connection between your Macintosh and the SQL Server, you will be ready to set up the external database options in Excel to use the proper database.

To configure the external database options in Excel, you'll need to set up the query that Excel will be making to the database you wish it to use. Follow these steps to set up the external database connection to extract data from the SQL Server using Excel:

1. Double-click on the icon for Microsoft Excel.

2. In Excel, click on the File menu and select Open.

3. Open the workbook for which you wish to set up the connection between Excel and SQL Server.

4. Once the workbook has been opened, click on the Data menu and select Create New Query from the Get External Data submenu.

5. Choose the data source that you created when configuring the ODBC DSN and click on OK, as shown in Figure 10.5.

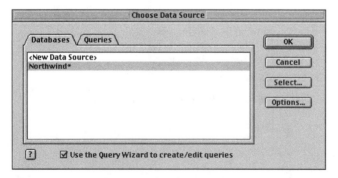

Figure 10.5 Select the ODBC data source that you wish to connect to.

6. From the VSI MS SQL Server dialog box that is now displayed, enter the username and password that you need to use when connecting to this database.

7. Once you have entered the correct username and password (see Figure 10.6), click on OK.

8. You will now see a list of all the tables that are present in the database. Choose the tables that you wish to access using Excel and then click on the OK button.

9. Once you have completed selecting all the tables that you want to use, you can now run queries and perform other database operations using the data stored in those tables.

Once you've established your connection between Excel and Microsoft SQL Server, you can then create connections to other SQL Server databases or other data sources such as FileMaker or Excel workbooks. You can also set up SQL Server to limit a user's access so that he or she is only able to read data from the database. Alternatively, you can set up access so users can actually change and manipulate data in the SQL Server database from Excel.

To configure the level of access that you wish to grant different users, talk to the administrator of your SQL Server and have him or her set up the various users and the database permissions that you wish them to have. For example, you might want some users to be limited strictly to viewing data in the database. To do this, simply have the SQL Server administrator give these users read only access to the database. For users that you wish to actually change the data, give them the rights needed to change the database.

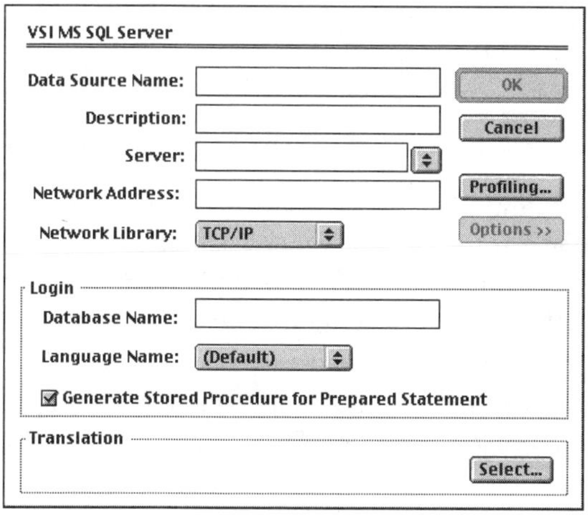

Figure 10.6   Type in the username and password needed to connect to the database.

319

Setting Up Outlook For Macintosh

While Microsoft Exchange has been the electronic messaging system preferred by many companies, up until recently, it was limited to Windows users only. However, with the release of Service Pack 2 for Microsoft Exchange Server 5.5, Microsoft has finally released a Macintosh-based client. Now, Macintosh users who wish to connect to and use the Microsoft Exchange email system can use Microsoft Outlook for Macintosh.

Using Outlook for Macintosh, you will be able to connect into the Microsoft Exchange server to send and receive email, handle address books, and send and receive contact information. However, some features, particularly the scheduling system, are not currently available to users of the Mac version.

At the present time, you will see two different versions of Outlook that run on the Macintosh.

Outlook Express, the email and newsgroup client that is bundled with Internet Explorer 4.5, is the version that you see most frequently as it is installed when you install Internet Explorer. The other version of Outlook is the version that comes with Service Pack 2 for Microsoft Exchange Server 5.5. This is the version that allows you to connect to the Exchange server from your Macintosh.

NOTE: *Although it hadn't shipped with new Apple computers and Mac OS releases when this book was being prepared, Microsoft has made Outlook Express 5.0 for the Macintosh available from their Web site, at **http://www.microsoft.com/mactopia**. This version offers an updated user interface and enhancements in all areas, particularly those involving scheduled email sessions and filtering, including improved filters designed for mailing lists and junk email. The new version also provides Hotmail and Palm Pilot support and a much more user-friendly way of handling Address Books. The information offered in this book about Outlook Express 4.5 may also be applied to the new version.*

As we want to allow your Macintosh users to connect to your Microsoft Exchange Server to send and receive email and other services, we will focus upon the installation and configuration of Outlook for Macintosh. To install and configure Outlook, complete the following steps:

1. Double-click on the Outlook Installer and complete the steps needed to install Microsoft's Outlook for Macintosh on your computer.

2. After you have installed Outlook for Macintosh on your Macintosh, you will need to configure it.

3. Open the Outlook Settings Control Panel that was installed by the Outlook installer and use it to configure the connection between your Macintosh and the Exchange server that contains your mailbox. (See Figure 10.7.)

4. Click on the Add button in MS Exchange Settings Control Panel, and choose the Microsoft Exchange Server from the list, as displayed in Figure 10.8.

5. Now, you will be asked to enter the name of the Exchange server that houses your mailbox. If you do not know the name of the Exchange server that your mailbox is located on, you will need to ask the Exchange administrator to look it up for you.

6. Next, enter the name of your mailbox. This is normally the same as your Windows domain username; however, some

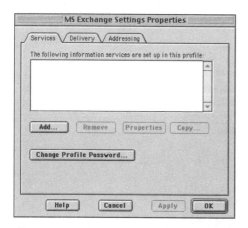

Figure 10.7   *To open the Outlook Settings Control Panel, click on the Apple menu, and scroll down to Control Panels. Then select the Outlook Settings Control Panel from the list of Control Panels.*

Figure 10.8   *Select the Microsoft Exchange Server to establish the connection to your Exchange server.*

companies have different policies. Should you not know the name of your mailbox, you will need to ask the Exchange administrator.

7. Now that you have finished entering the server name and the mailbox name that you wish to use, double-check to make sure that TCP/IP is the desired connection type.

8. Next, you will need to finish checking all the startup options that you want to use, as shown in Figure 10.9.

9. After you are satisfied that your settings are correct, click the Check Name button to test the connection between your Macintosh and the Exchange Server. Clicking on the Check Name button will bring up a dialog box asking for the username, domain that this username belongs to, and your password, as shown in Figure 10.10.

10. Type your username, the domain that your username belongs to, and your password. Once you have finished entering all this information, click on OK.

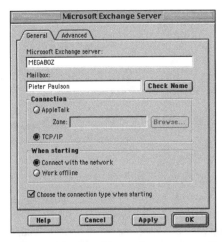

Figure 10.9   Configure all your connection options for your Exchange server.

Figure 10.10   Type in the User Name, Domain Name, and Password for the mailbox you are validating.

11. Outlook will then contact the Exchange server that you se-
    lected and will see if the mailbox that you specified exists on
    the server and if your username and password have access to it.
    If everything is correct, Outlook will underline the mailbox
    name in MS Exchange Control Panel.

12. Once you have finished validating this connection, you can add
    other mailboxes that you wish to access. Please see Figure
    10.11 for more information.

13. After you are done configuring your mailbox properties using
    the Microsoft Exchange Server dialog, click on OK to close the
    dialog box.

NOTE: *Only mailboxes that are located on the same Microsoft Exchange Server can be opened
at the same time in Outlook for Macintosh.*

---

14. Next, you will need to determine where you want to store your
    mail. To see all the delivery options available to you, click on
    the Delivery tab of the MS Exchange Properties dialog box.

15. You will once again be asked to type in your password so that
    the Control Panel can connect to the Exchange server. Once
    you have typed in your password, click on Connect to proceed.

16. Click on the location where you would like Exchange to store
    your electronic mail, as shown in Figure 10.12. To keep all of
    your electronic mail stored on the mail server, select the

*Figure 10.11   Create connections to all the other mailboxes that you wish to
view with Outlook.*

Mailbox option. To have your mail stored locally on your Macintosh or on a network volume, you must select the Private Folders option.

17. To complete the configuration process, click on the Addressing tab and choose the various address books that you want to use when using Outlook (see Figure 10.13).

18. After all the Exchange Settings are set the way that you want, click on OK to close the Control Panel.

19. Now, you need to locate the Microsoft Outlook program and launch it.

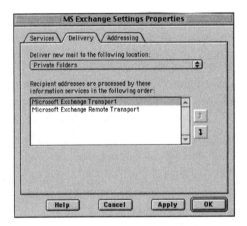

Figure 10.12   Set your mail delivery options for Outlook from this dialog box.

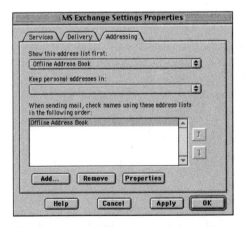

Figure 10.13   Choose the address books you wish to use in Outlook.

20. After starting Outlook, you will see a list of the mail folders for each mailbox located on the left-hand side of the window. On the right-hand side of the window you will see a list of all the messages in the mail folder that you have selected, as shown in Figure 10.14.

21. If you wish to use Outlook for Macintosh to keep your schedule, you will need to click on the calendar icon that is located in the Outlook toolbar.

22. Should Outlook not find a schedule file on your Macintosh, it will ask you what you wish to do next. If you have a schedule file located on your Macintosh or on a network volume, you can choose to connect to an existing file. Having a file on a shared network volume or another volume that is readily accessible to others on the network is a great idea if you wish others in your company to be able to view your calendar. Otherwise, it is usually best to simply create a Schedule + file on your Macintosh. Please look at Figure 10.15 for an example setup.

23. Looking at your Schedule, you can select between the daily view, a weekly view, and a monthly view.

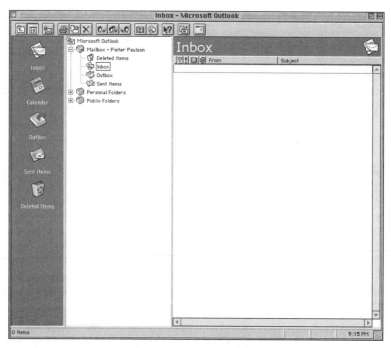

Figure 10.14   This is your email Inbox in Outlook.

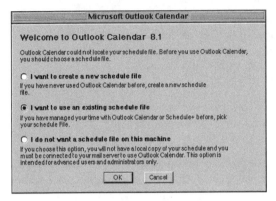

Figure 10.15   This illustration displays selecting sample Schedule + calendar in Outlook.

After you have examined all of the functions in Outlook and made sure that they are set as you expect, try sending email to yourself or have other people send you email so that you can make sure that Outlook is receiving email properly. Once you are certain that Outlook is receiving email properly, you are ready to begin using the program.

Using QuickMail To Send And Receive Email

Microsoft Exchange provides a wealth of useful features, possibly more than you might find suitable to your installation. If you decide that Microsoft Exchange is not well-suited to your needs, you may wish to look at another cross-platform email application to handle your messaging needs.

QuickMail from CE Software is an excellent choice for users that want a high-quality, well-rounded email system that runs on both Windows-based and Macintosh-based computers. While QuickMail does not offer all the options that are available using Microsoft Exchange, QuickMail is capable of handling all of your email needs quickly and easily.

As with Exchange, QuickMail is capable of handling a large number of user mailboxes as well as being able to direct mail in the system using a variety of user defined rules. QuickMail is also capable of sending and receiving email from the Internet or other email systems that you may have installed on your network.

The real beauty of QuickMail is that you can choose to run the email server portion of QuickMail on either a Macintosh or a Windows 2000 or NT-based server. This allows you to choose which server you want to use. You are not required to stay with a Windows NT or 2000 server as Exchange does. This choice of server platforms is definitely a plus for users on networks where Macintoshes are the principal platform.

Proxy Server 2.0 And Other Internet Access Products

Setting up your Macintosh to access the Internet is, depending upon how your network is set up, normally a very simple procedure.

On the majority of business networks, the connection between the Internet and your company network is controlled by a server that acts as a gateway or firewall between the wild and uncontrolled elements on the Internet and the controlled environment that is your company network.

When looking for a firewall, you can choose between a dedicated firewall product such as the Cisco PIX or the Axent Raptor firewall for Windows NT and products that are designed to perform other functions but also have firewall capabilities. Such products include Tiny Software's Winroute Pro and Microsoft Proxy Server 2.0, which are designed to provide a variety of Internet access options, one of which is the ability to provide firewall capabilities.

Pure or dedicated firewalls are servers whose sole purpose is to protect you and your network from being attacked or victimized by hackers and other unsavory folks on the Internet. These servers are designed to limit the network traffic that passes between your network and the Internet. When setting up a firewall, it is generally a good idea to follow the "less-is-more" philosophy. This means that you only configure your firewall to allow the minimum of network traffic needed to support the Internet applications that you want to run.

NOTE: *Before you try to set up your Macintoshes to connect to the Internet, you will need to get information on the type of connection that you have to the Internet and all the configuration settings that will need to be set on each Macintosh from your Network administrators.*

While not a dedicated firewall, products such as Winroute Pro and Proxy Server 2.0 are capable of acting as a firewall. When you set up the access rules that are available in both of these products you can quite effectively limit the traffic that goes to and from your network, much as a dedicated firewall would.

Both Winroute Pro and Microsoft Proxy Server are designed so that all the network traffic heading out to the Internet is directed through it. Winroute Pro, however, offers a much wider variety of options, especially for the Macintosh users on your network. Winroute is able to handle both your proxy-enabled Internet applications along with those that do not explicitly support a proxy server, by offering both a transparent native address translation service, NAT, and a wide variety of proxy services.

As part of Microsoft BackOffice, Microsoft Proxy Server is designed to provide users on the Windows 2000 network with access to the Internet. To perform this function, Microsoft has created four distinct components that are all integrated in a simple-to-use-and-administer application. The four components of Proxy Server 2.0 are:

- *The WEB or HTTP proxy server*—This is designed to access the Internet and pull down pages that users are requesting. Since this is also a caching proxy server, it will keep copies of the most commonly used Web pages and will serve them up to users who request a page that has been stored in the cache if it is still current.

- *SOCKS*—For non-Web applications, like FTP, the SOCKS proxy is designed to provide access to the Internet. Unfortunately, only those applications that are specifically designed to use the SOCKS proxy can work with it.

- *Security module*—The security module is designed to allow you to configure Proxy server to act much like a dedicated firewall. By allowing you to deny access to specific network traffic and even specific Web sites, you can set up Proxy Server to protect your network.

- *Winsock proxy*—Designed to allow Windows-based computers to seamlessly redirect network traffic destined for the Internet through the Proxy Server. However, while this proxy works great for Windows-based computers, there is no way for Macintosh users to use this proxy.

Configuring Macintosh Applications For Use With Microsoft Proxy

While many modern Macintosh Internet applications are capable of using the SOCKS server provided by Proxy Server 2.0, not all are. Should you find that your favorite Internet application is not able to use the SOCKS proxy, you should check to see if there is a newer version of the software that does support the feature. If there is not a version that supports SOCKS, then you may want to look at another application that performs the same function, but is also SOCKS-aware. It should be noted however, that not all Internet applications for the Macintosh are capable of using SOCKS and may never be.

NOTE: *Among the Mac programs that support SOCKS is the popular FTP program, Fetch. You are apt to find that a number of programs do not support the feature, and your best bet is to check the documentation to be certain what protocols are available.*

In most Macintosh Internet applications, you can set the Proxy configuration in either the preferences of the specific application or by using the Configuration Manager Control Panel that's installed when you Install Internet Explorer. To configure a proxy server in the Configuration Manager Control Panel, you will complete the following steps:

1. Select the Configuration Manager Control Panel from the Control Panels sub-menu located in the Apple Menu.

2. In the Configuration Manager, there is a list of the settings that you can configure. These options include your email settings (as shown in Figure 10.16), file download, and Web browser.

3. To configure your Macintosh to use the various proxies available on the network, click on the Proxies list item. Enter the IP addresses and port numbers of the various proxies that are configured on the network. For example, you would set the HTTP proxy to point at the IP address of the Web proxy and set 80 as the Port number that you wish to use.

NOTE: *While port 80 is the standard port used by Web browsers to talk to Web sites, some companies use a different port number so as to improve network security. By directing the Web proxies to use a non-standard network port, some companies believe that this helps to prevent unauthorized individuals from accessing their Internet connection. So, should you discover that pointing your Internet applications to use a proxy located on the standard port does not work, you will need to contact the Proxy Server administrator to find out what port the Proxy is configured to use.*

---

4. In order to configure your Web Browser (Internet Explorer in this example) to go through a Proxy (see Figure 10.17), click on the Enabled radio button and then choose HTTP as the protocol that you wish to direct through the proxy.

5. Next, click on the list of Methods and select Normal.

6. Then, enter the IP address of the Proxy Server and set the Port either to 80, the default TCP/IP port for HTTP, or one that your company has chosen.

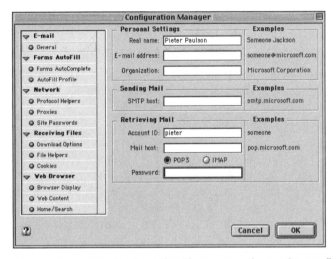

Figure 10.16   The Configuration Manager can be used to configure your Internet email.

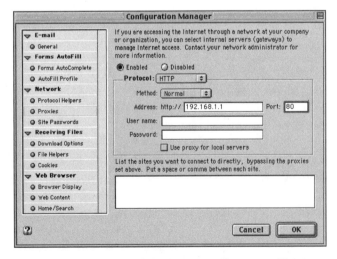

Figure 10.17   Use this dialog box to configure your Web browser to use the Web proxy.

7. To configure the other proxy servers, choose the protocol used by the application that you want to direct through a proxy. Using the example in Figure 10.18, you will select SOCKS from the list of available Methods and then enter the IP address of the Proxy Server and set the Port number to 21 or whatever your company has configured it to be.

8. To set up other applications, click on the protocol menu and select Other from the list of available options.

9. Next, select Methods|SOCKS and enter the IP address and port number of the SOCKS Proxy that is installed on your network.

10. After you have finished configuring all application proxies, click on OK to close the Configuration Manager Control Panel.

If you don't wish to use the Configuration Manager, you can manually set the proxy settings in each of your Internet applications that are proxy-aware. While setting up each application's network preferences is a good way of making sure that all the special options are set, it is labor intensive. It is also a bit more prone to error as you have to set up each application independently instead of just setting them once in the Configuration Manager. In the next section, we will provide examples on how to configure the proxy settings on some common Macintosh-based Internet applications.

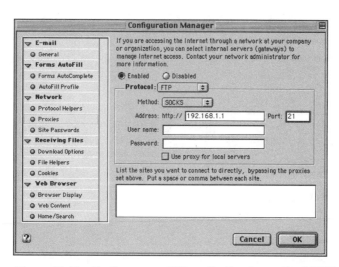

Figure 10.18   Configure your FTP application to use the SOCKS proxy.

Configuring Fetch 3 To Use A SOCKS Proxy

Fetch can easily be configured to use either the Microsoft Proxy Server's SOCKS proxy or any other SOCKS-compliant proxy. To configure Fetch to use SOCKS, please do the following:

1. Double-click on Fetch 3.0.3 (the version shipped when this book was written).

2. Once the program has launched, click on the Cancel button on the New Connection screen.

3. Click on Customize|Preferences.

4. In the Preferences dialog box, click on the Firewall tab to see the proxy settings.

5. To use the SOCKS proxy, click on the SOCKS checkbox and then enter the IP address of the SOCKS proxy server. The settings should match those shown in Figure 10.19.

6. Once you are finished, click on OK to close the preferences dialog box.

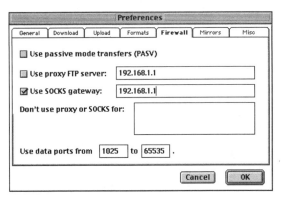

Figure 10.19   Set up the SOCKS proxy in Fetch 3.0.3.

Setting Internet Explorer 4.5 To Use A Web Proxy

Configuring Microsoft Internet Explorer 4.5, like Fetch is a very easy procedure. To set up Internet Explorer to use a Web proxy, complete the following steps:

1. Start Internet Explorer by double-clicking on its icon.

2. Once it has finished loading, click on Edit|Preferences.

3. In the Preferences dialog box, scroll down and click on the listing for Proxies located under Network.

4. Click on the Enabled checkbox to tell Internet Explorer to use a proxy server and then select HTTP as the protocol. After choosing the protocol, click on Methods|Normal.

5. Next, you will need to enter the IP address of the proxy server and set the port number to 80, or whatever it is set to on your network. Examine Figure 10.20 for more information.

6. After you have finished setting up the proxy, click on OK to close the Internet Explorer Preferences dialog box.

NOTE: *As this book was written, Microsoft was developing Internet Explorer 5.0 for the Macintosh (it will probably be released about the time this book appears). While Preference dialog boxes will change somewhat with the new version, the basic process of setting up proxies will involve essentially the same steps as outlined in this section. The biggest changes in the new version reflect the browser engine and support for the latest Web standards.*

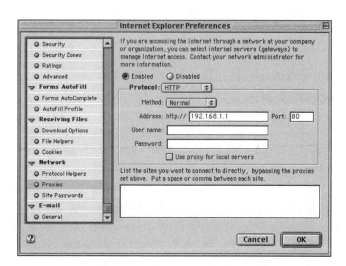

Figure 10.20   Set up Internet Explorer 4.5 to utilize a Web proxy.

Using Winroute Pro With Macintosh Internet Applications

Microsoft Proxy Server limits you to using Macintosh applications that can support either a Web or SOCKS proxy. Winroute Pro, on the other hand, allows you to use all of your Macintosh Internet-enabled applications. Winroute Pro has a variety of application proxies built in that seamlessly direct your Internet traffic to and from the Internet without having to use a specific proxy. This allows you to ignore the proxy settings and simply run Internet Explorer, Fetch, or any of your other Internet applications without having to configure them in any special way. Additionally, by making the proxy server effectively transparent to your Macintosh, Winroute allows all your Macintosh Internet applications to run and function, not just those that are capable of using a Web or SOCKS proxy.

Winroute Pro is also capable of translating private IP addresses to a real one by native address translation (NAT); users can use a private IP address on their local network and still connect to the Internet as usual. In addition to NAT, Winroute Pro can be used to protect your network from intruders by denying specific TCP/IP ports that are commonly used by hackers or to block specific applications that you do not wish users to access, such as Internet Relay Chat or others.

For small networks, Winroute can be used to distribute TCP/IP configurations to the computers on your network via its built-in DHCP server and limit which computers have access to the Internet and when. This feature in particular is of great use in limiting the ability of a user to work with different applications and the time that they spend online.

Configuring Winroute Pro For Macintosh Internet Applications

Configuring Winroute Pro to support a small network of Macintosh and Windows users is a fairly easy task. To set up Winroute to administer TCP/IP and establish NAT for your network, do the following:

1. To open Winroute Pro, click on Start|Program|Winroute Pro 4.0|Winroute Administration.

2. Once you have opened Winroute Administration, you will be asked to log in to Winroute Pro. Once you have entered in a valid Administrator username and password, click on OK. Once you are logged into Winroute Pro, click on Settings|Interfaces.

3. In the Interfaces/NAT dialog, click on the network interface that is connected to the Internet and then click on Properties button. See Figure 10.21 for additional information.

4. In the NAT dialog box, select the two checkboxes so that Winroute Pro will use the IP address provided by your ISP as the real address used in the native address translation process and to exclude this interface IP address when translating network requests.

5. Click on OK to continue.

6. Once you have finished configuring the interface, click on OK to close out this dialog box.

7. Next, click on the Settings|Advanced|Packet Filter.

8. In the Packet Filter dialog box, click on Add to add a new packet filter to Winroute. In Figure 10.22, you will see an example of how to set up a packet filter that blocks NetBIOS network traffic from coming in to your network from the Internet.

9. Once you have configured the settings for your incoming packet filter, you need to click on the outgoing tab and repeat the procedure to block traffic coming from your network that is undesirable.

10. When you have finished adding all of the packet filters you wish to install, click on OK. The packet filter dialog box should look like the one shown in Figure 10.23. For a list of the most common TCP/IP Port numbers, please look in the Glossary.

11. To configure the proxy portion of Winroute Pro, click on Settings|Proxy.

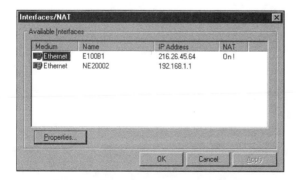

Figure 10.21   Here are the Internet Properties for Winroute Pro.

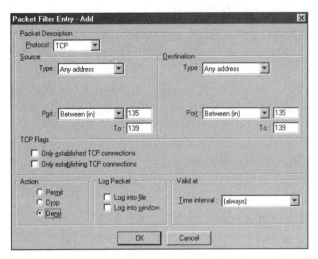

Figure 10.22   This dialog box is used to block specific network traffic from the Internet.

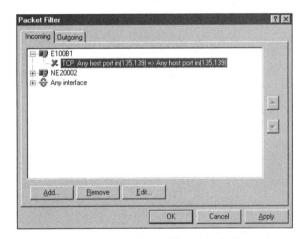

Figure 10.23   This is a typical Packet Filter dialog box configuration.

12. Once you are in the Proxy dialog box, set the proxy port to the port number you wish to use and adjust any of the other settings that you wish to change. Figure 10.24 shows a typical example of such a setup.

13. To limit the sites that users of this proxy can visit, click on the Access tab and click on Insert to add the Web sites that you wish to block, as shown in Figure 10.25. You can also specify which users and groups can view each restricted site so that teachers or parents may be allowed to view a specific group of sites, while children would be prevented from viewing those same sites.

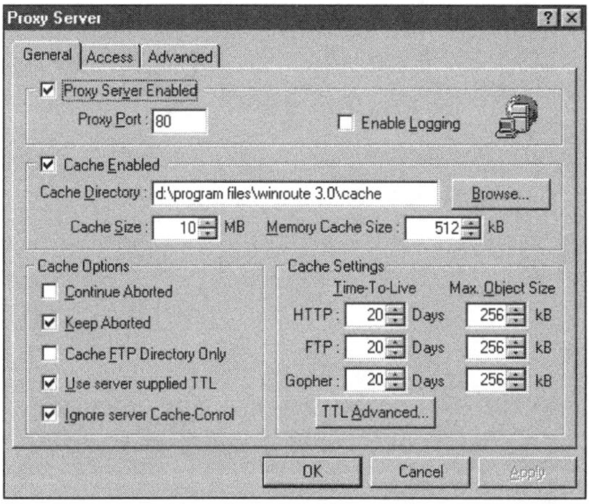

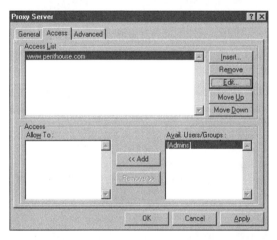

Figure 10.24   This is a typical setup for your Winroute Pro proxy dialog box.

Figure 10.25   This dialog box is used to limit access to specific Web sites that may contain unacceptable content.

14. Under the Advanced tab, you will find the settings needed to connect this proxy server to another or parent proxy server, thus allowing you to build a cluster or group of proxy servers. Once you have finished configuring the proxy, click on OK

15. Next, click on the Settings|DHCP to set up Winroute Pro to administer the TCP/IP configuration for your Windows and Macintosh workstations.

16. In the example shown in Figure 10.26, we have set up DHCP in Winroute Pro to lease TCP/IP addresses between 192.168.1.2 and 192.168.1.10 to all of the Windows and Macintosh workstations on the network. We have also configured it to specify the

337

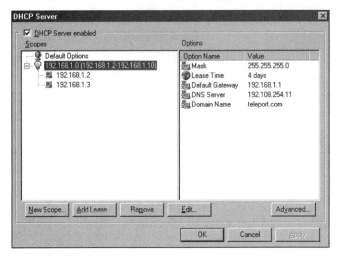

Figure 10.26   A typical DHCP setup dialog box for Winroute Pro.

DNS or Domain Name Server, Default gateway, and Domain Name used by each computer on the network. Once you have finished configuring DHCP, click on OK to continue.

17. If you wish to set up specific users and user accounts for use in limiting the access that folks have when using the Winroute Pro proxy, click on Settings|Accounts.

18. In the Accounts dialog box, you can add users directly or you can click on the Import NT Database to import a list of all the Windows 2000 users available to this server. See Figure 10.27 for a typical example.

19. If you wish to create a group of users to control access, click on the Groups tab in the Accounts dialog box and then click on Add to create a group.

20. Then, select the group and add the users you wish to include as part of that group, as shown in Figure 10.28.

21. Once you are done, click on OK to close the Accounts dialog box.

22. To close Winroute Pro, click on the Exit button in the upper right-hand corner of the window.

Once you have finished configuring Winroute Pro, you will be ready to start using it to provide your Macs with Internet access.

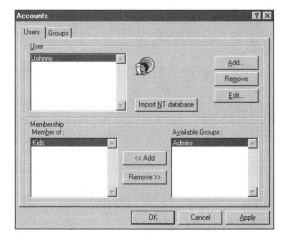

Figure 10.27   Use this dialog box to import a list of Windows 2000 users.

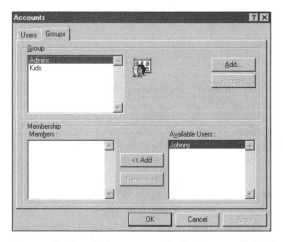

Figure 10.28   Add your users in the Groups dialog box.

Protecting Your Network From The Internet

When connecting your network to the Internet, one of the first things that you need to think about is security. The Internet is a wide-open environment and unfortunately, there are many individuals out there who are willing and able to attack the computers on your network. From the casual snooper interested in seeing what your network looks like to the cracker intent on stealing your company secrets, there are many different threats that you will need to protect against. This section covers the various threats that you may face and how you can configure your Firewall or Proxy to protect you.

The first thing that you should think about when setting up a firewall is what type of network access you will need to allow. Will you need to allow every user to be able to use AOL and any other Internet applications from their desk, or do you intend to limit the types of Internet applications that your users can use? Once you have decided which Internet applications will be supported, you will need to decide what other network services you wish to allow. These services are used by your routers and servers to provide information to other computers. However, while this may be useful inside your network, you do not always want that information to be made available on the Internet.

Finally, once you have determined the applications and services that you wish to allow to and from the Internet, you need to actually set them up. While we discussed how to set up these filters using Winroute Pro in the previous section, the information provided below is easily adapted to any of the other Firewalls or Proxies available on the market.

Common Internet Applications And Their Impact

The most common Internet application that you will be asked to provide to your users is electronic mail. Email is the primary reason that most companies connect to the Internet. Next on your users' wish list is undoubtedly going to be Web access so they can spend endless hours looking for the latest news and information online. Another service that is rapidly gaining in popularity is instant messaging. Instant messaging programs like ICQ and Microsoft's Instant Messenger allow users to hold conversations in real time over the Internet. Lastly, there are a wide variety of other Internet-based applications, such as FTP, RealAudio, Liquid Audio, and Pointcast that your users may desire access to.

Email

Electronic mail is a critical tool used by businesses large and small to communicate among their employees and with their customers. Email on the Internet is transferred from server to server using the Simple Mail Transport Protocol also known as SMTP. Mail servers on the Internet send and receive SMTP traffic using TCP port 25. Because email is a critical service, you will most likely want to create a hole in your firewall to let it through. However, like many heavily used services, there are many different ways of going about it. As such, it is best to make sure that your firewall is configured to only allow SMTP traffic to and from the Internet to your mail server and no others. This limits the ability of any cracker to compromise your network via email.

NOTE: *As you may have heard, there are now a whole group of email-based computer viruses. When connecting your email system to the Internet, it is very important that you make sure that your anti-virus software is kept current and that your users are well educated. Make sure that your users know not to open email attachments from people they do not know. Also, if possible, set your email reader programs so that they are not capable of executing macros or scripts that may be stored in an attachment. Following a few simple steps can save you hours of lost time trying to stamp out a virus infestation.*

For users on networks that do not have their own mail servers, but rely instead on your Internet Service Provider's email servers, you will want to make sure that your firewall is set up to allow your users to access them. The most common mail reader programs use the Post Office Protocol also known as POP to access the remote mail servers and pull down any email that is stored there. Another common protocol that seems to be gaining in popularity is the Internet Message Access Protocol or IMAP. IMAP is used by a variety of programs and by Windows CE devices to access mail servers.

Internet

Web browsers such as Microsoft's Internet Explorer and AOL's Netscape Navigator are tools that allow users to view and interact with World Wide Web servers all over the Internet. Using the Hypertext Transport Protocol, HTTP, and the secure version known as Secure HTTP, or HTTPS, Web browsers can download text, graphics, and even small programs from computers located all over the world. The information provided on these Web servers can range from recipes on someone's home Web page to information critical to the running of your company. In general, it is best to allow your users access to the World Wide Web as the information that is available online can be immensely useful. A very good idea, especially in business or educational environments, is to require that all users wanting access to the World Wide Web sign or otherwise agree to a written code of conduct that spells out what sites they can and cannot visit.

Instant Messaging

Like email, instant messaging programs like Microsoft's Instant Messenger and ICQ allow users to communicate quickly and efficiently with others on the Internet. While these tools are great for conversing with a friend or relative over the Internet, they are not business tools. As such, businesses need to be very careful about allowing the current instant messaging programs on their networks. One major concern, especially with ICQ, is that there are many people using ICQ who send out viruses and other inappropriate material to unsuspecting users. Additionally, the conversation that you hold on the Internet is not encrypted and as such can be intercepted by others on the Internet. Another major concern, especially with Microsoft's Instant Messenger, is that it is not licensed for commercial use.

Miscellaneous

Other programs that your users might wish to use range from Liquid Audio to Pointcast. Liquid Audio and RealAudio are programs that allow you to listen to music and other audio broadcasts on the Internet. While these programs are relatively benign, both of them have been shown to consume an inordinate amount of network bandwidth. This problem has resulted in many network administrators banning them from the network. The only problem with this is that both products now are capable of using HTTP to listen to broadcasts as well as their native protocol. So, if you are looking to block Liquid Audio or RealAudio from your network, you will need to not only block the ports used by each program's native protocol, but also watch network utilization to spot users who are trying to get around your ban by using them with HTTP. Pointcast is a tool that allows users to receive customized stock quotes and news from servers located on the Internet. However, Pointcast has been banned from many networks—despite its usefulness—because it frequently consumes too much network bandwidth.

Common Network Protocols And Their Ports

The following is a list of common network protocols that you will find in use on the Internet and some security suggestions for them. While this is not a complete list of all the protocols and port numbers, it does cover many of the most popular protocols that you will encounter.

- *SMTP*—Uses TCP port 25 to send and receive email. This is a well-known port and should only be made available to and from your mail server. IIS, by default, is installed with an SMTP server. Unless you are using it, you should block SMTP traffic to this SMTP server or use the custom IIS install to prevent its installation.

- *POP*—Uses either TCP port 109, for POP version 2, or 110, for POP version 3, depending on the version of POP server that is installed on the mail server. There is no POP version 1.

- *IMAP*—Uses either TCP port 143 for IMAP version 2 mail servers, or port 220 for mail servers using IMAP version 3. There is no IMAP version 1.

- *HTTP*—Uses TCP and UDP port 80 to communicate with Web servers and browsers.

- *HTTPS*—Uses TCP and UDP port 443 to conduct secure communications with Web servers and browsers. You will need to open this port if you want your users to access secure Web sites or if you wish to create a secure Web site for your clients.

- *Microsoft Instant Messenger*—Uses TCP port 1863 outgoing and gets traffic back on a random TCP port between 1024 and 65535.

- *America Online Instant Messenger and the AOL service*—Use TCP port 5190 to send information and then expects to receive traffic back on a random port between 1024 and 65535.

- *ICQ*—Uses UDP port 4000 to send and receive data.

- *Liquid Audio*—Uses either TCP port 18888 for outbound and UDP port 18888 for inbound data, or TCP port 18888 for outbound data and UDP port 18888 for inbound and outbound data. The liquid audio players and server can also be configured to work using TCP port 80.

- *RealAudio and Real Video*—Use TCP ports 554 and 7070-7071 or UDP ports 6770-7170 to send and receive data from either RealAudio/Video servers or users. Real recommends that you use UDP if possible for best performance.

- *Network News Transport Protocol (NNTP)*—Uses TCP port 119 to send and receive information from Newsgroup servers located on the Internet.

- *NetBIOS and Windows Remote Procedure Calls*—Use TCP and UDP ports 135-139. If you wish to make sure that people on the Internet cannot easily interfere with the Windows 2000 computers on your network, you must block these ports so they cannot be accessed from the Internet.

Troubleshooting

Troubleshooting problems connecting your Macintosh to Microsoft BackOffice and the Internet requires that you look at both your software and network configurations.

This section is broken into three basic sections: problems connecting to SQL server, problems with Microsoft Exchange, and problems connecting to the Internet. In each of these sections, we will cover a variety of the most common problems that you may encounter when implementing the solutions that we have described in this chapter.

Resolving Problems Encountered When Connecting To Microsoft SQL Server

Setting up the ODBC connector and configuring both your Macintosh-based application and the SQL server database can be a fairly detailed process. The first thing that you need to do before starting to deploy your solution is to talk to the database administrator and collect all the information that you will need.

For example, to create the user data source name, you will need the name of the server, the name of the database, and the username and password that are needed to access the database. You also need to make sure that the database administrator has set up the database to support your user data source name and configured everything properly. Once you have finished doing this, you can proceed to the actual implementation.

Here are some of the common problems that you will likely encounter when connecting your Macintosh OS application to a Microsoft SQL server via ODBC:

- *When creating the ODBC connector, you may sometimes encounter a problem when trying to select the server that hosts the database you wish to access*—The first thing that you should check is that the network library is set to use TCP/IP. If that setting is correct, you will need to check with the database administrator to make sure that database is set up so that it is visible as a data source. If both of these are set up correctly, then you should take a look at the network troubleshooting discussion in Chapter 9 to make sure that the Macintosh can see the server hosting the SQL server database.

- *Another common problem that you will likely encounter involves authenticating the username and password against a remote database*—The first thing that you should check when having problems authenticating against your database is to verify with the database administrator that you have the proper username and password. Pay special attention to the password, as it will frequently contain a mix of upper- and lowercase letters as well as some special characters mixed in to make the password more difficult to hack. If the username and password are still rejected, check to see if the database is using Windows 2000 to authenticate the username and password or if it is a user account that has been created inside SQL server. If you are using Windows 2000 authentication, make sure that the username has the Windows 2000 domain added to the front of the username. For example "Niflheim\Pieter" would be the username used instead of just "Pieter".

- *You have trouble viewing the data after you have set up your ODBC connector and hooked up to the database*—The first thing that you should check is the database itself. Contact the database administrator to make sure that the database is set up correctly and actually contains data. Also, have her check to see that the user you are connecting to the database has the proper rights to see the data. If the user is set up properly, then check to see that the ODBC connector you are using properly supports the version of SQL server that you are using. Some older ODBC connectors work fine with one version of SQL server, but will fail when trying to fetch data from a newer version of SQL server. If this is the case, you will need to make sure that you have the proper version of ODBC connector.

Resolving Problems When Connecting To Microsoft Exchange Server

When starting to troubleshoot problems connecting Microsoft Outlook to the Exchange server, you need to make sure that you have the correct setup information. You will want to make sure that you know the name and IP address of the Exchange server that houses the mailbox as well as the username, password, and domain that the mailbox is configured to use. The following are some common problems that you may encounter when connecting to Exchange from your Macintosh.

- *When setting up the connection to the Exchange server in the Outlook Settings Control Panel, you may find yourself having trouble verifying the mailbox configuration*—This is frequently caused when the Macintosh client is unable to reconcile the name of the Exchange server that you have entered to its IP address on the network. In many Windows 2000 networks, DNS is not used to register the names of servers and their IP addresses for non-WINS-capable operating systems such as Macintosh OS. To get around this, you can either enter the IP address of the Exchange server in place of the server name in the Outlook Settings or you can edit the Hosts file that is located in the System folder to add an entry for your Exchange server.

- *When setting up your Exchange calendar you may try to connect to a network calendar*—If you do, then you need to make sure that there is a Schedule+ calendar configured on the server you are trying to access. As the Macintosh version of Outlook is not capable of connecting to the Exchange network calendar used by the Windows users, attempting to connect to the calendar located on the Exchange server will frequently result in a connection failure.

  To use a network calendar, make sure that a Schedule+ network calendar is configured on the server or choose to use a local calendar file. In either case, you will still be able to retrieve all of your appointments stored on the Exchange server; you will only be able to view them in a graphical calendar format from the Schedule+ module.

- *Sometimes, you may find that you are unable to log into the Exchange server to collect your email*—When this happens, the first thing that you should do is make sure that your username, password, and domain name are all entered correctly. If they are, then the next thing that you should do is check your Windows 2000 domain account. You will also need to double-check if your account has become disabled due to too many failed login attempts.

Resolving Problems When Connecting To The Internet

Most problems that you will encounter when connecting to the Internet from your Macintosh are related to the configuration of either your Internet application or the TCP/IP Control Panel.

Before you start trying to isolate the source of your problem, you should make sure that you have the following information:

- IP address of the default gateway on your network subnet
- Subnet mask used on your subnet
- IP address of the proxy server or firewall used to connect you to the Internet

- IP address of the DNS server

- Port number of the proxy that you wish to use

Once you have this information, you will be ready to start the trouble-shooting process.

- *Sometimes, you will find that you cannot access certain Web sites because your Web browser says that they cannot be found*—This is usually due to either a misconfigured DNS server address in the TCP/IP Control Panel on your Macintosh or on the firewall or proxy server that you are using. If you are configuring DNS on your Macintosh, open the TCP/IP Control Panel and double-check that you have entered the proper DNS server IP address and the proper search domain name. This is the name of the domain that the DNS server you are connecting to is using. For example, if you use EarthLink Sprint for your Internet access, the search domain would need to be set to earthlink.net.

  If you do not configure a DNS server on your Macintosh, then you will need to talk to the network administrators about the DNS settings on the firewall and/or proxy server. Make sure that the DNS settings on these are set properly and that the search domains are also set correctly. If they are not, have them reset so that they are correct and then reboot the proxy server or firewall so that they pick up the new settings. If they are correct, you may wish to contact your Internet Service Provider to see if its DNS servers are configured correctly. One note of caution is that DNS on the Internet is not always accurate due to the fact that updates can take days to propagate through the various DNS servers that control name resolution on the Internet.

- *Another common problem occurs when you try to use an application through a SOCKS proxy*—The first thing that you should check are the proxy settings in either the Configuration Manager Control Panel or in the application's preferences. Make sure that the IP address and port number of the SOCKS proxy are set correctly. If they are, then you need to make sure that the Macintosh can talk to the proxy server over the network.

  If you are using the same proxy server as your Web proxy, using a browser can be a good quick test of the proxy server. If you can reach the proxy server, then you should check with the systems administrator to make sure that the SOCKS proxy is running and properly configured. One note of caution: some applications, notably early editions of Fetch 3.0, had SOCKS support built in, but it is not functional. If you are having trouble, make sure that your application really is capable of using a SOCKS proxy.

- *One problem that you may encounter when running Microsoft Proxy server or Winroute Pro as a firewall is that it will suddenly lose its connection to the Internet after a set period of time*—This problem is usually due to a misconfigured port filter on the proxy server. In cases where Microsoft Proxy Server is connected to an Internet Service Provider by either a dial-up connection or other type of connection that relies upon DHCP to provide it with an IP address, the DHCP server will set the expiration time of the IP address lease to a fairly short period of time. This allows the server to quickly reclaim IP addresses that are no longer in use. The downside to this is that the proxy server must continually be communicating with the DHCP server so that it can renew its IP address. If the port filters on the proxy server are configured to block access to UDP ports 67 and 68, the proxy server will be unable to talk to the DHCP server, and thus, will be unable to renew its IP address. This causes the server to lose its IP address after a certain period of time, and thus, its connection to the Internet.

  To resolve this problem, reconfigure the port filter on the proxy server to allow UDP traffic on ports 67 and 68. To improve security, you might try limiting this traffic from the ISP's DHCP server; however, this is a bit risky, because the ISP may move its DHCP server to another IP address without warning.

- *Misconfigured port filters are always something that you should check when trying to connect to the Internet using a new application*—Many applications, such as Liquid Audio, ICQ, AOL, and others, use special TCP or UDP ports to communicate over the Internet. If your firewall is configured to block these ports for security purposes, you will need to talk to your systems administrator about opening them up so that you can use your new application.

NOTE: *Before you examine the situation, it is a good idea to have a listing of all the TCP and UDP ports that need to be opened and in which direction they should be opened—into the network or out from the network. By consulting on this information, you can quickly check the sources of a potential problem.*

Glossary

10BaseT—The designation for standard 10Mbs Ethernet run over twisted pair network cable. 10BaseT is the most common form of Ethernet available today and has largely supplanted the other forms of Ethernet: Thicknet and Thinnet. 10BaseT utilizes either Category 3 or Category 5 four-pair twisted pair wire to send data up to 100 meters without the need for a repeater. The followup to 10BaseT is the newer 100BaseTX, which sends data at 100Mbs per second over Category 5 twisted pair cable. As the cost of 100BaseT network adapters and the associated hubs and switches continues to drop, expect that 100BaseTX will replace 10BaseT. On the horizon is 1000BaseT, also known as Gigabit Ethernet.

access list—A series of commands that determines what network traffic is either allowed or denied by the network interfaces on a router. Access lists can also be used to determine if certain information about a network will be distributed to the other routers on the network. In addition, they can shape the traffic on the network by directing certain types of traffic through specific network interfaces.

Address Resolution Protocol (ARP)—The network protocol that computers use when they wish to determine what network address is associated with a computer's Internet Protocol (IP) address. When a computer attempts to determine which computer on the local network segment is using a given IP address, it sends out an ARP broadcast with the IP address of the destination computer and the computer making the request. The computer that is using the IP address in question then replies to the requesting computer with the address of its network adapter. Once this conversation has completed, the two computers can communicate with each other.

Address Resolution Protocol (ARP) cache—Where Internet Protocol (IP) addresses are mapped to network adapter addresses after the initial ARP conversation has taken place. The entries in this cache are usually set to time out after a set period of time so that you can change the IP addresses of the various computers on the network without traffic being sent to the wrong computer by mistake.

America Online (AOL)—The largest Internet Service Provider (ISP) in the world, with over 18 million members. Headquartered in Vienna, Virginia, AOL provides Internet access to users across the world.

AppleShare—The name of Apple Computer's server software for Macintosh operating system (OS)-based computers. Like Windows NT Server, AppleShare lets users on the AppleTalk network log into it and then upload and download files from it.

AppleTalk—A network protocol developed by Apple Computer in the mid-1980s to provide networking services for Macintosh operating system (OS) computers. AppleTalk is available in two forms: AppleTalk Phase 1, which was developed in 1984, and AppleTalk Phase 2, which was released in 1988 to address many of the issues that plagued AppleTalk Phase 1. AppleTalk is available on all Macintosh-based computers and provides a quick and simple workgroup networking solution that can be set up in minutes.

AppleTalk Data Stream Protocol (ADSP)—The network protocol used by AppleTalk Phase 2 to move large blocks of data over the network. ADSP is most commonly seen on the network when you are copying files to and from file servers or backing up files over the network using Retrospect or some other backup utility.

AppleTalk Link Access Protocol (LAP)—The part of the AppleTalk network protocol that governs the transmission of data packets between two AppleTalk-based computers on the same network segment.

AppleTalk Phase 1—Was first introduced in 1984 as a quick and easy way to network Macintosh computers. Unfortunately, AppleTalk Phase 1 networks are limited to only 127 computers per network.

AppleTalk Phase 2—Was introduced in 1988 to address the limitations of AppleTalk Phase 1. Unlike AppleTalk Phase 1, AppleTalk Phase 2 networks can have up to 65,298 network segments, known as zones, and can have up to 254 AppleTalk devices per zone.

AppleTalk Transaction Protocol (ATP)—A reliable, connection-based transport protocol that supports file services of the AppleTalk Filing Protocol and print services provided by the Printer Access Protocol (PAP). For a good analogy, think of ATP as being the AppleTalk equivalent of Transmission Control Protocol (TCP).

AppleTalk Update-Based Routing Protocol (AURP)—The default AppleTalk routing protocol used on AppleTalk Phase 2 networks to distribute routing information between non-contiguous AppleTalk networks.

AppleTalk zones—A means to allow more AppleTalk devices on the same network segment than would normally be permitted by the limit of 254 AppleTalk devices per network. AppleTalk zones are also used in a manner somewhat like Windows workgroups, in that all the computers in a specific AppleTalk zone can see all the resources that are available on that zone.

auditing—An option available on Windows NT and Windows 2000 that allows you to log specific events on the server or workstation. By configuring auditing, you can track who created, modified, or deleted a specific file or who printed a file on the printer attached to your Windows NT or 2000 computer. The downside to auditing is that the logs and the stress it places on the server can become a problem if you are not judicious with your choice about what you audit and the detail you demand.

auxiliary port—On a Cisco router, the secondary serial port on the router used to access the router while it is in operation. By connecting a PC or Macintosh to the auxiliary port on the Cisco router using a serial cable, and then using a terminal program like ZTerm, you can directly access the command line interface (CLI) of the router as well as upload and download files to it.

binary numbers—A way to represent numerical values using a combination of 1s and 0s called bits. In most computers, numbers are represented by a block of 1s and 0s called bytes, which contain 8, 16, or 32 bits. For example, the number 5 is represented by 00000011. In this example, the first bit on the right-hand side of the byte is equal to 2^0, the next one is equal to 2^1, and so on, until you get to the last bit, whose value is equal to 2^7. By adding up all the 1s in the byte, you can get any number between 0 and 255.

bindings—The Windows NT and Windows 2000 abstraction that connects network protocols to specific interfaces and influences in what order they are accessed. By changing the order of the protocols and their bindings to the network adapter, you can influence the performance of each protocol on the network. You can also use bindings to limit what protocol is available on what network interface by selectively connecting and disconnecting a given protocol from the various network adapters.

Bootstrap Protocol (BOOTP)—A system used to distribute Internet Protocol (IP) addresses to computers on the network that need them. Computers that request an IP address send out a broadcast asking for an IP address from the BOOTP server. The BOOTP server then responds to the requesting computer with an IP address. BOOTP has largely faded in importance as Dynamic Host Configuration Protocol (DHCP) has become more widespread.

byte—The basic object of data that a computer uses. A byte, in a modern computer, consists of 8 or more bits, 1s or 0s that represent a binary number. *See also* binary numbers.

cable range—The numbers that you use when setting up AppleTalk zones on the network. The cable range that you assign to a network segment is then used to determine what number is assigned to a specific zone on that network segment. The total number of zones on the network is limited to the number of zones specified by the cable range.

caches—In network setups, areas in a router or computer where information is stored for fast retrieval. Caches are usually associated with data that is frequently used and thus must be readily available to the computer. Good examples of caches are the ARP cache, which stores information on what Internet Protocol (IP) address maps to what network address, and routing caches, which keep track of where to send packets on the network.

Challenge Handshake Authentication Protocol (CHAP)—The secure system that authenticates users as they log into a computer. CHAP uses a challenge response system that encrypts your password as it is being sent to the computer you wish to log into. It then sends back an encrypted response that your computer decrypts and uses to grant you secure access to the various resources on the network.

checksum—A number that is calculated based upon the data in a packet or file. Checksums are looked at as the data is being examined after transmission to see if the checksum calculated before transmission and the checksum calculated after transmission are identical, indicating that the data did not get corrupted.

Chooser—A Macintosh operating system (OS) program that controls the Macintosh's networking and printer connections.

command-line interface (CLI)—A way of interacting with a computer or router using commands that you type in via a keyboard. Unlike with Windows or the Macintosh operating system (OS)—where most interaction with the computer is based upon menu selections and clicking on items with your mouse—a CLI demands that you type in the commands that you wish to use. Good examples of a CLI are Unix and the Cisco Internetwork Operating System (IOS).

Compact Disc Read-Only Memory (CD-ROM)—A variant of the music CD that stores computer data. CD-ROMs are used extensively these days to distribute large programs such as the various Windows operating systems (OSs) and other large software applications like Microsoft Office.

COM port—Used to allow your Windows-based PC to connect to other serial devices, such as the console ports or auxiliary ports on a Cisco router. Also known as a serial port.

computer browser—The portion of Windows that displays what resources are on the network (such as printers and shared volumes) that are available to users in the Windows workgroup or Windows NT domain. On one computer in the workgroup or domain is a master browser, which actively scans the network for new resources and then distributes this information to the other computer browsers on the network.

computer name—The Network Basic Input Output System (NetBIOS) name that is associated with the computer.

console port—On a Cisco router, the primary serial port on the router used to access the router while it is in operation. By connecting a PC or Macintosh to the console port on the Cisco router using a serial cable, and then using a terminal program like HyperTerminal, you can directly access the command-line interface (CLI) of the router as well as upload and download files to it.

counters—Used by computers and routers to keep track of network traffic and other resources. In a router, counters are most commonly used to keep track of the number of network packets that have been sent and received on a given network interface. Counters are also commonly used to record the number of errors that occurred, or anything else of interest to the router.

creator types—A 4-byte code assigned to a Macintosh file that determines the application program that created it. The Macintosh operating system (OS) uses creator codes to determine which application should be launched when a user attempts to open a specific file.

Data Source Name (DSN)—The name of the data source that you connect to when you configure an Open Database Connector (ODBC) connection to a database. Frequently, the DSN that you use when connecting to a specific database is the name of the database.

Glossary

Datagram Delivery Protocol (DDP) packets—The network packets that transport the data between AppleTalk devices on the network. DDP-1 packets transfer data between two AppleTalk devices on the same segment of the network. For data that is destined to an AppleTalk device off the current network segment, AppleTalk uses DDP-2 packets, which can be routed over the network.

DAVE—A tool from Thursby Software Systems, Inc. that allows the Macintosh to communicate using the Network Basic Input Output System (NetBIOS) protocol used on Windows-based networks. DAVE also provides Macintosh users with a variety of tools to access resources on the Windows-based network.

Digital Versatile Disk Read-Only Memory (DVD-ROM)—A variant of the DVD you use to watch your favorite movies, modified to store computer data. DVD-ROMs, with a total capacity of approximately 5.2GB, are used to store massive amounts of data that cannot fit on CD-ROMs. Examples of DVD-ROMs are games such as Baldur's Gate or the Microsoft TechNet technical reference library.

domain—The organization to which servers and computers belong. For example, **www.microsoft.com** is a computer in the **microsoft.com** domain. Like the Domain Name Service (DNS), which controls domain information on the Internet and your local network, Microsoft Active Directory is based upon the domain structure. See also *Domain Name Service* and *Microsoft Active Directory*.

Domain Name Service (DNS)—The service on the network that matches up a computer's domain name with its Internet Protocol (IP) address. DNS servers receive requests from computers on the network that request the IP address of a server using a specific Internet domain name. For example, when you type in "**http://www. microsoft.com**", your computer contacts a DNS server to get the IP address assigned to the computer named www.microsoft.com. It then takes the IP address it receives from the DNS server and uses it to connect to the remote computer.

Dynamic Host Configuration Protocol (DHCP)—A network protocol that automates the process of assigning Internet Protocol (IP) addresses and other network-specific information to computers that request them on the network. A DHCP server on the network responds to requests from a computer on the network and then assigns an IP address to computers for a specified time. By only leasing the IP address to each computer, DHCP allows the IP addresses of computers that are no longer using them to be reclaimed and redistributed to other computers on the network.

Dynamic Host Configuration Protocol (DHCP) options—Settings that allow you to distribute network-specific configuration information—such as the Internet Protocol (IP) addresses of the Windows Internet Naming System (WINS) servers on your network, or the Network Basic Input Output System (NetBIOS) node type being used on the network—along with the IP address that the DHCP server distributes.

Dynamic Host Configuration Protocol (DHCP) scope—The Internet Protocol (IP) address ranges that you specify for the DHCP servers to distribute to computers that request an IP address.

duplex—The way that a computer transmits and receives traffic on the network. Half-duplex mode means that a computer must wait for all transmissions to it to cease before it starts sending data out. Full-duplex means that a computer can send and receive data at the same time. 10Mbs Ethernet is normally half-duplex, which means that it can only send or receive data, not do both at the same time. 100Mbs or Fast Ethernet supports full-duplex, allowing a computer to send and receive data at 100Mbs each way, bringing the actual throughput up to 200Mbs per second.

Enhanced Internetwork Gateway Routing Protocol (EIGRP)—A proprietary Cisco routing protocol that can distribute routing information about AppleTalk, Transmission Control Protocol/Internet Protocol (TCP/IP), or Internetwork Packet Exchange/Sequenced Packet Exchange (IPX/SPX) routes on the network. EIGRP is normally the preferred routing protocol when you will be distributing routing information only between Cisco equipment.

Ethernet—Was developed in the 1970s by Bob Metcalfe at Xerox PARC as a way to provide a high-speed connection between computers and printers. Over the years, Ethernet has become the principal network technology that links computers and other network-based devices on the local area network (LAN). Ethernet is most commonly seen in two varieties these days: standard Ethernet, which moves data at 10Mbs a second, and Fast Ethernet, which moves data at 100Mbs a second. Although not commonly available today, Gigabit Ethernet, which moves data at 1 billion bits of data a second, is starting to become more available and should be in common usage sometime in the next few years.

ETYPE—The type of Ethernet you are using. The various types of Ethernet that you are likely to encounter include Thick Ethernet, Thin Ethernet, 10BaseT, or Twisted Pair Ethernet and Fast Ethernet.

Glossary

Fast Ethernet—The version of Ethernet that transfers data at 100Mbs a second in half-duplex mode. Fast Ethernet can operate in full-duplex mode as well, so actual throughput using Fast Ethernet can reach 200Mbs a second.

File Allocation Table (FAT)—The original file system used by MS-DOS and the subsequent Windows operating systems, until the development of Windows NT. Hard drives formatted with FAT can see volumes with up to 2GB of data. To utilize partitions larger than 2GB, you must use either utilities that extend the FAT file system or the new FAT-32 file system developed for Windows 95 and Windows 98 (if you are using Windows NT, use the NT File System [NTFS file system]).

file extensions—The three-character suffixes on MS-DOS and Windows files that tell Windows what type of data the file contains. For example, a .doc file extension tells Windows that the file in question is a Microsoft Word document.

File Transfer Protocol (FTP)—Used to move files across the Internet, usually from a remote server to your desktop computer. FTP is commonly used to move files larger than 1MB because it is a more efficient protocol for moving data than Hypertext Transfer Protocol (HTTP). FTP uses Transmission Control Protocol (TCP) port 21 to send FTP commands between the sending and receiving computers, and a randomly assigned TCP port above 1024 to actually transfer the data. The most common FTP application on the Macintosh is known as Fetch.

file types—The 4-byte code that tells the Macintosh operating system (OS) what type of data is contained in the file. For example, a file type of TEXT indicates that the file contains text.

firewalls—Computers or routers that are configured to act as a gateway between your local area network (LAN) and the Internet. Firewalls can be anything from a Cisco router with some access lists applied to the interface that is connected to the Internet, to a Windows NT Server that runs firewall software such as Tiny Software's Winroute Pro, or even a dedicated computer such as the Cisco PIX firewall. By limiting the access that computers on the Internet have to your LAN, the firewall protects you from attack and intrusion by hackers and other unfriendly folks.

flags—Used by various operating systems (OSs) and programs to indicate specific conditions and settings.

gateway—A computer or router that directs traffic off the current network segment and out to the rest of the network.

hexadecimal numbers—Another method of describing the numeric value of a byte. Hexadecimal values are based upon base 16 math, where numbers range from 0 through F. To display the full value of a byte, you use two hexadecimal numbers. For example, to represent a byte with the value of 255, type FF. See also *binary numbers*.

HFS+—The upgrade to the Macintosh file system that increases the number of files that can be supported on a Mac drive, thus reducing the minimum file size on larger devices. Similar to FAT-32 under Windows. Sometimes known as Mac OS Extended.

Hierarchical File System (HFS)—The standard system for organizing files on the Macintosh operating system (OS). Similar to FAT-16 on the Windows platform. Sometimes known as Mac OS Standard.

HOSTS—A file located on a Windows- or Macintosh-based PC that contains the Internet Protocol (IP) addresses and the domain names of the computers on your network. This file allows the computer to resolve a computer's name to its IP address in the absence of a Domain Name Service (DNS) server.

Hypertext Transfer Protocol (HTTP)—The Internet Protocol (IP) network protocol that is used to move data from Web servers to your Web browser. HTTP utilizes Transmission Control Protocol (TCP) port 80 to send and receive information from a Web server and then to send back information to the Web server, allowing you to interact with it. It is a connectionless protocol, meaning that it sends or receives one piece of information and then closes down the connection. Although this made sense with small amounts of data like that present on the early Web pages, as Web pages grew, performance was apt to suffer. To improve HTTP's performance, HTTP version 1.1, which allowed whole Web pages to be downloaded without breaking the connection, was developed.

Hypertext Transfer Protocol Security (HTTPS)—The version of HTTP which uses Secure Sockets Layer (SSL) encryption when you are sending and receiving data from secure Web servers. HTTPS normally uses Transmission Control Protocol (TCP) port 443 to send and receive information. HTTPS can use either 40- or 128-bit encryption, depending on where the browser or the server is located.

HyperTerminal—The default terminal program that comes with Windows 95, Windows 98, and Windows NT.

ICQ—An instant message protocol that sends instant messages across the Internet. A related protocol, ICQW, also allows users to see when others are connected to the Internet and to set up multi-person conversations across the Internet.

Instant Messenger—A program from America Online (AOL) that sends instant messages across the Internet. This program also allows users to see when others are connected to the Internet and to set up one-on-one conversations with them. Special "branded" versions of Instant Messenger are provided by such companies as EarthLink, Netscape (a subsidiary of AOL), and MindSpring (which is in the process of being combined with EarthLink). Microsoft's variation on the instant messaging theme is called MSN Messenger. *See also* MSN Messenger.

Internet Control Message Protocol (ICMP)—The network protocol used to communicate message flow and error correction information between two computers. ICMP is also used by such tools as Ping and Traceroute to send and receive messages to and from the destination and host computer.

Internet Message Access Protocol (IMAP)—A network protocol that allows users to access and retrieve email from mail servers on both the local network and the Internet. Due to its modern design, IMAP is rapidly becoming the email client protocol of choice on many networks.

Internet Protocol (IP)—The network protocol that is used to send information over the Internet. IP was developed in the 1970s by Vincent Cerf and others to provide a reliable method of transferring data over the Internet. IP can send network traffic over many network media, from low-speed serial connections to multi-gigabit fiber connections.

Internet Protocol (IP) address—A unique address that is composed of 4 bytes. Class A addresses (1-126.x.x.x) use the first byte in the address to specify on which network the computer is located. Class B addresses (129-191.x.x.x) use the first 2 bytes of the address to define what the network is. Class C addresses (192-225.x.x.x), the most commonly assigned these days, use the first 3 bytes to assign the network to which the address is assigned.

Internet Protocol (IP) protocol types—The types of transport protocols that are defined on top of IP. These transport protocols include ones for data transfer—such as Transmission Control Protocol (TCP) and Universal Datagram Protocol (UDP)—and protocols like Generic Routing Encapsulation (GRE) that can be used for secure communication between servers or networks.

Internet Relay Chat (IRC)—A set of client software and servers that allows groups of users from all across the world to have interactive conversations in real time. Users who want to join an IRC chat use an IRC client to connect to server networks on the Internet. Once connected to one of the many IRC networks, users can create or join conversations on just about every subject known to man.

Internet Service Providers (ISPs)—The companies that provide users with a connection to the Internet. From huge ISPs such as America Online (AOL) to small local operations such as Teleport.com, ISPs allow users to dial up and connect to the Internet from their home or office.

Internetwork Operating System (IOS)—The operating system that all Cisco routers use. IOS allows you to control all aspects of the router, and the network traffic that flows through it.

Internetwork Packet Exchange (IPX)—The network protocol used on Novell-based networks to exchange data between workstations and servers. Like Internet Protocol (IP), IPX is a routable protocol in which IPX packets can be directed over the network from one network segment to another via routers and other network devices. Although IPX is a very good protocol, it has been largely supplanted, even on Novell networks, by IP.

IPHelper—The command used in a Cisco router's configuration that allows it to forward Boot Protocol (BOOTP) and Dynamic Host Configuration Protocol (DHCP) requests from one network segment to another segment on the same network.

JetDirect—The trade name of a series of network cards and their associated software created by Hewlett-Packard for use with its DeskJet and LaserJet printers. JetDirect cards provide the printer with an Ethernet port and allow it to send and receive data from a server or workstation that is configured to host the printer.

link—The indicator on both the network switch and adapter card that indicates that you have a completed circuit between the computer that houses the network controller and the network switch or hub that it is connected to.

Liquid Audio—A network transport that transfers audio information over the Internet. Liquid Audio is used by a variety of music-oriented sites on the Internet and maximizes the quality of the sound.

Glossary

LMHOSTS—A file located on your Windows-based PC or on a Macintosh-based computer with DAVE installed that contains the Internet Protocol (IP) addresses and the Network Basic Input Output System (NetBIOS) names of the computers on your network. This file allows the computer to resolve a computer's name to its IP address in the absence of a Windows Internet Naming Service (WINS) server.

local area networks (LANs)—High-speed networks, either in a single building or multiple buildings at a single site. LANs are almost always connected by some sort of high-speed networking infrastructure such as Ethernet.

LPT port—Used to allow your Windows-based PC to connect to other parallel port devices, such as a laser or inkjet printer. Also known as a parallel port.

Microsoft Active Directory—The new directory services technology that has been built into Windows 2000. Unlike the previous Windows NT domain model, which was limited to about 10,000 users or computers per domain, Active Directory handles an effectively infinite number of users and computers in its directory structure. For more information on Active Directory, visit **www.microsoft.com**.

Microsoft Challenge Handshake Authentication Protocol (MS CHAP)—The secure system that authenticates users as they log into a Windows-based computer. MS CHAP uses a challenge response system that encrypts your username and password as it is being sent to the Windows-based computer you wish to log into. It then sends back an encrypted response that your computer decrypts and uses to grant you secure access to the various resources on the network.

MSN Messenger—Microsoft's version of an instant messaging program. See also *Instant Messenger.*

name server port—The Transmission Control Protocol (TCP) port number used by Windows to distribute name server information from either Windows Internet Naming Service (WINS) servers or broadcasts on the network.

native address translation (NAT)—A system that allows packets originating from computers that use private Internet Protocol (IP) addresses to be modified so that they appear to be coming from a computer with a valid IP address on the Internet. Proxy servers such as Winroute Pro and Winroute Lite handle multiple connections to the Internet, all mapped through a single IP address.

Glossary

NetWare—The networking operating system produced by Novell. Although not as popular as it once was, NetWare is still commonly found running many business and school networks.

network adapter—The piece of electronics that connects a computer to the local area network (LAN). One example of a network adapter is the Ethernet port that is included on all current Apple computers (such as the iBook, iMac, PowerBook, and Power Macintosh) and many modern Windows-based PCs. Other types of network adapters include Token Ring, an older IBM network system, and LocalTalk, the original network solution that Apple developed for inclusion with the Macintosh.

Network Basic Input Output System (NetBIOS)—The system that Windows-based PCs use to exchange information and data over the network. Although Windows NT and Windows 2000 can use NetBIOS, they do not need it when communicating among themselves. NetBIOS is needed only to support legacy versions of Windows, such as 3.1, 95, and 98.

Network Basic Input Output System (NetBIOS) name cache—The cache on a Windows-based PC that stores the mappings of NetBIOS names to Internet Protocol (IP) addresses that it has learned previously.

Network Basic Input Output System (NetBIOS) node types—The various NetBIOS name resolution behaviors that you can configure workstations and servers to utilize. You can choose from the following NetBIOS node types: B-Type, M-Type, H-Type, and P-Type.

network browser—The application on your Windows-based PC that goes out and looks at the local network to see what servers, workstations, or other network resources are available for your workstation or server to connect to and use. A similar program became available on the Macintosh beginning with Mac OS 8.5, and was expanded with Mac OS 9 to include networking via Transmission Control Protocol/Internet Protocol (TCP/IP) across the Internet.

network hubs—Small electrical devices that connect several network connections. In order to prevent signal loss, Ethernet hubs, for example, amplify the network signal so that it does not become degraded as it goes through the hub to its destination. The downside to hubs is that they connect all the computers on the network and thus frequently cause performance degradation due to packet collisions.

Glossary

Network Monitor—The sniffer program that comes bundled with Window NT or Windows 2000. The version of Netmon that comes with Windows NT and Windows 2000 is limited to seeing only network traffic that originates from or comes to the server upon which it is installed. The version of Netmon that ships with Microsoft's Systems Management Server (SMS) does not have this limitation and can examine all the traffic that it intercepts.

Network Monitor Driver—The Windows NT and Windows 2000 network component that actually intercepts network packets destined for or sent by the computer. The Network Monitor program then examines these intercepted packets so that network problems can be quickly and easily identified.

Network Newsgroups Transfer Protocol (NNTP)—The network protocol that newsgroup servers use to distribute information on one newsgroup server to other newsgroup servers on the Internet. In addition, newsreader programs use NNTP when they connect to the news server and read the newsgroup messages on it.

network numbers—The numbers you use when setting up AppleTalk zones on the network. The network numbers that you assign to a network segment are then used to determine what number is assigned to a specific zone on that network segment. The total number of zones on the network is limited to the number of zones specified by the network numbers.

network segment—The portion of the network that is connected to a router. Network segments can range from a small two- or three-host network connected to an interface on a router to a large switched network with hundreds of computers all connected to a series of switches and then a router.

network switches—Small network devices that connect several network connections. In order to prevent signal loss, network switches amplify the network signal so that it does not become degraded as it goes through the switch to its destination. Switches, unlike hubs, do not connect all the computers on the network and thus avoid performance degradation due to packet collisions because they create a connection directly between the source and the destination.

New Technology File System (NTFS)—The file system that the Windows NT operating system (OS) uses. Microsoft developed NTFS as a high-performance file system with greatly improved security over its previous file systems: File Allocation Table (FAT) or High Performance File System (HPFS).

New Technology File System (NTFS) security—The file security functionality that is built into the Windows NT file system.

newsgroups—Internet-based bulletin boards where users from all over the world can converse and share information regarding a variety of topics. If you are looking for technical information about a problem that you are having with a computer or your network, for instance, checking the appropriate newsgroups and/or posting a message may well get you an answer. Also called UseNet.

Open Database Connector (ODBC)—A cross-platform system that allows computers running a variety of operating systems (OSs) to connect to and access databases. Using an ODBC connector on a Macintosh, users can connect to a Structured Query Language (SQL) server database that is running on a Windows NT Server and then access the data stored on it.

Open Systems Interconnection (OSI) model—A seven-layer abstraction that is very useful when you are looking at the different portions of the network. Starting at the physical wire, the OSI model looks like this: Physical Layer, Data Link Layer, Protocol Layer, Transport Layer, Session Layer, Presentation Layer, and Application Layer. The Physical Layer refers to the actual network connection such as Ethernet or Token Ring. The Data Link Layer controls the interaction between the computer and the network. The Protocol Layer is where protocols like Internet Protocol (IP) and AppleTalk reside. The Transport Layer is where Transmission Control Protocol/ Universal Datagram Protocol (TCP/UDP), AppleTalk Data Streaming Protocol (ADSP), and the other network transport mechanisms reside. The Session Layer is where things like Hypertext Transfer Protocol (HTTP), File Transfer Protocol (FTP), and RealAudio reside. The Presentation Layer is where data encryption and data compression operations occur. Finally, the Application Layer is where Web browsers and other programs that you interact with reside.

organizational unit—A sub-domain in a Windows 2000 active directory. For example, an organizational unit in the widget.com domain would be **nwterritories.widget.com**. Thus, users in the organizational unit **nwterritories.widget.com** would be known as **user@ nwterritories.widget.com**.

packet filters—Usually access lists on a router or on a firewall that allow you to specify what types of network traffic are allowed to pass. The term "packet filter" is used because each network packet that the network interface sends or receives is examined and then accepted or rejected based upon the filters that you have placed on the interface.

Glossary

363

parallel printer interface—The principal connection you use when connecting a printer to a computer. The parallel printer port is also known as the LPT port.

Ping—The Packet Internet Groper (Ping) is a tool used to send Internet Control Message Protocol (ICMP) packets to a remote computer or other network device. Ping is a great tool when you want to see if the remote computer you are trying to connect to is not responding. By pinging the remote computer and then watching the time it takes for packets to come back (if they do at all), you can get an idea as to how far the remote server is on the network and if it is responding.

Pointcast—A streaming media application that allows users to see stock quotes and other information such as news and sports scores as a ticker tape on your desktop. Although popular with many Internet users, Pointcast can consume an inordinate amount of network bandwidth.

Post Office Protocol (POP)—The primary network protocol that mail servers use to distribute email to users across the network. Programs such as Eudora and Pine connect to the central email server using POP, and once they have logged on to the mail server, they can receive email that has been stored on the server waiting for the user to retrieve it.

PostScript—A page description language developed by Adobe Systems in the early 1980s to improve the print quality of documents coming out of printers. In PostScript, the contents of a page are reduced to mathematical calculations, and as such, PostScript, is commonly regarded as being "device independent." This means that the quality of the printed document depends on the capabilities of the output device. Over the last 15 years, PostScript has evolved into the primary printer description language used by many printers.

PostScript fonts—Mathematical descriptions of a font that a PostScript-based printer can use to print out an accurate copy of the font in any size simply by scaling the font up and down.

PostScript Printer Description (PPD) file—Files that are used to tell your computer how to communicate with a specific PostScript printer to support its special features. For example, a PPD may tell your computer that the printer has multiple paper trays and allow you to select among them. You normally encounter PPDs only on the Macintosh, and they must be installed on the Macintosh for them to work.

print queue—The service on the computer or server hosting the printer that stores print jobs as they are getting ready for the printer to print them. Setting access rights on the print queue is very important so that you do not allow inappropriate users to delete another users' print jobs as they are stored in the queue.

Printer Access Protocol (PAP)—The AppleTalk transport protocol that moves data to and from AppleTalk-based printers. PAP sends data to the printer that is printing your file as well as sends back information regarding the status of the printer and if there are any problems you should know about.

printer drivers—Programs that tell your computer how to communicate with the printers on your network. Depending on how you have set up the Windows NT Server that hosts the printer, the printer driver is automatically downloaded to any Windows-based PCs when you set up a connection to the printer.

printer pooling—A technique that allows you to set up a group or pool of printers so that they are seen as one. This technique allows you to purchase a number of inexpensive printers and set them up in a pool so that the print jobs being sent to them are distributed among them.

private Internet Protocol (IP) addresses—A set of three IP address ranges that have been reserved for use on private networks. These three IP ranges—10.x.x.x, 172.x.x.x, and 192.168.x.x—are non-routable IP addresses, meaning that any network traffic with a network address within these three ranges is not sent to the Internet. Thus, users on a network that uses these private addresses must convert the addresses that their workstations use to IP addresses that can be sent out onto the Internet. They do so by using a proxy server, among other methods.

QuickTime—Apple Computer's multimedia protocol, which supports a variety of audio and video compression methods to create and play back such productions. QuickTime is available in both Macintosh operating system (OS) and Windows versions.

QuickTime TV—A service of QuickTime, similar to RealAudio, in which streaming audio and video presentations can be viewed from the Internet. It competes with RealAudio.

RealAudio—A popular Internet-based multimedia streaming protocol that allows users with a RealAudio or RealVideo player to hear audio and video productions direct from a Web site. It competes with QuickTime TV, which offers a similar capability.

Glossary

Reflections—A Windows-based terminal program created by WRQ software. Reflections is one of the best and most capable terminal programs available for Windows-based computers.

Remote Procedure Calls (RPCs)—Inter-computer communications that allow one computer to initiate an action on another computer. RPCs can be as mundane as asking for information about a server, or they can be more complex, such as copying a file between two computers. Programs such as User Manager for Domains commonly use RPCs to communicate with the domain server and to enter the changes that you desire.

Reverse Address Resolution Protocol (RARP)—A system that allows a computer to make a request for information about its network address. RARP sends out a broadcast that contains its Ethernet address to the computers on the network, where a RARP server picks up the broadcast and matches the Ethernet address against a list of Internet Protocol (IP) addresses. Once it has found a match, it sends back a message telling the computer what its IP address is. One of the big downsides of RARP versus Dynamic Host Configuration Protocol (DHCP) or Boot Protocol (BOOTP) is that you have to have an RARP server on each subnet because the RARP broadcasts do not get routed over the network as do BOOTP or DHCP packets.

route cache—A cache that contains network routes learned by either a computer or a router. You can add routes to the route cache by listening to the routing information that is passed over the network by such protocols as Enhanced Internetwork Gateway Routing Protocol (EIGRP), which allows the various routers on your network to distribute information on how to get from one part of the network to another and how long it takes to get there. Based on this information, a router can decide the most efficient path by which it should be sending the network traffic.

router—A specialized computer whose sole purpose is to move network traffic from one network segment to another. Routers can be of all shapes and sizes, from a simple NT Server to an extremely powerful dedicated router such as the Cisco 12000. Although an NT or Windows 2000 server might be able to handle the routing needs of a small network, it is not suited to the demands of a medium-sized business, let alone a large one.

Routing and Remote Access snap-in (RRA)—The Windows NT and Windows 2000 component that adds basic routing capabilities along with an enhanced remote access server. RRA can turn your Windows NT or Windows 2000 server into a general-purpose router.

Routing Information Protocol (RIP)—A general-purpose routing protocol used by almost every router available on the market, from a top-of-the-line Cisco 12000 to a simple NT router. RIP is a very simple routing protocol and does not carry extensive information regarding the paths that you can take to get data from point a to point b.

routing protocols—The communications protocols that routers use to distribute information about the network routes that they know. Two of the more common routing protocols are Routing Information Protocol (RIP) and Enhanced Internetwork Gateway Routing Protocol (EIGRP). To choose the proper routing protocol for your network, check with your router vendor.

RRAS—*See* Routing and Remote Access Server.

seed routing—The seeding of an AppleTalk network with a network number, also known as a cable range. By seeding the AppleTalk network's cable range, the Windows NT Server allows you to create zones on AppleTalk Phase 2 networks.

Sequenced Packet Exchange (SPX)—The transport protocol used by many Novell servers that support IPX/SPX. SPX is very similar to Transmission Control Protocol (TCP) in the Transmission Control Protocol/Internet Protocol (TCP/IP) network model. Although SPX is still used in many networks, it cannot be routed over the Internet and is being gradually replaced by TCP/IP.

serial printer interface—Sends data 1 bit at a time to the printer. Serial ports are also frequently used to connect computers to modems and cameras. Frequently known as COM ports.

Service Advertising Protocol (SAP)—A Novell protocol that identifies the services—such as printers and shared volumes—available on a network.

service packs—Updates that Microsoft and others release from time to time in order to fix bugs and add capabilities to their products. When you are working on Windows-based computers, it is very important to know what service packs are installed and which ones are needed to support the various options that you want.

Simple Mail Transfer Protocol (SMTP)—The network protocol that transfers mail between mail servers over the Internet. SMTP is a text-based protocol that runs over Transmission Control Protocol/Internet Protocol (TCP/IP) on port 25.

Glossary

Glossary

sniffer—A computer or a piece of software that records, analyzes, and then displays information about traffic on the network. Sniffers such as Netmon allow your computer to listen to the traffic being transmitted over the network and then pick out the traffic you are looking for. By looking at the traffic, you can then help isolate problem elements on your network.

sockets—A logical abstraction that programs connect to when utilizing the network. When a program connects to a network socket, it connects into the network subsystem that is present on the computer. It can then send and receive information from the network and other network-based applications.

SOCKS proxy—A standardized way for network-based applications to redirect their traffic so that it can be forwarded off the current network. SOCKS, like Winsock, is designed so that network traffic from a computer is directed to a proxy server which is connected to the Internet or another segment of the network. The proxy server then relays the network traffic to the Internet and then back again to the originating computer.

spooler—A program on the printer or on the server controlling the printer that stores up print jobs until the printer is ready to print them. A printer spooler allows multiple users to print to a printer all at the same time and then to have each printer job be stored and printed in the order that it came in. Some spooler programs prioritize the order in which print jobs are actually printed, based upon who has sent them and the priority that was assigned to them.

Structured Query Language (SQL)—A standardized command protocol that is used to query databases. SQL was developed by IBM in the mid-1970s and then commercialized in the late 1970s by Oracle. Microsoft SQL Server uses a dialect of SQL that is slightly different from the standard version; it contains several proprietary extensions developed by Microsoft to improve the performance of the database.

StuffIt—A data-compression program used on Macintosh-based computers. Stuffed files are compressed using mathematical algorithms to reduce the space that the files take up on the computer. Stuffed files are commonly sent over the Internet because they can check themselves for consistency when the file is being unstuffed. Similar to the ZIP protocol on the DOS and Windows platforms.

Systems Management Server (SMS)—A set of tools developed by Microsoft to distribute software to computers over the network and to perform a variety of other administrative functions over the network. Properly configured, SMS can allow a single administrator to distribute and install software to computers all over the network as well as to perform a variety of configuration and management functions remotely.

Telnet—A text-based network protocol that operates on Transmission Control Protocol (TCP) port 23. Telnet is frequently used when one wants to communicate with a computer or router on the network that uses a command-line interface (CLI). Telnet is the preferred tool to use when you are connecting to routers on the network because it allows you to connect to any router on the network from one workstation. You can also use Telnet programs to connect to other TCP ports, such as port 25—Simple Mail Transfer Protocol (SMTP)—to probe them, and see if the programs that use these ports are functioning as expected.

Transmission Control Protocol (TCP)—A connection-oriented network protocol that moves data over the local area network (LAN) or the Internet safely and reliably using Internet Protocol (IP). TCP relies upon a built-in error-correction system to identify problems in the transmission of data and to then correct them so that the file being transferred is transferred properly. TCP can also dynamically alter the speed of transmission to reflect changing network conditions or the load on either the sending or receiving computer.

TrueType—A printer technology that was developed in the 1980s and 1990s by Apple Computer as an alternative to Adobe's PostScript fonts. Like PostScript, TrueType describes fonts as mathematical expressions so that they can be scaled or manipulated without destroying the original font's proportions. Although originally designed for the Macintosh operating system (OS), it has actually become more popular on the Windows platform.

TrueType fonts—The default font types that are shipped with Macintosh- and Windows-based computers. Like PostScript fonts, TrueType fonts are mathematical representations of a given font and as such can be scaled up and down without losing the original font's proportions.

Universal Datagram Protocol (UDP)—A connectionless and unreliable Internet Protocol (IP)-based network protocol that is used to send small bits of information around the network or even over the Internet. Unlike Transmission Control Protocol (TCP), UDP does not have any error-correction mechanisms, nor can it dynamically adjust data flow to adapt to changing conditions. UDP is commonly used on networks to send small bits of information around the network or to send information that will not be degraded significantly if some of it is lost.

User Authentication Module (UAM)—A plug-in to the Chooser on a Macintosh that allows the Macintosh to securely connect to and authenticate with a Windows NT- or Windows 2000-based server using Challenge Handshake Authentication Protocol (CHAP).

Web Proxy—A standardized way for Web browsers and other applications that use Hypertext Transfer Protocol (HTTP) proxy to redirect their traffic so that it can be forwarded off the current network. Web proxies are designed so that network traffic from a computer is sent directly to the Web proxy that is connected to the Internet or another segment of the network. The Web proxy server then relays the network traffic to the Internet and then back again to the originating computer.

wide area network (WAN)—A network that spans more than one geographic area. WANs can include a network that is composed of several different offices spread out around town or a network that is spread out around the world. The common thread to all WANs is that the connections that bind each location are significantly slower than the connections that bind the servers and workstations at each location.

Windows Internet Naming Service (WINS)—A service on a Windows-based network that maps a computer's Internet Protocol (IP) address to its Network Basic Input Output System (NetBIOS) name. WINS is a service that you can install on any Windows NT Server. Once it is configured on the various workstations in your network, it automatically updates itself when computers are restarted. You can also configure WINS servers to exchange IP to NetBIOS mapping information with other WINS servers on the network, allowing WINS to function properly over a wide area network (WAN).

Windows workgroup—A loose association of Windows-based computers, each of which maintains its own list of users and groups. This means that, unless the share is set to allow access to everyone, or a user to have access to a server or workstation in the workgroup, he or she must have a user account on that server or workstation.

Windows workgroup groups—Groups that have been created on each member workstation or server that is in the workgroup. Although they can all be of the same name and have the same users listed within, the groups and the users they contain must be created locally on each workgroup server or workstation.

Windows NT domain—A collection of computers in a group whose organization and members are controlled by one or more computers known as domain controllers. Users in a Windows NT domain can connect to and authenticate against all of the servers and workstations in the same Windows NT domain or in a Windows NT domain that trusts the one the user belongs to. Having a central controlling authority for the Windows NT domain can allow you to centralize all of the user functions such as administering users and groups from any computer in the domain.

Windows NT domain controller—The central controlling authority for a given domain. The domain controller stores all of the user accounts and groups as well as records for all of the servers and workstations that are members of the domain. In each domain, there is a primary domain controller, which is the authoritative source for all information regarding the domain. Backing up the primary domain controller are backup domain controllers that contain exact copies of all the data on the primary domain controller and that can be turned into a primary domain controller if the primary domain controller fails.

Windows NT domain groups—Groups of users that are available to all the servers and workstations in the domain. By creating domain groups, administrators can create groups of users and then use these groups on the various servers and workstations in the domain to simplify administration and management.

Windows NT services—Optional operating system components that can be installed to provide specific functions. Windows NT services include such functions as a Domain Name Service, a Windows Internet Naming Server, or one of many other network and application services. Windows NT services can come from either Microsoft, as is the case of the services that are bundled with Windows NT, or a third-party software company.

Windows NT 4 Services for Macintosh—Network services that you can install on a Windows NT 4 Server to add Macintosh support to your Windows NT Server. Services for Macintosh adds AppleTalk to the list of protocols spoken by the server as well as adds printer sharing and file sharing capabilities, allowing the server to share printers and files with its Macintosh clients.

Winsock proxy—A Windows-based system for directing the traffic from network-based applications so that it can be forwarded off the current network. Winsock, like SOCKS, is designed so that network traffic from a computer is sent directly to a proxy server connected

Glossary

to the Internet or another segment of the network. The Winsock proxy server then relays the network traffic to the Internet and then back again to the originating computer.

wizards—Small programs in Windows 95, 98, NT, and 2000 that walk you through the process of setting up various Windows programs or components. You encounter wizards when you create a new printer connection or when you set up a new share volume under Windows 2000. By walking you through each step of the configuration procedure, wizards greatly simplify the configuration process.

ZIP—A compression program used on PCs, Macintoshes, and Unix-based computers. Zipped files are compressed using mathematical algorithms to reduce the space that the files take up on the computer. Zipped files are also frequently sent over the Internet because they can check themselves for consistency when the file is being expanded.

ZTerm—A shareware terminal program available for the Apple Macintosh family of computers. ZTerm offers most of the features you need in a terminal program. Being shareware, its price is quite reasonable.

Index

A

access-list commands, 101–102, 280–281

Access-lists. *See also* Permissions.
in configuring AppleTalk zones, 26
fine-tuning of AppleTalk, 110–113, 288–289
troubleshooting, 124

Access rights, 16, 210–211. *See also* Permissions.
customizing for multiple users, 43–47, 212–216
with Get Info window, 41–42
to printers, 59–60, 76–77, 233–239, 252

Accounts dialog box, 154, 155, 339

Adapters tab, in Network Control Panel, 19, 20

Add Printer Wizard, 53–54, 226–228
connecting to printers from Windows with, 72–74, 248–249
selecting printers with, 55–56, 228–232

Address configuration, 6

Address resolution cache. *See* Arp cache.

Address Resolution Protocol. *See* ARP.

ADSP, 84, 258–259

Advanced tab, in Properties page, 235, 236

Allow AppleTalk Access By Other Users, in printer configuration, 68

Allow Guests To Logon option, 30

Allow Workstations To Save Password option, 30

America Online. *See* AOL.

Antivirus software, email and, 157, 341

AOL, ports for, 343

AOL Instant Messenger, 158
ports for, 159, 343

Apple Macintosh computers. *See* Macintosh computers.

AppleShare file server, 15

appletalk access-group command, 99, 278

appletalk address command, 99, 278

appletalk cable-range command, 99–100, 278

AppleTalk commands, 103–104, 282
for displaying network data, 104–105, 282–284
enable mode, 103–105
for IOS AppleTalk administration, 101–103, 280–281, 281–284
for IOS AppleTalk configuration, 99–101, 277–279

Appletalk Data Stream Protocol. *See* ADSP.

appletalk discovery command, 100, 278

appletalk distribute-list command, 100, 278

appletalk event-logging command, 102, 281

appletalk getzonelist-filter command, 100, 278

AppleTalk language, 82–128
with Services for Macintosh, 17, 20

appletalk name-lookup-interval command, 102–103, 281

N

Windows 2000 Titles from Coriolis

Windows 2000 Server Architecture and Planning

By Morten Strunge Nielson
ISBN: 1-57610-436-2
$29.99 U.S. • $43.99 CAN

Discover the major capabilities of Windows 2000 Server, as well as Professional, and the fine points of the new Active Directory features. In-depth discussions on how to migrate or interoperate Windows 2000 from NT, NetWare, Unix, and various host systems are provided.

Windows 2000 Systems Programming Black Book

By Al Williams
ISBN: 1-57610-280-7
$49.99 U.S. • $74.99 CAN

Discusses crucial and little understood aspects of Windows 2000, such as multi-tasking, threading, alertable timers, APCs, and fibers. Also covers Active Directory Services, Microsoft Message Queue, over-lapped I/O, advanced memory management, networking, and security.

Windows 2000 Registry Little Black Book

By Nathan Wallace
ISBN: 1-57610-348-X
$24.99 U.S. • $37.99 CAN

Serves as a complete reference for any problem or change needed to Windows 2000 that requires manipulating the Registry. Covers Active Desktop, Asynchronous Transfer Mode, backup, encrypted file system, Internet printing, and more.

Windows 2000 Security Little Black Book

By Ian McLean
ISBN: 1-57610-387-0
$24.99 U.S. • $37.99 CAN

Discusses potential security holes in the Windows 2000 system and how to prevent them. Covers desktop security, as well as server security. Emphasizes security issues raised by high bandwidth connections to the Internet with and without firewalls.

Windows 2000 Reducing TCO Little Black Book

By Robert E. Simanski
ISBN: 1-57610-315-3
$24.99 U.S. • $37.99 CAN

Teaches how to use each feature of TCO, which will result in reduction of operating costs in any organization. Explains how to detect, gather, and analyze hardware and software inventory remotely. Provides over 250 immediate solutions.

Windows 2000 Mac Support Little Black Book

By Gene Steinberg and Pieter Paulson
ISBN: 1-57610-388-9
$24.99 U.S. • $37.99 CAN

Focuses on difficult Mac/Windows 2000 and Mac/NT integration issues. Covers migration of Mac systems to Windows 2000, as well as migrating data back from Windows 2000 to Mac. Gives special emphasis to networking addresses.

Black Books. Solutions. Now.™

CORIOLIS™
Technology Press

The Coriolis Group, LLC

Telephone: 800.410.0192 • International: 480.483.0192 • www.coriolis.com
Coriolis books are also available at bookstores and computer stores nationwide.